MING DYNASTY TALES

MING DYNASTY TALES

A Guided Reader

Edited by
Victor H. Mair and Zhenjun Zhang

BLOOMSBURY ACADEMIC
LONDON · NEW YORK · OXFORD · NEW DELHI · SYDNEY

BLOOMSBURY ACADEMIC
Bloomsbury Publishing Plc
50 Bedford Square, London, WC1B 3DP, UK
1385 Broadway, New York, NY 10018, USA
29 Earlsfort Terrace, Dublin 2, Ireland

BLOOMSBURY, BLOOMSBURY ACADEMIC and the Diana logo
are trademarks of Bloomsbury Publishing Plc

First published in Great Britain 2022

Copyright © Victor H. Mair and Zhenjun Zhang, 2022

Victor H. Mair and Zhenjun Zhang have asserted their right under the Copyright, Designs and Patents Act, 1988, to be identified as Editors of this work.

Cover design by Catherine Wood
Cover image: *Elegant Gathering in the Apricot Garden*, After Xie Huan (Chinese, 1377–1452). (© Purchase, The Dillon Fund Gift, 1989 / The Metropolitan Museum of Art)

All rights reserved. No part of this publication may be reproduced or transmitted in any form or by any means, electronic or mechanical, including photocopying, recording, or any information storage or retrieval system, without prior permission in writing from the publishers.

Bloomsbury Publishing Plc does not have any control over, or responsibility for, any third-party websites referred to or in this book. All internet addresses given in this book were correct at the time of going to press. The author and publisher regret any inconvenience caused if addresses have changed or sites have ceased to exist, but can accept no responsibility for any such changes.

A catalogue record for this book is available from the British Library.

Library of Congress Cataloging-in-Publication Data
Names: Mair, Victor H., 1943- editor. | Zhang, Zhenjun, 1956-editor.
Title: Ming dynasty tales : a guided reader / Victor H. Mair and Zhenjun Zhang.
Description: London ; New York : Bloomsbury Academic, 2022. | Includes bibliographical references and index. | English with some Chinese.
Identifiers: LCCN 2021037299 (print) | LCCN 2021037300 (ebook) | ISBN 9781350263291 (hardback) | ISBN 9781350263284 (paperback) | ISBN 9781350263307 (epub) | ISBN 9781350263314 (pdf) | ISBN 9781350263321
Subjects: LCSH: Chinese fiction–Ming dynasty, 1368-1644–Translations into English. | Short stories, Chinese–Translations into English. | Tales–China.
Classification: LCC PL2658.E8 M56 2022 (print) | LCC PL2658.E8 (ebook) | DDC 895.13/0108046–dc23/eng/20211102
LC record available at https://lccn.loc.gov/2021037299
LC ebook record available at https://lccn.loc.gov/2021037300

ISBN:	HB:	978-1-3502-6329-1
	PB:	978-1-3502-6328-4
	ePDF:	978-1-3502-6331-4
	eBook:	978-1-3502-6330-7

Typeset by Integra Software Services Pvt. Ltd.
Printed and bound in Great Britain

To find out more about our authors and books visit www.bloomsbury.com and sign up for our newsletters.

CONTENTS

Notes on the Editors and Contributors … vii

Introduction … 1
    Victor H. Mair and Zhenjun Zhang

Tale 1
"Jinfeng Chai Ji" 金鳳釵記
(The Golden Phoenix Hairpin)
    By Qu You 瞿佑 Translated by Paul W. Kroll … 7

Tale 2
"Cuicui Zhuan" 翠翠傳
(The Tale of Cuicui)
    By Qu You Translated by Zhenjun Zhang and Sidney
    Sondergard … 19

Tale 3
"Taixu Sifa Zhuan" 太虛司法傳
(The Account of the Legal Administrator of
the Grand Void)
    By Qu You Translated by Kelsey Seymour … 39

Tale 4
"Lüyi Ren Zhuan" 綠衣人傳
(The Tale of the Lady in Green)
    By Qu You Translated by Yunwen Gao … 51

Tale 5
"Fengwei Cao Ji" 鳳尾草記
(The Record of a Phoenix-Tail Fern)
    By Li Changqi 李昌祺 Translated by Qian Liu
    and Joanne Tsao … 63

Tale 6
"Furong Ping Ji" 芙蓉屏記
(The Record of the Lotus Screen)
    By Li Changqi Translated by Weiguo Cao … 87

Tale 7
"QIUQIAN HUI JI" 鞦韆會記
(THE TALE OF THE SWING-PLAY GATHERING)
    By Li Changqi Translated by Jing Wang   113

Tale 8
"YAO GONGZI ZHUAN" 姚公子傳
(THE TALE OF YOUNG MASTER YAO)
    By Shao Jingzhan 邵景詹 Translated by Chen Wu   131

Tale 9
"FUQING NONG ZHUAN" 負情儂傳
(THE FAITHLESS LOVER)
    By Song Maocheng 宋懋澂 Translated by Zhenjun Zhang   143

Tale 10
"ZHU SHAN" 珠衫
(THE PEARL SHIRT)
    By Song Maocheng Translated by Jing Hu   159

Select Bibliography   173
Index   178

Notes on the Editors and Contributors

Weiguo Cao received his PhD from the University of Wisconsin-Madison. His research interests include early Chinese narrative and historical works, the development of Chinese fictional writing, and the translation of ancient Chinese texts. He has taught at Arizona State University and is now Clinical Associate Professor at Washington State University. His publications include annotated translations of several chapters of Sima Qian's *Shi ji, The Grand Scribe's Records*, vols. 2 and 5.1 (Indiana University Press, 2002 and 2006), as well as annotated translations of Tang tales: "The Tale of Hongxian" in *Tang Dynasty Tales: A Guided Reader* (World Scientific, 2010) and "A Supplement to Jiang Zong's 'Biography of the White Ape'" and "Records of Constructing the Grand Canal" in *Anthology of Tang and Song Tales: The* Tang Song chuanqi ji *of Lu Xun* (World Scientific, 2020).

Yunwen Gao received her PhD from the University of Southern California and is now assistant professor at the Centre for China Studies at the Chinese University of Hong Kong. Born and brought up in Shanghai, she is especially drawn to the culture and language of the local and the regional manifest in literature, film, and oral performance in the Wu fangyan (topolect) speaking region. Currently, she is working on her book manuscript titled "Language, Soundscape and Identity Formation in Shanghai Fangyan Literature and Culture." It examines the changing discourse and cultural significance of Wu fangyan writing in the history of Shanghai literature and culture from the late Qing period to the present.

Jing Hu received a Master's degree in Comparative Linguistics from Peking University and another Master's degree in Chinese Linguistics from the University of Wisconsin-Madison. She is currently teaching Chinese at the University of Pennsylvania. Before coming to UPenn, she had taught Chinese at Smith College and Yale-NUS College for over a decade. Her publications include annotated translations of "The Story of Li Zhangwu" and "The Story of Lady Feng of Lujiang" in *Anthology of Tang and Song Tales: The* Tang Song chuanqi ji *of Lu Xun* (World Scientific, 2020), as well as articles in the *Journal of Chinese Teaching and Research in the U.S., Tradition and Modernization, Tradition and Transition: Teaching Chinese Culture Overseas,* etc.

Paul W. Kroll is Professor Emeritus of Chinese at the University of Colorado, Boulder. He has published widely on medieval Chinese literature and cultural history and is also the author of *A Student's Dictionary of Classical and Medieval Chinese* (Brill, 2014; rev. ed. 2017).

Qian Liu, PhD, is East Asian Studies Librarian at the Arizona State University Library and affiliated faculty of the School of International Letters and Cultures (SILC) and the Center for Asian Research (CAR). She has publications in Medieval Chinese literature and history, print culture, and international exchange programs.

Victor H. Mair, Professor of Chinese Language and Literature at the University of Pennsylvania, has been teaching there since 1979. He specializes in Buddhist popular literature as well as the vernacular tradition of Chinese fiction and the performing arts. Beginning in the early 1990s, Professor Mair has led an interdisciplinary research project on the Bronze Age and Iron Age mummies of Eastern Central Asia. Among other results of his efforts during this period are six documentaries for television (Scientific American, NOVA, BBC, Discovery Channel, History Channel, and German Television), a major international conference, numerous articles, and a book, *The Tarim Mummies: Ancient China and the Mystery of the Earliest Peoples from the West* (Thames and Hudson, 2000). He is also the author of numerous other publications (including several anthologies from Columbia University Press) and is the editor of Sino-Platonic Papers, the ABC Chinese Dictionary Series (University of Hawai'i Press), and the Cambria Sinophone World Series. He blogs frequently for Language Log.

Kelsey Seymour received her PhD in East Asian Languages and Civilizations from the University of Pennsylvania in 2018. Her research focuses on the intersection of religious experience, music, linguistics, and memory in pre-modern Chinese Buddhist chanting. In particular, she is interested in what religious literature can reveal about sound perception and sensory experience. She has held research fellowships at Academia Sinica in Taipei, the Max Planck Institute for the History of Science in Berlin, and Yale University. Her publications include annotated translations of "The Record of the Ancient Mirror" and "A Record of Nocturnal Spirits near Dongyang" in *Anthology of Tang and Song Tales: The Tang Song chuanqi ji of Lu Xun* (World Scientific, 2020).

Notes on the Editors and Contributors

Sidney L. Sondergard, Piskor Professor of English and Asian Studies Emeritus, St. Lawrence University, is the sole translator of the complete *Liaozhai Zhiyi* 聊齋志異 [*Strange Tales from Liaozhai*] (Jain Publishing, 6 volumes, 2008–2014) in English, and co-translator of conservationist/naturalist Zhang Jinxing's *Yeren Meihuo* 野人魅惑 [*The Lure of the Wild Men*] (Jain Publishing, 2018) with Li Lin 李琳.

Joanne Tsao (PhD) teaches at Arizona State University. She has published translations and articles, including "The Creation of the Bronze Bird Terrace-scape in the Northern and Southern Dynasties Period" (*Early Medieval China* 23, 2017). Tsao's book *The City of Ye in the Chinese Literary Landscape* (Brill, 2020) was released on the cusp of the pandemic outspread in the US in 2020.

Jing Wang received her PhD in Chinese literature from the University of Wisconsin-Madison. She has taught at Carnegie Mellon University and the University of North Carolina-Charlotte, and is now Senior Lecturer and Associate Director of the Chinese language program at Princeton University. Her research interests include Tales in the Tang-Song period and Chinese language pedagogy. She has published *Song Dynasty Tales: A Guided Reader* (World Scientific, 2017; co-authored with Zhenjun Zhang) and *First Step: An Elementary Reader for Modern Chinese* (Princeton University Press, 2014; co-authored with C.P. Chou). She has also published articles on Tang tales, the teaching of classical Chinese, and teaching Chinese language through film.

Chen Wu earned her BA in Chinese Language and Literature (2006) and MA in Classical Chinese Philology (2009) from Fudan University and her PhD in Pre-modern Chinese Literature (2016) from the University of Wisconsin-Madison. Her PhD dissertation is titled "How a City Speaks: Urban Space in Chang'an and the Construction of Tang Dynasty Narratives." Since 2013, she has been teaching modern and classical Chinese in the Department of East Asian Languages and Cultures at Columbia University. Her research interests include classical Chinese, medieval Chinese narrative writings, and the interrelation between city and literature.

Zhenjun Zhang received his MA from Peking University and PhD from the University of Wisconsin-Madison. He is currently Professor of Asian Studies and World Languages, Cultures, and Media at St. Lawrence University. His research interests focus on pre-modern Chinese literature, especially fiction and its interaction with history, religions, and culture. His English publications include *Anthology of Tang and Song Tales: The* Tang Song chuanqi ji *of Lu Xun* (World Scientific, 2020; co-edited with Victor Mair), *Hidden and Visible Realms: Early Medieval Chinese Tales of the Supernatural and the Fantastic* (Columbia University Press, 2018), *Song Dynasty Tales: A Guided Reader* (World Scientific, 2017; co-authored with Jing Wang), and *Buddhism and Tales of the Supernatural in Early Medieval China: A Study of Liu Yiqing's* Youming lu (Brill, 2014). He is also the author of *Chuantong xiaoshuo yu Zhongguo wenhua* 傳統小說與中國文化 (Guangxi Normal University Press, 1996) and *Jingu yu chaoyue: cong Sanyan Erpai kan Zhongguo shimin xintai* 禁錮與超越：從"三言二拍"看中國市民心態 (Guoji wenhua, 1988; co-authored with Mao Defu) as well as editor of several series of Classical Chinese novels and Daoist texts.

Xin Zou received her BA (2008) from Peking University, and her MA (2010) and PhD (2017) in Chinese Literature and MS (2018) in Curriculum and Instruction from the University of Wisconsin-Madison. She is currently Lecturer in East Asian Studies at Princeton University. Her research focuses on classical Chinese literature and cultural history, especially the interaction involving social-political changes, language, and literature. She has published several journal articles and annotated translations as well as a book chapter; she is currently working on a book manuscript tracing the literary production and transmission of anecdotes from the Tang to the Northern Song dynasty. Xin Zou is also interested in language reform in modern China and Chinese language pedagogy, and she has co-authored *Eyes on China: An Intermediate-Advanced Reader of Modern Chinese* (Princeton University Press, 2019).

INTRODUCTION

Chinese Classical language tales, or *wenyan xiaoshuo* 文言小說, started to thrive during the Six Dynasties 六朝 period (220–589), which has traditionally been classified into two genres: *zhiguai* 志怪 (accounts of anomalies) and *zhiren* 志人 (records of people). While *zhiren* works are mainly anecdotes of notable figures, *zhiguai* is defined by Kenneth DeWoskin as "the generic name for collections of brief prose entries, primarily but not exclusively narrative in nature, that discuss out-of-the-ordinary people and events."[1] These two genres are often considered the earliest forms of Chinese *xiaoshuo* 小說 (fiction).[2]

Chuanqi 傳奇 (transmission of marvels), or "tale," is a substantial achievement in early fiction in classical Chinese, and it represents a much more advanced genre compared with its predecessor, the Six Dynasty *zhiguai*. The *chuanqi* thrived in the Tang 唐 dynasty (618–907), impressing readers with their much more elaborate plots, polished language, and, significantly, their "conscious creation" by their authors—that is, they were deliberately creating fiction.[3]

It is believed that the Qing (1644–1911) masterpiece by Pu Songling 蒲松齡 (1640–1715), *Liaozhai zhiyi* 聊齋志異 (Strange Tales from Liaozhai), reaches the peak of classical Chinese tales. However,

---

1. See DeWoskin's entry on "Chih-kuai" in William H. Nienhauser, Jr., ed., *The Indiana Companion to Traditional Chinese Literature*, 2nd ed. (Taipei: SMC Publishing Inc., 1987), p. 280. For a more detailed discussion of the genre of *zhiguai*, see Zhenjun Zhang, "The Zhiguai Tradition and the *Youming Lu*," in his *Hidden and Visible Realms*, pp. xxvi–xlvi and Robert Ford Campany, *Strange Writing: Anomaly Accounts in Early Medieval China*, pp. 21–32.

2. See Lu Xun 魯迅 (1881–1936), *Zhongguo xiaoshuo shilue* 中國小說史略 (Beijing: Renmin wenxue chuban she, 1973), pp. 29–44. Lu Xun's argument has become authoritative and influential since the publication of his book, though it has been challenged in recent years.

3. The term *chuanqi* also refers to the plays of the Ming and Qing 清 dynasties, a performance genre that carries over the concept of "transmitting the strange" in similar themes found in classical tales.

represented by Qu You's 瞿佑 (1347–1433) *Jiandeng xinhua* 剪燈新話 (New Stories Written while Trimming the Wick), the first officially banned yet internationally acclaimed Chinese tale collection, Ming dynasty (1368–1644) tales worked as the bridge between the brilliant Tang (and Song) tales and Pu Songling's *Strange Tales from Liaozhai*.

Jiandeng xinhua presents twenty tales written in classical Chinese, very much in the tradition of Tang *chuanqi* stories, plus another two in an appendix, twenty-two in all. Most are relatively brief, running between 1200 and 1600 characters, with a few somewhat longer. Several of them, such as "The Golden Phoenix Hairpin," revise and develop the outlines of stories that were known from earlier classical tales and *zaju* 雜劇 plays. Like the Tang tales, Qu You's tales are written in compact, elegant language, aimed at the educated elite, in contrast with the more broadly popular and widely disseminated tales of the *huaben* 話本 and *pinghua* 平話 traditions that were written in vernacular language. The tales of Qu's followers, such as Li Changqi 李昌祺 (1376–1452) and Shao Jingzhan 邵景詹 (fl.1560), are generally the same as Qu's in nature.

While Tang tales and Pu Songling's *Strange Tales from Liaozhai* have drawn much attention in the West,[4] classical tales of the Song and Ming have long been neglected. Although some poorly translated pieces are found in Christopher Levenson's *The Golden Casket Chinese Novellas of Two Millennia* (Penguin Classics, 1964), the English translations were based on a German rendition of the Chinese original, and there are many inaccuracies and errors, with some parts even omitted. It seems that the only Ming tales that previously have been formally translated into English are "The Golden Phoenix Hairpin," in *Traditional Chinese Stories* (pp. 400–03) and "The Regulator of the Ultimate Void" in *Renditions* (No.69 [2008]: 35–40).

But this situation is changing. Some of the most recent endeavors aimed at changing this situation include Alister Inglis's *The Drunken Man's Talk*, a translation of Luo Ye's 羅燁 *Zuiweng tanlu* 醉翁談錄 (Seattle: University of Washington Press, 2015), as well as Zhenjun Zhang and Jing Wang's *Song Dynasty Tales: A Guided Reader*

---

4. The most recent publications of Tang tales include: William H. Nienhauser, Jr., ed., *Tang Dynasty Tales: A Guided Reader*, Vols. 1–2 (Singapore: World Scientific Publishing Co., 2010–2015), Alexei Kamran Ditter et al., *Tales from Tang Dynasty China: Selections from the* Taiping guangji (Indianapolis/Cambridge: Hackett Publishing Co., 2017), and Victor H. Mair and Zhenjun Zhang, eds., *Anthology of Tang and Song Tales: The* Tang Song chuanqi ji *of Lu Xun* (Singapore: World Scientific Publishing Co., 2020).

(Singapore: World Scientific, 2017), which includes English renditions of twelve Song tales. Although *The Drunken Man's Talk* is not purely a collection of classical tales—as it also includes jokes, poems, and legal rulings—most of its texts are tales.

This new volume is part of the effort to make changes; it is the first annotated English translation of ten selected Ming dynasty tales in classical Chinese, with an introduction and commentaries on each tale in the form of "Notes and Reading Guide." Besides its significance in the history of Chinese fiction, this volume opens a window into the colorful life of the Ming and presents as well a gloomy picture of the chaos during the transition between the Yuan 元 (1260–1368) and Ming dynasties.

Like a breath of fresh air, classical tales brought significant changes to the field of literature of the Ming dynasty, especially early Ming. In about a hundred years from the beginning of the Ming dynasty, Chinese literature, including poetry, prose, fiction, and drama, was dedicated to praising peacefulness and promoting Confucian teachings such as loyalty, filiality, chastity, and righteousness. This trend was disrupted by Qu You's *Jiandeng xinhua* and the works of his followers such as Li Changqi's *Jiandeng yuhua* 剪燈餘話 (Supplementary Stories Written while Trimming the Wick), Shao Jingzhan's *Mideng yinhua* 覓燈因話 (Tales of the Searching Lamplight), and Song Maocheng's 宋懋澂 (1569–1622) *Jiuyue ji* 九籥集, etc. These tales are mostly filled with realistic emotions, with vivid and detailed narration.

A prominent theme of Ming dynasty tales is romantic love. The tales included in this volume, such as the "Cuicui zhuan" 翠翠傳 (The Tale of Cuicui), the "Fengwei cao ji" 鳳尾草記 (The Record of a Phoenix-Tail Fern), "Furong ping ji" 芙蓉屏記 (The Record of the Lotus Screen), and "Qiuqian hui ji" 鞦韆會記 (The Tale of the Swing-play Gathering), are all romantic love stories. While some of these love stories feature traditional themes, such as parents' breaking a promise (The Tale of the Swing-play Gathering) and romantic tragedy due to the different social statuses of the lovers (The Record of a Phoenix-Tail Fern), a prominent, new characteristic of these tales is portraying the pain of youth brought about by the social turbulence and warfare between the Yuan and Ming dynasties. In "The Tale of Cuicui," the love between Cuicui and her husband, Jinding, is destroyed by the warfare as she falls into the hands of the rebel General Li. "Qiuxiang ting ji" 秋香亭記 (Autumn Fragrance Pavilion) also tells of a tragic love story during the turbulence. Through the mouth of the ghost girl, "Lüyi ren zhuan" 綠衣人傳 (The Tale of the Lady in Green), directly pours the miserable suffering of women during the warfare.

Love between ghost girls and human beings is a noted sub-theme of Ming tales. The term "ghost" (*gui* 鬼) is derived from the belief that a person becomes a ghost after death.[5] While in early Chinese texts the ghosts always seem to have supernatural powers and therefore inspire awe in people, the portrayal of ghosts in the Six Dynasties *zhiguai* is quite different: the ghosts are not only shown in their divine aspect but are also full of the emotions of human beings. This feature continued in the tales of Tang, Song, Ming, and Qing. In Tang tales, "Li Zhangwu zhuan" 李章武傳 (The Tale of Li Zhangwu) is a touching love story between a man and a ghost lady; but such a story did not become popular until the Song and Ming dynasties. The tales included in this volume, such as "Jinfeng chai ji" 金鳳釵記 (The Golden Phoenix Hairpin) and "The Tale of the Lady in Green," are both good examples. A variant of this theme involves a girl who cannot marry her lover until she dies. Early examples, such as "Wuwang xiaonü" 吳王小女 (King Wu's Little Daughter) and "Hejian jun nannü" 河間郡男女 (The Boy and Girl from Hejian), are found in the Six Dynasties tales. "The Tale of Cuicui" from Qu You's *Jiandeng xinhua* is a new example that features this motif.

Although the ghost girl in these love stories is as beautiful as the descended goddess in the stories between human beings and goddesses, which were popular in the tales of the Han 漢 (206 BCE to 220 CE) and Tang dynasties, the tone of the motif in ghost wife stories is always sad. While the descended goddess symbolizes the ideal woman in the mind of tale authors, or Chinese literati, the ghost girl represents the ugly fact of women being treated as inferior compared with men for thousands of years in Chinese history; if we say that the goddess in the tales is the incarnation of beauty, then the ghost girl is definitely the incarnation of resentment (*yuan* 怨). The images of resentful women are closely related to the lowly social status of women in traditional China as well as to numerous women's tragedies caused by Neo-Confucianism 宋明理學 during the Song and Ming dynasties.[6]

Quite a few Ming dynasty tales feature important and influential motifs. Noted examples include the "detached-soul" motif in "The

---

5. *Ren si yue gui* 人死曰鬼. "Jifa" 祭法 of *Liji*. See *Liji zhengyi*, in Ruan Yuan 阮元 (1764–1849), ed., *Shisanjing zhushu* 十三經註疏 (Beijing: Zhonghua shuju, 1980), 46. 1588.

6. Cf. Zhenjun Zhang 張振軍, *Chuantong xiaoshuo yu Zhomgguo wenhua* 傳統小説與中國文化 (Nanning: Guangxi daxue chuban she, 1996), pp. 99–102.

Golden Phoenix Hairpin," a "couple's reunion" motif in "Lotus Screen" and "The Pearl Shirt," and the "faithless lover" motif in "The Faithless Lover." All of them had a significant impact on literary works of later times, especially the vernacular short stories in the storytelling tradition and drama (for details, see "Notes and Reading Guide" to each tale).

Regarding writing style, Ming dynasty tales mostly tend to mimic the language and narrative style of Tang tales. Some of them, especially those in Qu You's collection such as "The Tale of Cuicui," "The Tale of the Lady in Green," and "Teng Mu zuiyou Jujingyuan ji" 滕穆醉遊聚景園記 (Teng Mu's Drunken Excursion to Assembled Scenery Park) are all excellent works. Similar to Song dynasty tales, however, Ming dynasty tales were undervalued since Lu Xun's 魯迅 (1881–1936) remarks on Qu You's *Jiandeng xinhua* in his *Zhongguo xiaoshuo shilue*: "Both [its] titles and artistic conception [tried to] follow those of Tang tales, but its writing is extremely superfluous and weak, so [it] does not match that [of the Tang tales]" 文題意境，并撫唐人，而文筆殊冗弱不相副.[7] We would say that "extremely weak" is certainly not always true of Qu You's tales. Some of them are quite vivid and moving, showing their own charm compared with Tang tales. The description of Cuicui being unable to reunite with Jin Ding and of Jin Ding's subsequent death in "The Tale of Cuicui," for example, is touching and powerful:

> When the scholar received the poem, he could tell from it that Cuicui was promising him to die, so he no longer had hope, which made him feel all the more depressed and gloomy till he succumbed to a serious and protracted illness.
>
> Cuicui pleaded with the general and was allowed to pay her respects once, but by then the scholar was already critically ill. She took his arm and helped him sit up, and as he raised his head to glance sideways at her, tears filling his eyes, with a long sigh he suddenly died.

Inclusion of poems and lyrics is a prominent feature of Ming dynasty tales. Modern scholars such as Sun Kaidi 孫楷第 have criticized this phenomenon, "[When Qu] You wrote *Jiandeng xinhua*, he attached poems and lyrics to the narrative, even reaching thirty pieces in one tale. But based on the text, they are not necessary and looked like only

---

7. Lu Xun, *Zhongguo xiaoshuo shilue*, 22: 178.

showing off. [Li] Changqi followed him in writing *Jiandeng yuhua*."[8] This observation is true to Ming dynasty tales as a whole, but it is not an accurate assessment of Qu You's collection for the following reasons: (1) Not all of his tales include poems and lyrics, and (2) most of the included poems and lyrics are necessary. It seems that Lu Xun also considers this practice a shortcoming (calling it "superfluous") of Qu You's work. But modern scholars have observed that in *Jiandeng xinhua*, the inserted poems and proses are proper, not tiresome. Criticizing its writing as superfluous and weak but neglecting the narrative function of the insertions in the text is unfair.[9]

It is clear that some of the poems in *Jiandeng xinhua* are erotic, with detailed depictions of love, which might be influenced by Zhang Zhuo's 張鷟 "You xianku" 遊仙窟 (Wandering in the Grotto of Immortals), and that could be one of the reasons why the collection was banned by the government. However, our observations show that the poems and lyrics inserted in Qu You's collection are not superfluous; on the contrary, they perform at least the following functions that are also found in vernacular fiction and beyond: (1) depiction of scenery, (2) depiction of character's appearance, (3) depiction of details of actions— including the intimate actions of lovers—and (4) depiction of the psychological state of characters. All of these are new features that are rarely found in Tang tales; the last two functions are also rarely seen in vernacular fiction, in which these two functions are replaced by direct *baihua* 白話 depictions. In Qu You's tales, depiction of the psychological state of characters, a function generally lacking in classical language tales, is done perfectly through insertion of poems and rhapsodies. Good examples include "The Tale of Cuicui" and "Teng Mu's Drunken Excursion to Assembled Scenery Garden."

Victor H. Mair and Zhenjun Zhang

8. 佑為《剪燈新話》, 乃以正文之外贅附詩詞, 其多者至於三十首, 按之實際, 可有可無, 似為自炫。昌祺效之, 作《餘話》。See Sun Kaidi, *Riben Dongjing suojian xiaoshuo shumu* 日本東京所見小說書目 (Beijing: Renmin wenxue chuban she, 1981), pp. 126–7.

9. 插入詩文適可而止, 并不令人生厭, 不考慮內容需要片面指責其文筆冗弱有失公允。Xu Shuofang 徐朔方 and Sun Qiuke 孫秋克, *Mingdai wenxueshi* 明代文學史 (Hangzhou: Zhejiang daxue chuban she, 2006), p. 27.

Tale 1

"JINFENG CHAI JI" 金鳳釵記
(THE GOLDEN PHOENIX HAIRPIN)

By Qu You 瞿佑
Translated by Paul W. Kroll

During the Dade reign period (1297–1308),[1] there lived in Yangzhou a rich man by the name of Wu who was a district defense commandant. He lived next to the Loft of Vernal Breezes, and was a neighbor of Master Cui, an official with whom he had a deep bond of friendship. Cui had a son named Xingge and Wu had a daughter called Xingniang, both of whom were still in infant's clothes. Cui sought the girl as a future wife for his son, and when Wu gave his consent, Cui presented him with a golden phoenix hairpin as a pledge. Shortly thereafter Cui was transferred to a post in a distant region, and for fifteen years not a word was exchanged between the two families.

At this time the girl reached her nineteenth year in the seclusion of her chambers. Her mother said to Wu, "The young master of the Cui family has been gone now for fifteen years with no news at all, and Xingniang has fully matured. I don't believe that we should hold to the previous accord and waste her youth." Answered Wu, "But I've given my word to my friend; the covenant has already been made. How can I go back on it?"

The girl, for her part, yearned for the arrival of her betrothed, became sick, and was confined to her bed. Within half a year she died. Her parents wept in grief.

As Xingniang was being prepared for burial, her mother, holding the golden phoenix hairpin, stroked the corpse and said tearfully, "This is a token from your husband's family. Now that you are gone, what use is there in my keeping it?" Thereupon she fastened it in her daughter's hair, to be interred with her.

---

1. This was the second of two reign periods of Emperor Chengzong of the Yuan dynasty, who took the throne in 1295.

Two months after the burial, young Cui arrived. Wu received him and inquired of his affairs, to which Cui replied, "My father died in the post of prefectural judge of Xuande prefecture.² My mother, too, passed away several years ago. Having now completed the mourning period for them, I've hastened here in spite of the long distance." With tears falling, Wu told him, "It was Xingniang's misfortune to fall ill because she yearned for you so. Two months ago, she died without fulfilling her wishes. She has already been buried."

Wu thereupon conducted him into the girl's chambers and burned sacrificial money before her memorial tablet, to inform her spirit of Cui's arrival. Every member of the household wept bitterly. Then Wu said to Cui, "Your parents are dead, and your home is so far away. Now that you are here, please make yourself at home at my place. The son of an old friend is just like my own son. You needn't be a stranger to me because of Xingniang's death." He then ordered Cui's baggage moved in, and the young man settled down in a small studio, beside the gates of the family compound.

Half a month passed, and the Qingming Festival came. Because of the recent death of Wu's daughter, the entire family paid a visit to her grave. Xingniang had a younger sister by the name of Qingniang, who was in her seventeenth year, and she also went along on that day. Only Cui remained at home to look after things.

When the family returned in the evening, the sky was already darkening. Cui greeted them, standing to the left of the gate. When the first of the two sedan chairs had entered and the second was before him, something seemed to fall out of it with a tinkling sound. He waited until the sedan chair had passed and then hurried over to pick it up. It was a golden phoenix hairpin. He wanted to return it to the inner quarters immediately, but the central gate had already been secured and he could not gain entrance. So he went back to his little studio, where he sat alone before a lighted candle, reflecting on his unconsummated betrothal and his loneliness. Considering that there was no future in living with someone else's family this way, he sighed deeply.

Just as he was about to retire for the night, he suddenly heard a light knocking at the door. He called out to see who it was, but there was no reply. After a short pause, the knocking resumed. This sequence was repeated three times before Cui finally unlatched the door and peered out. Standing there was a lovely young girl who, upon seeing the door

---

2. Present-day Xuanhua district, Hebei, northwest of Beijing.

open, hitched up her long skirt and stepped into the room. Cui was shocked, but the girl lowered her head and with bated breath spoke to him in a low voice: "Don't you recognize me? I'm Xingniang's younger sister, Qingniang. A while ago I threw a hairpin from the sedan chair. Did you retrieve it?" She then pulled Cui toward the bed, but Cui, remembering her father's hospitality, refused, saying, "I wouldn't dare." And he firmly resisted her repeated advances.

Suddenly the girl's face flushed, and she raged at him:

> My father has treated you with the propriety he would show his own brother's son and has taken you into his own household. But now in the deep of night, you've enticed me here! What are you up to? If I report this to my father, he will surely take you to the magistrate and he will not let you off!

Cui, taken aback by this threat, could only comply with her wishes. When dawn came, she departed.

From this time on, each evening she would come in secret to the little studio next to the gates and each morning would depart in secret. A month and a half passed in this way. One night Qingniang said to Cui:

> I live in the ladies' quarters while you live in an outside studio. Fortunately, no one has yet learned of this affair, but I only fear that 'a good cause will meet many obstacles and the wedding day can easily be delayed.' For if one day our secret is discovered, I'll be condemned by my family, shut up, and caged like a parrot. Then, 'once the duck is struck, the male of the love-birds will be frightened as well.'[3] Even though I'm quite willing to face this, I'm afraid that your good name would be compromised. It would be best to flee with whatever is dear to us before the matter is discovered. Rendering ourselves unknown in far-off villages and hiding our identities in other districts, we can grow old together without care and never be separated.

Cui was rather pleased with her suggestion and said, "What you've said is indeed sensible. Let me think about." Whereupon he mused:

---

3. This adage means that when one person is punished, the fears of someone else will also be called forth. Qingniang suggests that her punishment will inevitably involve Cui as well.

I'm an orphan, miserably alone, and have long lacked close relatives and friends. Even though I wish to flee with her, where could we go? But once I heard my father remark that our old servant Jin Rong was a faithful and honorable man. He dwells now in Lücheng, in Jinjiang prefecture,[4] and tills the earth for a living. We shall throw ourselves on his kindness; surely he will not refuse us!

The next night, the two of them left at the fifth watch, carrying with them only the simplest baggage. They hired a boat and stopped at Guazhou, whence they continued to Danyang.[5] There they inquired of the villagers and succeeded in finding Jin Rong, who had prospered with his family and become wealthy, while he himself had been made headman of the village. Cui was delighted and went directly to Jin's place, but at first he was not recognized. However, when he mentioned his father's name, official rank, and native place, and his own childhood name, Jin finally remembered him. Jin then set up a memorial tablet for his deceased master and wept. He then seated Cui and respectfully made obeisance to him, saying, "Here is my former young master." Cui fully informed him of his reason for coming, whereupon Jin had the main quarters cleared and lodged the two there. He attended them as though he were attending his former master, providing them with all the clothing and food they required.

They resided with Jin for nearly a year, at which time the girl said to Cui:

> At first I dreaded the censure of my parents, so I, like Lady Zhuo,[6] fled with you. I did so because there was no other way out for us. But now the old grain has been consumed and the new grain is sprouting—time passes like a flowing stream, and a year has nearly gone by. All parents love their offspring, and if we return now of our own accord

---

4. About forty miles southeast of Yangzhou, across the Yangzi.
5. Guazhou is about ten miles south of Yangzhou, on the north bank of the Yangzi. Danyang is across the river, and another twenty miles off. In fact, they are not actually going very far away, barely a two days' journey. But since Cui has spent his life since infancy in the north and Qingniang has rarely left her house, they will not be known here.
6. She is comparing herself with Zhuo Wenjun 卓文君, who, being wooed by Sima Xiangru 司馬相如 (179–117 BCE) who would later become a famous poet at the Han-dynasty court, eloped with him from her home in Chengdu.

they will be so happy to see us once again that they certainly will not reproach us. No kindness is greater than that of our parents who give us life, so how can they bear to break off from their children? Why not go and see them?

Cui assented, and together they crossed back over the Yangzi, returning to the girl's native town.

As they drew near her home, she said to Cui, "Having run off for a year, I fear I may meet my father's wrath if I go with you. It would be best if you go on ahead and take a look first. I shall moor the boat here to await word from you." As Cui was about to leave, she called him back and gave him the golden phoenix hairpin, saying, "If my father doubts you, show him this."

When Wu heard that Cui was at his gate, he was overjoyed and went out to welcome him, making unexpected apologies: "My lack of hospitality must have caused you such uneasiness that you subsequently departed for elsewhere. It is all my fault! I hope you will not take offense." Cui prostrated himself and, not daring to look up, repeatedly asked for Wu's forgiveness.

Wu said, "What crime have you committed to call forth such alarming words? Please, explain yourself and allay my doubts."

To which Cui replied:

Behind drawn curtains your daughter and I carried on a secret affair. Our affection for each other grew, and, turning our backs on the name of righteousness, we committed the offense of having a clandestine relationship. Without informing you I took her as though a wife and we stole away to hide in a far-off village. The months stretched on, and for a long time we made no effort to be in touch with you. But though our affection is more devoted even than that of husband and wife, how can one forget the kindnesses of father and mother? Humbly I implore you to behold the depth of our feelings and forgive our serious offense, so we may grow old together and be forever united. The blessing of your fond love and our happy family life are what we seek. I hope you will take pity on us.

On hearing this, Wu replied in amazement, "But my daughter has been bedridden for almost a year, unable to take thin gruel, and even needing help to turn over. How can you talk like this?"

Cui assumed that Wu was afraid of having disgrace brought to the family and so was covering up the truth in order to put him off. But he answered, "Qingniang is at this moment in my boat. You can send someone to bring her here."

Although Wu did not believe him, he commanded a servant to hasten there. When the servant came to the boat, there was no one there, and upon his report Wu became angry and berated Cui for indulging in such a sham pretense. Cui then brought forth from his sleeve the golden phoenix hairpin and showed it to Wu. When Wu beheld it, he was utterly confounded: "This token was interred with my deceased daughter, Xingniang. How could it possibly turn up here?"

Amidst their confusion and perplexity, Qingniang unexpectedly rose from her bed and came directly to the hall. She made obeisance to her father and said:

> I am Xingniang, whose ill fortune it was to leave you so early in my life and be cast into the wilderness. But my predestined bond with the young master of the Cui family was not yet broken. I've come here now desiring only to have my beloved younger sister Qingniang continue the union. If you concur with this wish, her ailment will be cured instantly; if not, she will expire now before you.

The entire household was petrified. They could see that the body was indeed that of Qingniang, but the voice and mannerisms were those of the deceased Xingniang.

Her father rebuked her: "You are already dead. By what right do you return to the human world and cause this turmoil?"

She replied:

> After I died, the Courts of the Underworld found me guiltless of any crime and therefore did not restrain me with the usual prohibitions. I was put under the tutelage of Lady Houtu,[7] and put in charge of forwarding messages. Since my earthly destiny had not been fulfilled, I was granted a special leave for one year in order to consummate my marriage with Master Cui.

Her father, hearing the urgency of her words, assented. She immediately composed her countenance and made obeisance to him in gratitude. Then she clasped Cui's hand, sighing tearfully over their parting: "My

---

7. The cult of Lady Houtu 后土 began to be popular during the Tang period and remained alive up to the twentieth century, especially in the Yangzhou area.

parents have granted my wish. Be a good son-in-law, and take heed not to forget your old love because of the new." After speaking these words, she cried bitterly and fell to the ground. She appeared dead.

Quickly a herb broth was forced between her lips, and in a brief while Qingniang revived. All symptoms of her sickness were gone, and her actions seemed normal. When asked about what had happened, she apparently remembered nothing, as if she had just awakened from a dream. An auspicious day was then chosen for her marriage with Cui.

Moved by Xingniang's affection, Cui sold the hairpin in the marketplace, and with the twenty taels of silver he got for it, he purchased incense, candles, and paper money for offerings and presented them at the Abbey of the Carnelian Blossom. There he enjoined a Daoist priest to erect an altar and carry out a three-day *jiao* ceremony in thanksgiving to her.

Xingniang appeared to him once more in a dream and said, "Owing to your prayers, I have gained my salvation. My love for you is undying, even though we are separate in the worlds of light and of dark. I feel deeply grateful and have great admiration for you. My younger sister is gentle and meek; please treat her with kindness." Cui awoke in wonderment and grief.

From that time on there was no further communication between the two of them.

Aiya! How strange it is!

NOTES AND READING GUIDE

Paul W. Kroll and the Editors

The collection of classical-language tales from which this story comes, *Jiandeng xinhua* (New Tales under the Trimmed Lamp), was the work of Qu You (1341–1427), who hailed from the Hangzhou area. Qu came to adulthood during the last years of the Yuan dynasty and would later serve briefly as a secretary for one of the many Ming princes, but he did not succeed in climbing the official ladder. However, several of his literary works became well known, particularly his *Jiandeng xinhua*, completed in 1378, which in the following decades would spawn two sequel collections by other hands.

The tale translated here is a detached soul story. It is believed that the "Pang E" 龐阿 in Liu Yiqing's 劉義慶 (403–444) *Youming lu* 幽明錄 (Records of the Hidden and Visible Realms) is the earliest detached soul story in Chinese literature. It reads:

> In Julu commandery,[8] there was a man by the name of Pang E who was handsome and carried himself well. The Shi family of that same commandery had a daughter who took a liking to him after she chanced to see him from the inner quarters of her house. Not long thereafter, Pang E saw this girl coming to pay him a visit.
>
> Pang E's wife was a very jealous woman, and when she heard this, she ordered her maidservant to tie up the girl and send her back to the Shi family. However, when they were halfway there, the girl transformed herself into a wisp of smoke and disappeared.
>
> Thereupon the maidservant went straight to see the Shi family and told them about this. The father of the Shi family was shocked and said, "My daughter has never even stepped outside this house. How can you spread such slander as this?"
>
> From then on Pang E's wife took even more care to keep an eye on him. One night she came across this girl again in the study, whereupon she herself tied her up and took her back to the Shi family.
>
> When the father saw her, he stared dumbfoundedly and said, "I just came from inside and saw the girl working with her mother. How could she be here?" He then ordered a maidservant to call the girl to come out. As soon as the girl came out, the one who had been tied up previously vanished like smoke.

---

8. Julu 巨鹿, present-day Jin 晉 county, Hebei.

The father suspected that there must be an abnormal reason for this, so he sent the mother to ask the girl about it. The girl said, "Last year I once stole a glance at Pang E when he came to our house, and ever since then I have felt confused. Once I dreamt that I went to visit Pang E, and when I reached the entrance to his house, I was tied up by his wife."

Mr. Shi said, "How could it be that there are truly such strange matters as this in the world! Indeed, whenever one's sincerest feelings are affected, the spirit will manifest itself in mysterious ways. Thus the one who disappeared must have been her *hun* soul."

After this, the girl made a vow that she would never marry. Some years later, Pang E's wife suddenly contracted a terrible illness, and neither doctors nor medicines were able to save her life. Only then did Pang E send betrothal gifts to the girl and make her his wife.

鉅鹿有龐阿者，美容儀。同郡石氏有女，曾內睹阿，心悅之。未幾，阿見此女來詣阿，阿妻極妒，聞之，使婢縛之，送還石家，中路遂化為煙氣而滅。婢乃直詣石家，說此事。石氏之父大驚曰："我女都不出門，豈可毀謗如此？"阿父[婦]自是常加意伺察之，居一夜，方值女在齋中，乃自拘執以詣石氏，石氏父見之愕貽，曰："我適從內來，見女與母共作，何得在此？" 即令婢僕於內喚女出，向所縛者奄然滅焉。父疑有異，故遣其母詰之。女曰："昔年龐阿來廳中，曾竊視之。自爾仿佛即夢詣阿，及入戶即為妻所縛。" 石曰："天下遂有如此奇事！夫精情所感，靈神為之冥著，滅者蓋其魂神也。" 既而女誓心不嫁。經年，阿妻忽得邪病，醫藥無徵，阿乃授幣石氏女為妻。[9]

Generally speaking, this is a romantic dream combined with a detached soul story, which is not seen in previous texts.[10]

9. The translation here is from Zhenjun Zhang, *Hidden and Visible Realms: Early Medieval Chinese Tales of the Supernatural and the Fantastic* (New York: Columbia University Press, 2018), pp. 6-7. The Chinese version is from Lu Xun, ed., *Guxiaoshuo gouchen* 古小說鉤沉, p. 417, and Li Fang 李昉 (925-996) et al., eds., *Taiping guangji* 太平廣記, 358. 2830.

10. For a discussion on the origin of the detached soul motif, see Zhenjun Zhang, "On the Origins of Detached Soul Motif in Chinese Literature," *Sungkyun Journal of East Asian Studies*, Vol. 9, No. 2 (2009): 178, or his book *Buddhism and Tales of the Supernatural in Early Medieval China: A Study of Liu Yiqing's Youming lu* (Leiden: Brill, 2014), pp. 205-21.

But "The Golden Phoenix Hairpin" derives from a Tang *chuanqi* called "An Account of a Detached Soul" ("Lihun ji" 離魂記) by Chen Xuanyou 陳玄祐 (fl. 780), an otherwise little-known author. That tale was much longer than the "Pang E" anecdote in *Youming lu*, but was still written in a rather unadorned style, with minimal dialogue, and is barely a third as long as Qu You's tale. "Lihun ji" borrows the structure and motif of "Pang E." It narrates the story of an official named Zhang Yi 張鎰, whose little daughter Qianniang 倩娘 was extremely beautiful. Her cousin, Wang Zhou 王宙, was a handsome boy. Zhang Yi said several times that he would allow Wang to take Qianniang as his wife in the future. But when they had grown up, Zhang Yi chose instead to marry Qianniang to a newly selected official. Filled with grief, Wang said goodbye to the Zhang family and went to the capital by boat. On his way, Wang Zhou saw Qianniang; they traveled to Shu 蜀, lived together for five years and had five children. Afterward, they went back home. Her father told them that Qianniang had been ill in her boudoir for years. Hearing that Wang Zhou had returned, the girl made herself up, went out to welcome them, and became one with the Qianniang from the boat.

In the late thirteenth century this story was refashioned and expanded for the *zaju* stage twice—once by Zhao Gongfu 趙公輔 (fl. 1280) whose version is no longer extant, and again by Zheng Guangzu 鄭光祖 (fl. 1295) the text of whose play "Qiannü's Detached Soul" ("Qiannü lihun" 倩女離魂) has come down to us.

Qu You's "Account of the Golden Phoenix Hairpin" is a wholesale reworking of the earlier versions, with names changed, new characters added, and fresh incidents and details, though the core plot remains. Qu You's major innovation was to provide the tale with two live daughters, whereas in the Tang tale one of them had died before the action commences and in the *zaju* there is but one daughter. Someone has remarked that "'The Golden Phoenix Hairpin' attaches the soul of the dead to an innocent girl and, by driving the soul of the living, achieves a breakthrough in the marriage dilemma, enabling the dead to express her intent fully and the living to continue her marriage seamlessly."[11] This is generally true.

---

11. 《金鳳釵記》以亡魂附身、驅動無辜者生魂之方式完成對於婚戀困境的突破,使早逝者心意既得以充分傳達,亦使存世者婚姻得以無暇延續。See Chen Baowen 陳葆文, *Gudian xiaoshuo gushi leixing xuanxi* 古典小說故事類型選析 (Taibei: Wunan tushu, 2019), p. 251.

Qu You's "The Golden Phoenix Hairpin" has been influential. In his *Jiandeng yuhua* (Supplemental Tales Written under the Trimmed Lamp), Qu's follower Li Changqi (1376–1452) wrote a tale titled "Jia Yunhua huanhun ji" 賈雲華還魂記 (The Returning of Jia Yunhua's Soul), in which the girl Yunhua fell in love with scholar Wei Peng. Due to some reasons, they parted, and Yunhua died in sorrow. Later on, Wei Peng became an official. Yunhua attached her soul to Song Yue'e, the daughter of another official, and married Wei. The plot is almost the same as that in "The Golden Phoenix Hairpin," though the story is much longer, with many poems.

Two and a half centuries later, near the end of the Ming era, Qu You's tale itself was modified by Ling Mengchu 凌濛初 (1580–1644)—primarily by much increasing and elaborating the details of individual scenes, but without substantive change—and included as the twenty-third story in his first collection of vernacular tales, *Pai'an jingqi* 拍案驚奇. The "detached soul" story thus has a nearly millennium-long history of development in Chinese literature, and Qu You's version is an important link in this chain.

Tale 2

"CUICUI ZHUAN" 翠翠傳 (THE TALE OF CUICUI)

By Qu You
Translated by Zhenjun Zhang and Sidney Sondergard

Cuicui, surnamed Liu, was a girl from a commoner's family in Huai'an.[1] She was born clever, able to understand the Confucian classics.[2] Her parents didn't oppose her aspirations and allowed her to attend school. Among her classmates there was a son of the Jin family, named Ding and the same age as Cuicui, who was also bright, handsome, and refined. Their classmates made fun of them, saying, "You two are the same age, so you ought to be husband and wife." And the two also began secretly to regard themselves in this way.

Once Scholar Jin sent a poem to Cuicui, which read,

Twelve railings encircle the Seven Treasure Terrace,
When the spring breeze arrives, sunny weather emerges.
The east garden's peach trees and the west garden's willows,
Why don't you move so you can be planted together in one place?

Cuicui responded,

I've always felt sorry for Zhu Yingtai[3];

---

1. Present day Huai'an County in Jiangsu province.
2. *Shishu* 詩書, *The Classic of Odes* and *The Classic of Documents*, here refers to Confucian classics in general.
3. Zhu Yingtai 祝英臺 appears in "The Butterfly Lovers" in folklore, dating back to the Eastern Jin dynasty. It is said that Yingtai, dressed as a boy, studied together with Liang Shanbo 梁山伯 for three years. Later Liang realized that she was a female and thus proposed marriage with her, but she was betrothed to another man already. After Liang died in melancholy, Yingtai passed by his tomb and offered sacrifice while mourning him. Suddenly the tomb opened and Yingtai jumped into it. From then on, a pair of butterflies were seen frequently flying together, and they were believed to be the souls of Liang and Zhu.

Why was her melancholy bosom so unwilling to open [to her lover]?
I hope the god of spring gives more care,[4]
Moving and planting the flowers and trees earlier, facing the sun.

Later on, as Cuicui grew older, she no longer went to study. When she turned sixteen and her parents proposed a marriage for her, she just wept sorrowfully and wouldn't eat. When they earnestly asked her why, she initially refused to say anything; after a long time, she explained, "The man has to be Jin Ding, who lives to the west of us, and I've already betrothed myself to him. If you don't listen to me, I'll die and that is all. I swear I won't enter the gate of any other family." Her parents had no alternative, so they acquiesced to her.

However, the Liu family was wealthy, and the Jin family was poor. Even though their son was intelligent and handsome, Jin's family status simply wasn't equal to the Liu family's. When a marriage broker arrived at the Jin home, they declined as expected because of their poverty, for they felt too ashamed to dare accept the proposal.

The marriage broker told them:

> The young woman of the Liu family desires resolutely to marry Jin Ding, and her parents have also agreed to this. But if you decline on the grounds of your poverty, you'll disappoint her sincere willingness and lose the chance of such a good marriage. Now you should reply to them in words such as, 'Our poor family has a son who knows a little bit about classics and rites. Your noble family seeks to have him become your son-in-law, how dare we not approve this? But he was born in our humble home and has felt contented with poverty and low status for a long time. If you were to demand betrothal gifts of him, as well as the matrimonial rite, I'm afraid we wouldn't be able to comply in the end.' For the sake of their beloved daughter, they wouldn't mind.

Ding's family heeded her suggestion.

The marriage broker reported on her mission, and Ciuciu's parents responded, "Seeking for wealth in marriage is the way of barbarians. We only want to select a son-in-law, so we disregard any other concerns. But the Jin family has too little wealth and we have plenty. If our daughter marries into their family, she won't be able to endure the discrepancy.

---

4. Dongjun 東君, god of spring, is also considered god of the sun.

2. The Tale of Cuicui   21

It is better that Jin Ding marries into *our* family." The marriage broker went back again and applied this argument, and the Jin family was very pleased. Thus they selected a day for the marriage, and all of the money and silk, as well as betrothal gifts such as lamb and geese, were handled by the girl's family.

After Jin Ding entered Cuicui's home and the couple kowtowed to each other in the wedding ceremony, the two people joined together—and their happiness can only be imagined! That evening, Cuicui sent Jin Ding a lyric that she'd composed while lying on her pillow to the tune of "The Immortals by the River."[5] It read:

> In the study, we have previously shared the same writing brush and inkstone,
> Old friends are now a newly married couple.
> The bridal chamber and wedding candles form a perfect spring!
> Your sweat moistens butterflies' pink dust,[6]
> Your body is enveloped with fragrant musk powder.[7]
>
> Entangled with rain and clouds[8] is not what I'm accustomed to,
> On the pillow I shyly knit my eyebrows from time to time,
> But please never mind, taking pity on me in different ways.
> From now on I wish, my darling,
> You'll be dearer and dearer to me day by day.

She invited the scholar to continue the lyric. He responded by echoing the stanza structure of her lyric and following its rhyme:

> Remember preparing lessons together in the study,
> My bride is none other than she.
> A small boat arrives, visiting Wuling in the spring,

---

5. Translation of *Linjiang xian* 臨江仙.
6. [Hu]die fen [蝴]蝶粉, "the pink dust on the wings of butterflies," implies virginity alongside its parallel term, fenghuang 蜂黃, "yellow powder on the body of bees." Luo Dajing 羅大經 (1196–1252?) of the Song dynasty quotes the *Daozang jing* 道藏经 in volume 14 of his *Helin yulu* 鶴林玉露: "After mating, the pink dust on the wings of butterflies fades and the yellow powder on the body of bees/wasps disappears" 蝶交則粉退,蜂交則黃退. See *Helin yulu* 2nd print (Beijing: Zhonghua shuju, 1997), p.2.
7. Shexiang chen 麝香塵, women's fragrant make-up powder.
8. Tiyu youyun 殢雨尤雲, entangled with rain and clouds, is a metaphor for lovemaking.

A divine abode near the Purple Palace,[9]
A world separated from human society.

Swearing by sea and mountains, your heart already promised,
A few light smiles and gentle frowns,
Still you repeatedly talk to me.
In my mind there is no other thought,
After coming to your home, who else could I love?

As for the happiness of the two getting along together, nothing is sufficient to describe it—even peacocks ascending into red clouds, or mandarin ducks swimming in crystal clear water.

But before even a year had passed, Zhang Shicheng and his brothers rose up in arms in Gaoyou,[10] capturing all of the prefectures along the Huai River. Cuicui was also captured by General Li, a military officer under Zhang.

At the end of the Zhizheng reign period,[11] Zhang Shicheng had opened up a vast separatist territory spanning north and south along the river[12] and also controlled western Zhejiang. Then he reconciled with the Yuan court, expressing his willingness to respect the Yuan emperor's authority.[13] The way was then opened for people to travel without hindrance.

The scholar thus took leave of his parents and parents-in-law to search for his wife, swearing that he would never return until he found her. When he traveled to Pingjiang,[14] he heard that General Li was defending Shaoxing[15]; when he reached Shaoxing, he learned that General Li's soldiers had been switched to being quartered in Anfeng[16]; turning around, he headed to Anfeng, where he found out that they had gone back to be stationed in Huzhou.[17]

    9. Zifu 紫府, "Purple Palace," refers to the immortal residence in Daoism, as the *xianju* 仙居.
    10. As part of the anti-Yuan Red Turban rebellion, rebel Zhang Shicheng 張士誠 (1321–1367) captured the city of Gaoyou (in modern Jiangsu province) in 1353 and the next year established his kingdom, Dazhou 大周 there.
    11. 1341–1367.
    12. Zhang established this area as the kingdom of Dazhou in 1354 and named himself its king.
    13. Zhengshuo 正朔, the first day of a year or the new calendar promulgated by the first emperor of a dynasty, is taken as sign here of his authority.
    14. Present-day Suzhou in Jiangsu.
    15. Present-day Shaoxing in Zhejiang province.
    16. Present-day Shou County in Anhui province.
    17. Present-day Huzhou City in Zhejiang province.

2. The Tale of Cuicui

The scholar came and went all along the Huai River, enduring all kinds of dangers and difficulties. While time elapsed, his pockets and bags were also emptied, but even so his will to find Cuicui never slackened. He walked through wilderness and slept out in the open, begging people for assistance, so he was able to reach Huzhou.

General Li held power with an exalted position, his authority blazing brightly. The scholar stood for a long time outside the walls of his residence, hesitating as he watched, finding himself prompted to move forward but unable to do so, wanting to ask questions but not daring to do so. The gatekeeper found his actions rather strange and asked him what he wanted.

"I'm from Huai'an," he replied. "Since the confusion there, I heard that one of my younger sisters is in this noble residence; so a thousand *li* couldn't keep me away. I've come in hopes of seeing her again."

The gatekeeper then asked, "If that's so, what's your name? How old is your sister and what's she look like? I want to get as many details as possible so I can look carefully into the matter."

The scholar told him, "My surname's Liu, my proper name is Jinding and hers is Cuicui. She knows how to read and can also write. At the time we were split up, she was seventeen. Calculating the years that have passed, she's now twenty-four."

Upon hearing this, the gatekeeper told him, "There's a Huai'an lady named Liu in the mansion whose age is like what you're describing. She's well-read and pretty adept at poetry, a very intelligent person, so she's been given special favor in the general's house. If what you say is true, I'll go inside and tell them. But for now, you just wait here." Then he hurried in to report.

In moments, he reemerged and led the scholar inside to see the general, who sat at the head of the hall. The scholar kowtowed twice and then stood up to relate his reason for coming to see his sister. The general, an honorable warrior, had no suspicions about trusting Ding's story, thus he sent his inner servant to go tell Cuicui, "Your brother has arrived from your hometown, so you should come out to see him."

When she received his instructions, Cuicui came out and the two exchanged the outward signs of courtesy between brother and sister. Apart from asking questions about their parents, they couldn't utter a single word, but could only stand there, face to face, all choked up.

"You've come from so far away," the general remarked, "taking the roads of an arduous journey, you must be fatigued physically and mentally. You can rest within these walls and I'll find a place for you later on." Right then he took out a new suit of clothing and asked Ding to put it on. Furthermore, he set up things like a curtain, bed clothing, and a mat in a small study near the western gate and let him settle in there.

The next day, he informed the scholar, "Your sister can read well. Are you also proficient in your reading skills?"

Ding replied, "Though I'm from the country, I'm pursuing Confucian studies as a means of livelihood and taking book-learning as my foundation. I have cursorily read all of the classics, histories, and books of the masters, as well as anthologies by individual authors. These are what I usually practiced upon, so there's no doubt about it."

Overjoyed, General Li told him:

> I was unable to go to school during my childhood, and I've just taken advantage of the rebellion to rise quickly. Now I'm entrusted with duty by the times. My followers are numerous, and visitors always fill my home, but there's no one here to welcome and entertain them; the letters have started piling up on my desk, yet there's no one here to reply to them. You may serve in my office as a secretary, which you are qualified to do.

The scholar was an intelligent man, gentle by nature, and his talent was also outstanding. While serving in the general's office, he disciplined himself strictly; in association with those above him and those below him, he made them all happy; while writing letters on behalf of General Li, he always expressed Li's ideas fastidiously and thoroughly. General Li was greatly pleased to have acquired such a man and so treated him very generously.

But the scholar had originally come to seek his wife, and after seeing her before the hall, he'd had no additional chance to do so. Her bedroom was deep inside the compound, completely isolated from the outside. Despite wanting to express his thoughts to her, there was no convenient way for him to do so.

Several months slipped by imperceptibly till the time for preparing winter clothes,[18] and a western wind began to stir as sunset and dew turned to frost. Alone in his study, Jin Ding was unable to sleep all night, so instead he composed a poem:

> The beautiful flowers moved inside the jade railing,
> The spring scenery is no longer to be viewed.

---

18. Shouyi 授衣, preparing, or giving, winter clothes. It also refers to the ninth month, when winter clothing needs to be prepared. "Qiyue" 七月 in the *Shijing* 詩經 (Classic of Odes): "In the seventh month, the [planet] Mars passes the meridian; in the 9th month, clothes are prepared/given" 七月流火,九月授衣.

How could one in the place of delight know the bitterness of one in anxiety;
It is easy to depart but hard to meet again!
When can we return home together, like the lost horse of the Northern Pass?
Tonight, however, I'll dance alone in the hall!
How deep is your misty chamber and cloudy windows?
What a shame! We now can only waste the bright full moon![19]

Once it was finished, he wrote it onto a piece of paper and sewed it into the collar of his garment. Then taking a hundred copper coins, he gave them to a servant, and told him, "Since the weather's already turned cold and my clothes are very thin, please give this to my sister so she can wash it and sew it up for me to keep out the cold." As requested, the servant took the clothing in to give to her.

Cuicui understood his meaning and undid the stitching, where she found the poem, which greatly increased her distress. Choking back sobs as she wept, she finished her own poem, also sewing it back inside the clothing, and returned it to the scholar. The poem read:

Since our native place became a battlefield,
How many old sorrows have turned to new anguish!
My heart is broken, yet my feelings for you have never stopped,
I won't be with you while I live, but I will after death.
Constantly I hoped to let you, like Deyan, hide a broken mirror,[20]
Finally, I caused you, my Zijian, to write a poem about a swimming dragon,[21]

---

19. According to Chinese tradition, when the moon is full, it is a good time for family reunion. It was indeed a shame that the moon was full at that time, when Jin Ding was separated from his wife.

20. Scholar Xu Deyan 徐德言 of the Southern dynasties lost his wife, the princess of Lechang 樂昌, during turmoil, and they were finally reunited by both hiding half of a broken mirror.

21. Cao Zhi 曹植, styled 子建, was the younger brother of Emperor Wen of Wei 魏 (Cao Pi 曹丕; r. 220–226) during the Three Kingdoms period (220–280) and a famous poet. One of his best-known works is the "Rhapsody on Goddess of the Luo River" 洛神賦, in which the goddess is depicted as "dancing lightly as a startled swan and moving gracefully as a swimming dragon" 翩若驚鴻,宛若游龍.

The idea in the mind of Green Pearl and Emerald Jade,[22]
Unexpectedly, has reached me today!

When the scholar received the poem, he could tell from it that Cuicui was promising him to die, so he no longer had hope, which made him feel all the more depressed and gloomy till he succumbed to a serious and protracted illness.

Cuicui pleaded [with] the general and was allowed to pay her respects once, but by then the scholar was already critically ill. She took his arm and helped him sit up, and as he raised his head to glance sideways at her, tears filling his eyes, with a long sigh he suddenly died. General Li pitied him and had him buried at the foot of Daochang Mountain.[23]

Cuicui attended the funeral service and then went back, but that same night she fell sick and refused to take any medicine, tossing and turning in her bed for almost two months, till one day she informed the general:

> It has already been eight years since I abandoned my family to follow you; I've drifted away to an unfamiliar place where there are no relatives when I raise my eyes. I had just one brother, and now he's dead. I'm ill and will not recover, thus I beg you to bury my bones alongside my brother's, so he'll be there to support me in the underworld and I won't be a wandering, lonely soul there.

As her words ended, she died.

In order not to violate her wishes, the general laid her to rest on the left side of the scholar's tomb, as though there were two graves there, one on the east and the other on the west.

By the beginning of Hongwu's reign,[24] Zhang Shicheng had already been exterminated.

---

22. Green Pearl 綠珠 was the favored maid of Shi Chong 石崇 (249–300) of the Jin, and Emerald Jade 碧玉 was the favored maid of Qian Zhizhi 喬知之 of the Tang. Both of them were taken by a powerful man, but each committed suicide for the sake of her old lord.

23. Three miles south of modern Huzhou city in Zhejiang.

24. Founder of the Ming dynasty, the Hongwu Emperor reigned 1368–1398; Zhang Shicheng died in 1367.

Cuicui's family had a former servant who did business as a trader, and as he was on the road to Huzhou, he passed by the foot of Daochang Mountain and saw the red-lacquered gate of a magnificent house, set off by locust trees and willows—and there stood Cuicui with Scholar Jin, leaning against his shoulder.

They quickly called for the former servant to come inside, where they asked about whether their parents were still living, and about old affairs in their hometown.

"Lady," asked the servant, "how did you and the young master come to live here?"

Cuicui replied, "It started with the havoc caused by war. I was captured by General Li, and when my husband came from far away to try to locate me, General Li didn't stand in the way, so he returned me to my husband and then we came to live here."

"I am leaving today to return to Huai'an," the former servant told her, "so you may want to write a letter to your parents."

Cuicui invited him to stay overnight, cooked him some fragrant Wuxing[25] sticky rice and a soup made from fresh carp of Shaoxi,[26] and took out Wucheng[27] wine for him to drink.

The next day, Cuicui wrote a letter to her parents that read,

> Humbly acknowledging my parents who gave birth to me, it's difficult for me to repay their infinite benevolence. Marital harmony has long been shown as the righteousness of the three obediences.[28] With their relationship so well-established, yet current events have made things so difficult!
>
> Formerly, the sun of the Han was in decline, and the aggressive atmosphere of Chu became very fierce.[29] Since the authority held the handle of the Tai'e sword in a wrong way,[30] the rebels acted

---

25. Present-day Wuxing district of Huzhou city in Zhejiang province.

26. Tiaoxi 苕溪, Tiao River, originates from Tianmu Mount in Zhejiang and enters Taihu lake 太湖 at Huzhou.

27. Present-day Huzhou city in Zhejiang.

28. The three authorities to whom women were traditionally obliged: before marriage, to obey the father; once married, to obey the husband; and after the husband's death, to obey the son.

29. The depiction here is not in accord with history, as the Yuan rulers were Mongolian, not from the Han people.

30. The meaning here is to give others a hold over oneself. Tai'e sword 太阿劍 is a legendary sword that symbolizes power.

without restraint or authority, like children playing with weapons in the pond.[31] Just like big pigs and long snakes, they preyed on each other; everyone, male and female, fled for their lives.[32] I could not die gloriously when made homeless by war, so instead I lived hastily an ignoble existence. I ran around frenetically with the warhorses, and always followed the troops on a long journey. As I look up into the high heavens, unable to fly free even if I had eight wings, and think of my hometown, my three souls have been torn from me repeatedly.[33]

Good days are easy to pass, how pitiful that the green simurgh[34] became companion to the woodcock; an unhappy couple became enemies, fearing the crows who strike at the crimson phoenix. Though I treated him[35] with courtesy to please myself, in the end I became sentimental, and sadness grew. In the light of the moon, the cuckoo cried; in the spring breeze, I dreamed of the butterflies.

But time passes, things move along, and after suffering comes happiness.

Now, General Li followed Yang Su, who saw the broken mirror and sent another's wife home,[36] and Wang Dun, who opened the door to his seraglio and released his maidens.[37] At Penglai Island, I fulfilled my previous promise, and at Xiaoxiang I reunited with my husband.[38]

I am self-pitying for what a harsh fate has been stored up for me, but I don't resent seeking for a spring that came so late.

31. Huangchi nongbing 潢池弄兵, refers to people overstating their ability and rebelling.
32. Xiongfeng cidie 雄峰雌蝶 here refers to crowds of people, male and female.
33. The Daoist concept of three *hun* (三魂) includes the *shuangling* (爽灵) or "bright soul," the *youjing* (幽精) or "secretive soul," and the *taiguang* (胎光) or "light of fetus."
34. Qingluan 青鸾, a legendary divine bird resembling the phoenix.
35. A reference to General Li.
36. This is the same story mentioned in footnote 20. Once captured, the princess Lechang ended up as minister Yang Su's 楊素 concubine, but eventually he learned of the mirror halves and restored her to her husband, Xu Deyan.
37. Wang Dun 王敦 (266–324), a general and prime minister of the Eastern Jin, was notorious as a womanizer. Accepting the remonstration of his retainer, one day he opened his back door and released several dozens of his maids and concubines.
38. The *Classic of Mountains and Seas* 山海經 lists Penglai Island as one of five islands that were reputedly the homes of the immortals.

The willow branch of Zhang Terrace was already broken by others,[39] but the [change of] peach blossoms of Xuandu Temple still didn't change the mind of Mr. Liu.[40]

I suppose that a sunken bottle cannot be found, and a broken hairpin cannot be rejoined. How could I expect the given-away jade and lost pearls to be returned?[41] It's almost the same as the maid

39. Zhangtai 章台, "Zhang Terrace," was a street in Chang'an filled with brothels. "Zhang Terrace willows" refers to prostitutes or women who cannot remain faithful to their husbands. Based on Xu Yaozuo's 許堯佐 "Liu shi zhuan" 柳氏傳 (The Tale of Miss Liu), the famous Tang dynasty poet Han Yi's 韓翊 favorite concubine, Miss Liu, was taken by a foreign general, Shazhali 沙吒利. Han sent her a poem which read:

"Zhang Terrace Willow, Zhang Terrace Willow,
Yesteryear so green and fresh, do you now still live or no?
Even if bough after bough seem to trail down as of old,
Some surely were pulled down and plucked by other hands."
"章台柳,章台柳!昔日青青今在否?
縱使條條似舊垂,亦應攀折他人手。"
Miss Liu responded with the following poem:
"What willow branches, in their fragrant season
Year after year hate: being given to those who part.
Though just one leaf has followed the wind in response to autumn,
Even if my lord should come, how should I be worth plucking!"
"楊柳枝,芳菲節,所恨年年贈離別。
一葉隨風忽報秋,縱使君來豈堪折!"

See Richard Lynn's translation in Victor Mair and Zhenjun Zhang, eds., *Anthology of Tang and Song Tales: The Tang Song chuanqi ji of Lu Xun* (Singapore: World Scientific, 2020), pp. 86–7.

40. The famous Tang dynasty poet Liu Yuxi 劉禹錫 (772–842) was banished from the capital Chang'an as a local governor twice, but each time when he returned he would go to enjoy the peach blossoms at the Xuandu Temple, leaving a popular poem each time. The later one includes such a line, "The former Mr. Liu has come again now" 前度劉郎今又來.

41. Bifan 璧返 refers to the historical story about Lin Xiangru 藺相如, the clever and brave prime minister of the Zhao State during the Warring States period, who brought Mr. He's jade back to Zhao from Qin; Zhuhuan 珠還 refers to lost pearls that were returned. According to *Hou Han shu* 後漢書 (Vol. 76), Hepu 合浦 commandery produced pearls, but because the corrupted officials there gathered them excessively, they were transferred to another place. When the new governor, Meng Chang, re-established the old harvesting policy, the pearls all returned.

Yuxiao's two-incarnation marriage,[42] but that hardly compares to the Lady of Red Whisks who married her own man right then.[43] Heaven gave me a convenience, and it was not by accident. I heat the glue and connect the broken instrument's string—restoring harmony again through firm attachment[44]; entrusting a fish belly with a letter in it, I send you my news.[45] I wasn't able to serve you, now I just express my greetings to you.

When Cuicui's father and mother received her letter, they were overjoyed. Her father immediately rented a boat and, with a servant, went from Huai'an to Zhejiang, then rushed straight to Wuxing. When they reached the place at the foot of Mount Daochang, where the couple had stayed in the past, they found it deserted and overgrown with weeds, with fox and rabbit tracks across the paths. The houses that were seen in the past were merely a pair of graves, one on the east and the other on the west. When they were puzzled and about to make inquiries, it happened that a Buddhist monk passed by with a tin staff, so they bowed respectfully and asked him their questions.

He said to Cuicui's father, "These are the graves where General Li buried Scholar Jin and the young woman, Cuicui, so how can anyone be living here?" Mr. Liu was frightened terribly, looking at the letter again—now it was just a blank piece of paper.

42. When Wei Gao 韋皋 of the Tang was young, he visited governor Jiang and fell in love with one of his maids, named Yuxiao, but when he left and didn't return for seven years, Yuxiao died of melancholy. Many years later, Wei Gao became the governor of Xichuan, and on his birthday someone presented him with a beautiful girl also named Yuxiao, whose appearance was the same as the former Yuxiao and on her finger was the ring he formerly sent the girl as a gift. So their marriage was called a two-incarnation marriage.

43. Hongfu 紅拂, the Lady of the Red Whisks, was a maid of general Yang Su (544–606) of the Sui dynasty. She fell in love with Li Jing 李靖, a heroic young man who was presenting advice to Yang as a visitor, and she fled with him at night and they became husband and wife.

44. To connect the broken instrument's string implies recovering or repairing a broken marriage.

45. Sending a letter through a fish belly is frequently found in old poems of the late Han, for example: "A guest has come from afar, who gave me a pair of carps. I asked my child to cook the carp, and inside it he found a one-foot long silk letter." 客從遠方來,遺我雙鯉魚。呼童烹鯉魚, 中有尺素書。

By that time, General Li had been executed by the reigning dynasty, so they had no way to get any details from him. Cuicui's father wept over her grave, saying:

> You deceived me with a letter, telling me to come a thousand *li* to this place because you wanted to see me. Now I'm here, but you've concealed all traces of yourself. When you were alive, I was already your father, so why must we be separated after your death? If your soul is numinous, don't be stingy and deny me a look at you. That will clear up all of my doubts.

That night, he stayed at the gravesite.

Following the third watch, he discovered Cuicui and Scholar Jin kneeling and kowtowing before him, crying piteously in deep sorrow. Cuicui's father wept with them and asked what had happened, and then she described the whole story to him:

> Back then, during the internal strife, soldiers rose up in the neighboring commandery. I couldn't devote myself to virginity like the daughter of the Dou family,[46] and then I was taken by a general like Shazhali.[47] I endured humiliation and an ignoble existence, separated from my hometown and homeland. I felt angry that, being a lady as feeble as an orchid, I was matched by such a stupid broker, who knew only to grab the maid from the Shi family,[48] but never cared about the woman from Xi State who kept constant silence.[49] I called at the gate of the Nine Heavens but found no way to get through, and one day for me was like three autumns.
>
> My husband hadn't forgotten about our past happiness together, so he had been especially diligent in traveling great distances to search for me. He pretended we were brother and sister as he gave out our

---

46. In Fengtian county during the Tang, two girls of the Dou family, Boniang 伯娘 and Zhongniang 仲娘, jumped off a cliff to avoid being raped by robbers.
47. See note 5 above.
48. Refering to Green Pearl, the maid of Shi Chong.
49. During the Spring and Autumn period, King Wen of Chu annihilated the state of Xi 息 and took its beautiful queen, Lady Xi, back home. Lady Xi gave birth to two sons for him but kept silence for years. When King Wen asked her why, her reply was, "As a woman, I married two husbands. Since I could not die for integrity, what else could I say?" (The 14th year of Duke Zhuang, *Zuozhuan* 左傳).

names, thus we were only granted a look at each other; a couple separated despite our feelings of love, there was no way for us to associate with each other. Finally, Jin Ding fell ill and died first, then, suffering over our great wrongs, I also perished. We hoped that we would be buried together; luckily we fulfilled that wish and thus were able to return together. This is a general summary; as for the details, they are beyond depiction.

Her father replied, "I came here originally wanting to take you home, in order for you to take care of me. But now that you've already passed away, I'll just take your bones and move them to our ancestral burial ground, so my trip won't be entirely wasted."

Cuicui wept again as she declared:

When I was alive, unfortunately, I wasn't able to care filially for my parents; after death, I had no chance to be buried in my hometown. However, the way of the earth cherishes tranquility and the reasoning of the spirit values stability, so moving my body would actually be a disturbance. Furthermore, the rivers and mountains here are beautiful, and the vegetation luxuriant and glorious. Since we have already been buried here peacefully, moving is not what I want.

She thus embraced her father while crying loudly. Her father was suddenly startled awake, realizing it had been a dream.

The next day, he made animal sacrifices and poured wine libations at the graves, then with the servant returned to the boat and went back home.

It is said that, to the present day, a passerby can still point out the locations and tell you that they're the graves of Jin Ding and Cuicui.

NOTES AND READING GUIDE

Zhenjun Zhang and Sidney Sondergard

This tale is from Chapter 3 of Qu You's *Jiandeng xinhua*. Among the moving love stories in the collection, "The Tale of Cuicui" is one of the most brilliant pieces and has long been favored by scholars and selected for inclusion in a variety of collections.

I. Tragic Love in the Turbulence of Warfare

Tragic love in the turbulence of warfare is a prominent theme in Ming dynasty tales. Noted pieces featuring this theme include "Qiuxiang ting ji" 秋香亭記 (Autumn Fragrance Pavilion) and the "Lüyi ren zhuan" 綠衣人傳 (The Tale of the Lady in Green). But the representative work is beyond doubt "The Tale of Cuicui."

In this tale Liu Cuicui falls in love with her classmate and marries him happily, but in the turbulence of war at the end of the Yuan dynasty, she falls into the hands of a general. Her husband travels thousands of miles to search for her but is unable to reunite with her until they have both died. Through detailed depiction of the miserable experience of this couple, the tale reflects the disaster and pain brought about by the lasting warfare between the Yuan and Ming dynasties.

Liu Cuicui, born into a family of wealthy commoners, is a social anomaly as a woman who is naturally adept at study, understands the Confucian classics as deeply as any of her male age peers and is also a talented poet. The equally skilled young scholar she studies with and privately chooses as her future mate, Jin Ding, is from a poor family whose economic disparity with the Liu family makes it impossible for them to accept a marriage proposal without feeling shamed. Because of Cuicui's devotion to love, the Lius, wanting Cuicui to be happy, accept the advice of a marriage broker offer to have Jin Ding marry into their family, rather than Cuicui marrying into the Jin family. This tactic seems to dissolve all worries, and the future seems bright for the young couple.

Unfortunately, the advent of the Red Turban Rebellion leads to Cuicui being taken captive by rebel forces while scholar Ding is forced to search for her with few resources for support. His extraordinarily wide-ranging pursuit reduces him to begging, but his resolve to find his wife never wavers. His loyalty elevates him to the level of heroism for the reader as he continually puts aside his own sufferings in order to determine Cuicui's whereabouts. He pretends to be her brother when he learns that she is living in the household of rebel General Li, adopting the identity of Liu Jinding, a hybrid name that actually reflects his marriage into the Liu family, but is allowed to see her only briefly, robbing them—and the reader—of the joy of reconciliation.

Learning that the young man is a scholar of talent like Cuicui's (who is treated with special respect by the General and his household due to her literacy and poetic skill), the illiterate General Li hires him to serve as his private secretary. Jin Ding takes his work seriously and performs it proficiently, despite his constant obsession to be reunited with Cuicui. Because he acts so selflessly and responsibly, the reader feels encouraged to hope that his efforts will be rewarded at some future point so he and Cuicui can continue their lives together.

Realizing after several months that they simply will not have the opportunity to be together again, they secretly exchange poetic expressions of their despair over the situation. Jin Ding sickens and by the time Cuicui receives permission to visit him, it is too late—and she, too, dies at the conclusion of his funeral service.

If the story ended here with the General burying them side by side, it might be considered tragic, a dark turn to the apparent fairy tale romance of the opening section of the narrative. But then it wouldn't truly be a *zhiguai* tale.

It takes the discovery by a former servant of the Liu family that Cuicui and Ding are apparently alive and living at the foot of Mt. Daochang— where they were buried by General Li—to initiate a supernatural turn in the story. Cuicui writes a lengthy letter for the servant to deliver to her parents, expressing both her sorrow over the exigencies of fate and her regret that she has been unable to fulfill her filial duties to them. Her father's excited journey to Daochang leads him not to a happy homestead, but instead to a pair of overgrown graves.

Overwhelmed by grief and disappointment, he weeps over Cuicui's grave and chides her for sending them false hope and demands that she appear to them. When the young couple appear that night, it is to explain everything they had faced during the years of their separation. Once again, the story seems poised for some kind of reconciliation— only to have the father awaken suddenly after being embraced by his daughter. Recognizing that it had been a dream, he makes sacrifices and libations before returning home.

The story records the tragedies of personal and political upheavals in a time of regime change and ends on a note that is implicitly positive: like "The Tale of Cuicui" itself, which confers a kind of immortality to Liu Cuicui and Jin Ding, the location of their graves, according to the story's narrator, are still known even "to the present day" to passersby.

II. Elegent, Effective, and Detailed Depictions

With the charm of its concise, passionate narration, gorgeous rhetoric, and beautiful wording, the author of this tale tries to follow the style of narrative of Tang dynasty tales. The inclusion of poems, parallel sentences, and allusions adds literary color and shows the characteristics of writings by literati authors.

The depictions of the couple's first meeting after they had been lost to each other, and of Jin Ding's death, are among the most touching ones:

> When she received his instructions, Cuicui came out and the two exchanged the outward signs of courtesy between brother and sister. Apart from asking questions about their parents, they couldn't utter a single word, but could only stand there, face to face, all choked up.
>
> When the scholar received the poem, he could tell from it that Cuicui was promising him to die, so he no longer had hope, which made him feel all the more depressed and gloomy till he succumbed to a serious and protracted illness.
>
> Cuicui requested to visit the general and was allowed to pay her respects once, but by then the scholar was already critically ill. She took his arm and helped him sit up, and as he raised his head to glance sideways at her, tears filling his eyes, with a long sigh he suddenly died.

The following poem by Cuicui is not only moving, but also applies allusions brilliantly:

> Since our native place became a battlefield,
> How many old sorrows have turned to new anguish!
> My heart is broken, yet my feelings for you have never stopped,
> I won't be with you while I live, but I will after death.
> Constantly I hoped to let you, like Deyan, hide a broken mirror,

Finally, I caused you, my Zijian, to write a poem about a swimming dragon.
The idea in the mind of Green Pearl and Emerald Jade,
Unexpectedly, has reached me today!

No matter whether through narration or poem, the depictions of events and psychological status of people here are beyond doubt more detailed comparing with those in earlier classical tales. It is likely that this is from the influence of vernacular stories in storytelling tradition, as some scholars suggest.[50]

III. The Influence of This Tale

Because of its contents, the moving love story, and its splendid writing, "The Tale of Cuicui" immediately became influential, even during the Ming dynasty.

The vernacular story, "Li Jiangjun cuiren jiu, Liu shi guicong fu" 李將軍錯認舅, 劉氏女詭從夫 (General Li Accepts a Brother-in-law by Mistake, the Daughter of Li Family Follows Her Husband Slyly), in Ling Mengchu's (1580–1644) *Erke pai'an jingqi* 二刻拍案驚奇 (Sequel to Slapping the Table in Amazement, Second Collection), is derived from it. However, apart from some detailed depictions, such as how the general urged Cuicui to give up her resistance, which are added, the plot of Ling's vernacular version of the story is basically the same as it is in the classical tale.

In addition to Ling's work, the Ming dynasty drama, *Jin Cui hanyi ji* 金翠寒衣記 (Records of Jin and Cui's Cold Clothes) by Ye Xianzu 葉憲祖 (1566–1641), is also derived from "The Tale of Cuicui." Differing from the tale, however, the drama features a happy ending: on the street Jin Ding stops the horse of the general of the Ming, Xu Da 徐達, and complains to him, thus Xu has General Li killed and allows Jin Ding to reunite with his wife Cuicui.[51] It has been suggested online that Ye Xianzu's play was one of the sources of Ling Mengchu's story. This is clearly inaccurate.

---

50. See Wu Zhida 吳志達, *Zhongguo wenyan xiaoshuoshi* 中國文言小説史 (Jinan: Qi Lu shushe, 1994), p. 690.

51. See Zhou Yibai 周貽白, *Mingren zajuxuan* 明人雜劇選 (Beijing: Renmin wenxue chubanshe, 1956), pp. 453–71.

2. The Tale of Cuicui

In the Qing dynasty work, the tale in "Lingtou shu" 領頭書 by Yuan Sheng 袁聲 (fl. 1692), after death and living as a couple in the netherworld, with the assistance of a Buddhist both Cuicui and Jin Ding are revived and reunited as living people. Moreover, by passing the civil service examination, Jin Ding finally becomes an official in the government.[52]

---

52. See juan 23, *Quhai zongmu tiyao* 曲海總目提要, in *Zhongguo zhexueshu dianzihua jihua* 中國哲學書電子化計劃, https://ctext.org/wiki.pl?if=gb&chapter=574797

Tale 3

"TAIXU SIFA ZHUAN" 太虛司法傳 (THE ACCOUNT OF THE LEGAL ADMINISTRATOR OF THE GRAND VOID)

By Qu You

Translated by Kelsey Seymour

Feng Dayi, whose personal name was Strange, was a madman in the Wu and Chu regions.[1] He was rather pompous and smug and never believed in ghosts and spirits. Whenever there were demons that would possess grasses or trees to scare people and frighten the masses, he would just push up his sleeves to confront them. When he got there, he would bully and insult them by either burning their shrines or sinking their idols, going forward bravely without consideration of anything. Because of this, people also praised him as courageous.

In the *dingchou* year of the Zhiyuan reign period,[2] he moved to the eastern gate of Shangcai.[3] Once, for a certain reason he went to an old village nearby. It was a time immediately after the ravages of warfare, and the place was entirely empty with no one residing. There were only yellow sands and white bones as far as the eye could see.

Before he had arrived [at his destination], the sun was already setting in the west and dark clouds were gathering from all directions. Since there was no inn, where could he stay overnight? On the side of the road there was an old pine forest, so he went in and leaned up against a tree for a little rest.

Owls and snipes cried in front of him; jackals and foxes howled from behind him. In the next moment, there was a flock of crows flying

---

1. The middle and lower Yangzi River valley, which belonged to the Wu and Chu states during the Spring and Autumn period.
2. There were two Zhiyuan 至元 reign periods during the Yuan, both of which contained a *dingchou* year. The first was in 1277, during the reign of Kublai Khan, and the second was in 1337, during the reign of Ukhaantu Khan.
3. In present-day Henan province.

wing to wing that descended, either standing on one talon cawing, or flapping their wings and dancing about; their cries were sinister as they tightly surrounded him. There were also eight or nine corpses lying rigid around him. A chill wind hissed by; a swift rain suddenly arrived.

When the sound of thunder suddenly clapped, the corpses around him arose. Seeing Feng under the tree, they rushed toward him. Feng hurriedly clambered up the tree to avoid them, and the corpses circled around below. Whether hissing, cursing, sitting, or standing, they loudly said to each other: "Tonight we must get this guy! Otherwise, we will be punished."

After a little while, the clouds cleared and the rain stopped, the moonlight pierced through, and he saw a *yaksha* coming from far away.[4] It had two horns on its head, its whole body was blue, and it cried out as it strode forward, arriving directly under the trees. It gathered up the corpses with its hands, plucked their heads off, and ate them, as if it were swallowing melons whole! When the *yaksha* was done eating, it lay down with its belly full, and the sounds of its snores shook the earth.

Feng thought that he had better not stay there for too long, so taking advantage of the *yaksha* being soundly asleep, he climbed down from the tree and fled. He had not gone more than a hundred paces when the *yaksha* was already at his heels! He ran with a death-defying effort and was still almost caught.

He came upon an abandoned temple and hurriedly cast himself inside. The east and west corridors were both in ruin, and only in the main hall was there still a Buddha statue that was quite enormous. He saw that there was an opening on the Buddha's back. Since he couldn't think of anything else, he threw himself into the hole, nestling in the Buddha's belly.[5] He thought to himself that he had finally found a place to rest, and he need no longer worry.

Suddenly he heard the Buddha statue drum on his belly and laugh, saying: "They chased you and couldn't catch you; I didn't chase you and you arrived on your own accord. Tonight I have this tasty morsel! No need to eat that vegetarian fare!"

---

4. In the Buddhist tradition, *Yakshas* can be either protective or malevolent, but in Chinese texts they are frequently depicted as violent demonic spirits that can fly and consume other ghosts and humans.

5. The irony of literally taking refuge in the Buddha (*guiyi fo* 歸依佛) should not be lost here!

The Buddha then got up with a rumble, but his footsteps were extremely heavy. He went forward about ten paces before he was blocked by the doorway threshold and suddenly tumbled down onto the ground. The statue frame shattered and became strewn rubble.

Feng managed to get out, and he still boasted: "What kind of ghost are you, tricking me? Now you're getting your recompense!" Then he went out of the temple and left.

In a field in the distance, a light glimmered where several people were greeting each other and sitting down. Feng was greatly delighted, and he rushed toward them. When he got there, it turned out that they were all headless. Of those who had heads, they had either lost an arm or lost a foot! Feng fled without looking back.

The ghosts angrily said: "We were just here drinking heartily. This guy has some gall, daring to come here and butt in! We should just catch him and dice him up for dinner!" Then they lurched and howled, some flinging dungballs at him, others casting human bones at him. The headless ones lifted up their heads to chase him.

The path before him was blocked by a river. Feng crossed through the turbulence; when the ghosts reached the river, they didn't dare cross. When he had gone just over a half *li*, Feng looked back. He could still hear a clamor sounding incessantly behind him.

Soon after, the moon had set, and he could no longer distinguish the path. He lost his footing and fell into a hole. It was deep and bottomless; it was the ghost pit. Chilly sand stung his eyes, and a frigid air chilled him to the bone. A group of ghosts gathered around him. There were some with red hair and two horns, some with green fur and two wings, some with bird beaks and tusks, some with ox heads and beast faces; all of them had bodies as [dark as] indigo, and flames spewed from their mouths. When they saw Feng arrive, they applauded to each other: "The enemy is here!"

Then they fastened his neck into iron shackles, tied his waist with a leather cord, led him to the throne of the Ghost King, and reported: "This is precisely the wild man who did not believe in ghosts and spirits and insulted us when he was in the mortal realm."

The Ghost King angrily reproached him:

> You possess a complete body and have knowledge. How could you not have heard of the extensive power of ghosts and spirits? Confucius was a sage, but he still said that you should venerate them, though you should keep a distance from them. The great *Book of Changes* spoke of 'loading a cart of ghosts,' and the 'Lesser Court Hymns' of

the *Book of Odes* speaks of 'behaving as ghost and spirits.' Other texts like the *Zuozhuan* chronicle the dream of Duke Jing of Jin[6] and the matter of Boyou[7] which all deal with these creatures [ghosts]. What kind of person are you that you alone claim ghosts do not exist? We have long suffered your insults! Now we are fortunate to have encountered you; how could I willingly give up [without punishing you]?"

Then he ordered the ghosts to strip Feng of his cap and garments and lash him with a whip until he was dripping with blood. He begged for death, but it was not allowed.

The Ghost King then said to him: "Would you rather we grind you up with mud to make a sauce, or would you rather we stretch your body to a length of three *zhang*?"[8] Feng thought to himself, how could mud make a sauce? So he chose to have his body stretched to three *zhang*.

The ghosts then seized him and placed him on top of a stone platform. They continuously rolled and kneaded him with their hands, as if rolling dough, and unconsciously he began to slowly stretch. When they finished and pulled him up, he was indeed three *zhang*, delicate and thin as a bamboo pole. They all laughed and insulted him, calling him a "long-pole monster."

The King again said to him: "Would you rather be boiled with rocks to make a mush, or would you rather be squashed down to a height of one *chi*?"[9] Feng had just suffered being lengthened, and he could not stand on his own, so he chose to be squashed down to one *chi*. The ghosts again forced him onto a stone platform. Just like pressing dough, they pushed him down with extreme force, causing his bones and joints to snap and crack. Then they gathered him up, and he was indeed one *chi* and round like a giant crab. They all laughed and insulted him, calling him a "crab monster." Feng tottered on the ground, unable to bear the pain.

On one side there was an old ghost who clapped his hands and laughed heartily, saying: "You didn't believe in ghosts and monsters

---

6. Duke Jing 景 of Jin dreamed of a vengeful spirit after killing officials in the state of Song.

7. After being killed in battle, the ghost of Boyou appeared in a dream to give the death dates of his defeaters Si Dai 駟帶 and Gongsun Duan 公孫段.

8. 9.6 m, 31.5 feet.

9. About one foot.

before; but why do you have this form today?" He then asked his companions: "Although he has been so rude, he has also greatly suffered disgrace. We should show some pity, please pardon him!" Then he lifted Feng by his hands and shook him. In a moment he recovered his original shape.

Feng pleaded to return [to the mortal realm], and the ghosts replied: "Since you came all the way here, we can't let you go empty-handed! We each have something to give you, so that the mortal realm can know about us." The old ghost said: "In that case, what would you like to give to him?"

One ghost said: "I will give him cloud-brushing horns." Then two horns were placed on Feng's forehead, lofty and parallel to each other. One ghost said: "I will give him a whistling-wind beak." Then an iron beak was attached to his lips, as pointy as a bird's bill. One ghost said: "I will give him hair of vermillion splendor." Then he dyed Feng's hair with red water; it all became disheveled and stood on end, and the color was like fire. One ghost said: "I will give him eyes of jade radiance." Then he took two green pearls and inlaid them in Feng's eyes, glowing a deep jade color.

The old ghost then sent him out of the tunnel, saying: "Please take good care of yourself! As for the teasing you've just suffered from us lowly ghosts, please do not take offense!"

Although Feng managed to get out, he still had the cloud-brushing horns, the whistling-wind beak, the hair of vermillion splendor, and the eyes of jade radiance, as if he himself had become a bizarre ghost.

When he got home, his wife and children would not dare recognize him. He went out to the market and everyone gathered around to gawk at him, thinking that he was a monster; small children cried in fright and fled. Thereupon he shut himself up in his home and refused to eat. He died of resentment.

When he was about to die, he said to his family:

> I was imprisoned and harassed by the ghosts, and now I am going to die! Would you please place some additional paper and brushes in the coffin? I am going to sue them from the Celestial Court. Within several days there will be a marvel in Caizhou.[10] This will be the moment that I get justice, and you can then make a libation in my honor.

10. In present-day Henan.

When he finished speaking, he died.

After three days, on a clear day, there was a sudden burst of wind and rain. Fog poured out into the four directions, and there were claps of thunder and bolts of lightning, their sound shaking the universe. Tiles flew off the roofs, and big trees were uprooted. A whole night passed before it started to clear up. Then the pit that Feng had fallen into became submerged in an enormous pond, inundated several *li* across. The water was all red.

Suddenly a voice spoke from within the coffin: "The lawsuit has been successful! The ghosts have all been completely executed! Also because of my righteousness, the heavenly ministry has appointed me as the Legal Administrator of the Court of the Grand Void. This is a very grand and important position, and I will never again return to the mortal world."

His family offered sacrifices and buried him; a sound spread loudly, as if there was a supernatural occurrence.

NOTES AND READING GUIDE

Kelsey Seymour

The short tale "The Account of the Legal Administrator of the Grand Void" (*Taixu sifa zhuan* 太虛司法傳) appears as the second entry of the fourth volume of Qu You's seminal collection *New Stories Told while Trimming the Wick* (*Jiandeng xinhua*).[11] With his grotesque depictions of ghosts and torture, Qu You here embraces the horror elements of strange tales (*zhiguai*). He introduces the reader to a murky setting on the edges of society, rife with supernatural, malevolent beings. The protagonist, a skeptical scholar by the name of "Unusual Feng" (Feng Dayi 馮大異), has his worldview abruptly overturned when he comes face to face with the very beings he ridiculed and refused to believe in—ghosts. Three of the themes that stand out in this tale are belief vs. skepticism, justice, and unnaturalness.

I. Belief vs. Skepticism

The tale begins with an introduction to Unusual Feng, explaining that he does not believe in ghosts and spirits. His disbelief allows him to go as far as slandering supernatural beings and even desecrating their sites. The reason behind his skepticism is never explained, but it is the driving force behind the entirety of the plot.[12]

---

11. For additional translations and annotations of this story, see: Iizuka Akira 飯塚朗, trans., "Tengoku no saibankan ni natta otoko no hanashi" 天国の裁判官になった男の話 (太虛司法傳) [The Story of the Man Who Became a Heavenly Judge], in *Sentou shinwa* 剪燈新話 [New Stories Told While Trimming the Wick] (Tokyo 東京: Heibonsha 平凡社, 1965), pp. 206–14; Qiao Guanghui 喬光輝, ed., "Taixu sifa zhuan" 太虛司法傳 [The Account of the Legal Administrator of the Grand Void], in *Qu You quanji jiaozhu* 瞿佑全集校註 [The Annotated Complete Works of Qu You], Vol. 2 (Hangzhou: Zhejiang guji chubanshe, 2010), pp. 792–8; Judith Zeitlin, trans., "The Regulator of the Ultimate Void by Qu You," *Renditions: A Chinese-English Translation Magazine*, No. 69 (2008): 35–40.

12. Stories about ghosts confronting skeptics to prove their existence are not unprecedented. The story of Ruan Zhan 阮瞻 in the Liu-Song 劉宋 period compilation *You ming lu* 幽明錄 is one such example. As in this story, the ghost debating with Ruan Zhan makes the argument that one should believe in ghosts because they are discussed by past sages. See Zhang Zhenjun, "On the Origins of Detached Soul Motif in Chinese Literature," *Sungkyun Journal of East Asian Studies*, Vol. 9, No. 2 (2009): 178.

Forced to spend a night in the woods, Feng spends the first half of the story encountering things that are not as they appear. First, under the rather poorly chosen tree where he decides to sleep for the night, the nearby corpses turn out to be not quite as immobile as he expected. After fleeing from the woods, he takes refuge in the Buddha, literally, by hiding in the belly cavity of a large Buddha statue. Believing a statue to just be a statue, he is again alarmed to discover that it is in fact conscious, capable of movement, malevolent, and hungry (for him). Managing to escape only through luck, he again flees to an open field where he spots some people in the distance. At this point the pattern has been established: upon closer inspection, these beings are again not what they appear. From afar they seem to be humans, but as he approaches, he sees that they are the living dead, malformed and disjointed with missing limbs and heads.

In the second half of the tale, Feng falls into a ghost pit, a hellish space cut off from the human world and ruled by a frightening ghost king. Here he learns that his lack of belief and consequent actions have offended the whole ghost realm. The ghost king berates him for his lack of belief and lectures him on his shoddy reading of the Classics. All of the great, lofty figures from the past believed in ghosts and the supernatural, the ghost king argues, how could you alone not believe? The evidence is right there in the texts!

Interestingly, here the standard of evidence is the content of the Classics, not the lived experience of Feng in the hours prior to his trial in the ghost pit, nor any prior experiences he may have rejected due to a lack of sufficient evidence. Seeing might be believing, but reading is better. More reliable than the world observed with his eyes or other senses, knowledge from the right texts reveals truths that cannot be uncovered or verified by the senses alone. After all, nothing he observed during the terror-filled time period prior to his fall in the pit was truly what he had originally observed.

II. Justice

The theme of justice appears in various ways in this tale, most notably in the narrative and descriptive parallels to accounts of postmortem trials, in the ghosts' vengeful actions for the wrongs they suffered, and in Feng's final lawsuit to seek justice for his torture and humiliation.

Tales of individuals being spirited away to the underworld to face trial have existed since at least the earliest *zhiguai* collections. The plots more or less follow the same trajectory: the main character dies and finds himself before a judge in the underworld. There, he is asked to explain the deeds of his life so that his sins can be accounted for and punishment doled out accordingly. The main character is often without sin or can make up for past evil deeds by expressing devotion to the Buddha. Thereupon, he is allowed to return to the world of the living and tell others of his experience, but not before first witnessing the gruesome torture and imprisonment of others who were not so lucky.

Feng does not die when he falls into the ghost pit, but the similarities are unmistakable between his experience and other postmortem trial tales. He is brought before a judge—the ghost king—where he is questioned for his wrongs against the ghost community. Perhaps in a subversion of the postmortem trial tale, unlike most lucky protagonists Feng is sentenced to torture. After the torture is carried out, he is released back into the human world.

Feng's actions in the human realm—his disbelief in ghosts, as well as his desecration of sites and constant badmouthing of the supernatural—have earned him some notoriety among the ghostly community. As soon as the first corpses he encounters speak, "Tonight we must get this guy! Otherwise, we will be punished," the reader is left with the impression that the ghosts have been planning and attempting (and possibly failing) to capture him for some time. Qu You briefly takes the reader into the minds of ghosts: they are furious, volatile, and vengeful over the indignity they have suffered, but at moments it makes sense. They want justice for being wronged.

However, by the end of the story we learn that humans are allotted more justice than ghosts. After the original wrong-doer Feng dies, he files a postmortem lawsuit against the ghosts for the torture he was subjected to. The result is that the ghosts are sentenced to death for their deeds, and Feng is even rewarded handsomely with a bureaucratic appointment in the afterlife, despite his ignorance of the Classics and his actions during his life. Reflecting on the judgment issued by the ghost king and the judgment issued by Celestial Court, one might question the difference between revenge and justice. Both the ghosts and Feng sought to retaliate against perceived wrongs. Is the difference then in the content of their grievances or is the difference in the sentencing authority? Has justice truly been served?

III. Unnaturalness

Perhaps Ming readers did not give much thought to the double standards of human and ghost justice, and instead readily accepted the wrongness of ghosts. After all, ghosts—especially the ghosts in this tale—were scary, malicious, harmful, grotesque, and most of all inhuman. In this tale, unnaturalness begins with distance to human order.

Feng's strange encounters take place when he is outside of human society. He comes across a razed village where human presence has been wiped out, and then ventures into the wild, further still from the traces of previous human presence. At first he is not aware of it, but he is treading a border space between the human and ghost realms: still in the human realm but outside the reach of ordered human society; not yet in the ghost realm, but in a space inhabited by ghosts that continually grow more visible. To make matters worse, the encounters occur at night, when it is dark, and humans are meant to be sleeping. Consequently, his physical vision to his surroundings dims, and he is increasingly faced with matters that humans are unconscious of.

Eventually he leaves this peripheral zone and crosses the border into the ghost realm when he falls into the ghost pit. The ghost pit is revealed to be a maximally unnatural space where the laws of anatomy and the rules of life and death no longer apply. Opting for the torture of being stretched to a length of three *zhang*, Feng finds himself placed on a giant platform where he is rolled noodle-thin like a piece of dough. His bones do not break, he remains conscious, and most surprisingly, he survives the distortion of his body. The situation is the similar when he is subsequently squished down to a height of one *chi*. His bones snap in this case, but he is still able to hobble around like a crab. Finally, he is returned to normal in an instant when a ghost lifts and shakes him, and the full length of his body unfolds out like the stretching of the bellows of an accordion.

The damage from the torture is impermanent, but the ghosts also choose to permanently disfigure Feng before allowing him to return to the human realm. They bestow Feng with several "gifts," which are in fact irreversible attachments to his body. Each attachment is presented to him as an enhancement with a supernatural-sounding name, as if it were a magical object being passed on from an immortal. But rather than turning Feng into some kind of extraordinary human, they instead grotesquely disfigure him. This is clear from the horrified reactions to his appearance once he arrives back in the human world. The people in his town's marketplace flee from him, and his family refuses to acknowledge him. In this sense, he is permanently cut off from the human community he strayed away from, even after he is able to return to it, and as a consequence he accepts that the separation is irreversible by locking himself away from society for the remainder of his life.

IV. Conclusion

When we read that Qu You self-censored the collection of stories in *New Stories Told while Trimming the Wick* due to obscene language even before it was formally censored by the government, perhaps this is the type of story he intended to conceal.[13] While it lacks "obscene language" in the sense of expletives and sexual content, the gory and suspenseful subjects are not for the faint of heart, let alone topics for refined and polite conversation.[14] The descriptions of each of the horrors encountered by Feng are grotesque—forests littered with corpses, monsters that swallow heads whole, and dank ghost pits where prisoners are subject to torture.

Moreover, the experiences of injustice, imprisonment, and fear experienced by Unusual Feng were not unfamiliar to Qu You, who witnessed the death of numerous famous vassals when he was young and he himself spent time in prison during the Yongle emperor's reign.[15] That Unusual Feng was able to get justice for his torture, even

---

13. Qu You self-censored because of his own almost obscene language. His works were later banned formally in 1442–1466 after the official Li Shimian expressed distaste, believing they would corrupt people. See Kang-I Sun Chang and Stephen Owen, eds., *The Cambridge History of Chinese Literature, Vol II: From 1375* (Cambridge: Cambridge University Press, 2010), pp. 7, 9–10.

14. Qu You himself recognized that many of the themes in the volume would be perceived as immoral by certain audiences. However, in his preface he states that even "immoral" themes (e.g., eroticism, the supernatural) are found in the classics, such as the *Book of Poetry* and the *Spring and Autumn Annals*. He argues that even fictional popular tales can have a moral component. See Cynthia Brokaw and Kai-wing Chow, *Printing and Book Culture in Late Imperial China* (Berkeley: University of California Press, 2005), p. 157. His audience would have primarily consisted of *haoshizhe* 好事者 ("connoisseurs" or "collectors"). See Brokaw and Chow, *Printing and Book Culture in Late Imperial China*, p. 165.

15. Qu You was sent to prison by the Yongle emperor for reasons unrelated to his literary pursuits. When the younger brother of the emperor was caught for allegedly plotting treason, Qu You was included in the collective punishment of his advisors. Some scholars have argued that themes of the underworld and dragon kingdoms in Ming fiction have served as allegories for the cruelty of the Ming government, while others have claimed them as challenges to Confucian values. See Sun Chang and Owen, *The Cambridge History of Chinese Literature*, pp. 8–9. This argument is also made by scholars such as Huang Min 黃敏 in *Mingdai wenyan duanpian xiaoshuo xuanyi* 明代文言短篇小說選譯, pp. 42–54.

if it took something as extreme as a postmortem lawsuit, may very well have been wishful fantasizing for justice on Qu You's part for his own hardships. By following Unusual Feng through a night of terror and suffering, Qu You invites his readers to share in the feelings of fear and inequity, ultimately asking: Wouldn't you want justice too?

Tale 4

"LÜYI REN ZHUAN" 綠衣人傳
(THE TALE OF THE LADY IN GREEN)

By Qu You

Translated by Yunwen Gao

Zhao Yuan, a native of Tianshui,[1] lost his parents while he was young, and he had not married yet. In the Yanyou era (1314–1320) [of the Yuan dynasty],[2] he traveled as a student to Qiantang,[3] and sojourned upon Ge Hill[4] near

---

This translation is based on the tale in volume 2 of Qiao Guanghui's 喬光輝 *Qu You quanji jiaozhu* 瞿佑全集校注, pp. 817–22. I have also consulted the text in Zhou Yi's 周夷 *Jiandeng xinhua wai erzhong* 剪燈新話外二種, pp. 107–11; An Pingqiu 安平秋, et al., ed., *Jiandeng xinhua* 剪燈新話, pp. 237–44; and National Chengchi University Classical Fiction Research Center, eds., *Jiandeng xinhua*, pp. 23–7.

1. Tianshui 天水 is located in modern-day Guansu Province. According to Zhou Yi, the author indicated here that the Zhao clan was a prominent clan of Tianshui. Zhao Yuan was not necessarily born and brought up in Tianshui. See Zhou Yi, ed., *Jiandeng xinhua wai erzhong*, p. 110.

2. Yanyou 延祐 was the second era name adopted by Emperor Renzong of Yuan (r. 1311–1320). Emperor Renzong, named Ayurbarwada 愛育黎拔力八達, was the fourth emperor of the Yuan dynasty. He was the first Mongol emperor able to read and speak Chinese and shifted the emphasis toward China. During his reign, a limited imperial exam system was reestablished. He was a patron of literature and painting. He was sympathetic to Chinese Confucian traditions. See Patricia Ebrey, Anne Walthall, and James Palais, *Pre-modern East Asia to 1800: A Cultural, Social, and Political History* (Boston and New York: Houghton Mifflin Company, 2009), pp. 198–201.

3. Modern Hangzhou in Zhejiang Province.

4. Ge Hill 葛嶺 is located north to the West Lake in Hangzhou, Zhejiang Province. It was said that Ge Hill was named after Ge Hong 葛洪 (283–343), an Eastern Jin dynasty scholar and alchemist, whose renowned work is *Baopuzi* 抱朴子 (Master Who Embraces Simplicity).

the West Lake, adjacent to the former residence of Jia Qiuhe (1213–1275), the Southern Song chancellor.[5]

Living alone, Zhao Yuan felt bored. One day at dusk, he wandered in front of the gate. He saw a lady walking toward him from the east. She was about fifteen or sixteen, dressed in green, with double-loop topknots. Although she was simply adorned, her beauty was exceptional. Zhao Yuan gazed at her for quite a long time.

The next day, while going out he saw the lady again. This happened several times, and she would come each day around dusk. Zhao Yuan asked her frivolously, "You come here every day. Where do you live?" The lady smiled and bowed, saying, "My house is next to yours. You just don't know where it is."

Zhao Yuan tried to flirt with her, and she responded happily. Therefore, he let her stay with him and spent the night together intimately. The next morning, she left but returned at night. Something happened like this for more than a month, the two loved each other passionately.

Zhao Yuan asked for her name and whereabouts. She said, "You have just obtained a beautiful lady. Why must you know these?"

Zhao Yuan kept asking, hence she replied, "Since I often wear green, you can just call me the Lady in Green." She still refused to reveal her address.

Zhao Yuan thought that she might be a concubine from a noble household who feared being caught for her nightly escapades once she revealed her identity. He believed in his speculation and loved her even more.

One night, while Zhao Yuan was drunk, he pointed at her clothes jokingly and said, "This is truly like the lines [in the *Shijing*], 'Green

---

5. Jia Qiuhe 賈秋壑, better known as Jia Sidao 賈似道, courtesy name Shixian 師憲, was a chancellor of the late Southern Song dynasty. He was the younger brother of a concubine of Emperor Lizong 理宗 of Song. Jia was in office since 1260 and assassinated after his court failures in 1275 in the Cotton Tree Nunnery at Zhangzhou. He built a residence at Ge Hill. One of the halls in the residence is named Qiuhe Hall 秋壑堂, hence Jia got the name Jia Qiuhe. See *Song shi* 宋史 (Beijing: Zhonghua shuju, 1977), pp. 474: 13779–13787 and Qu You's "A Visit to Tiantai" 天台訪隱錄 in *Jiandeng xinhua*. See Qiao Guanghui, ed., *Qu You quanji jiaozhu*, Vol. 2, pp. 705–14.

4. The Tale of the Lady in Green 53

is the upper robe, green the upper, and yellow the lower garment!'"[6] Humiliated, the lady did not visit in several of the following days.

The next time she came, Zhao Yuan asked her why.[7] She replied:

> I originally wanted to be with you till my death. However, you have treated me like a maidservant. That made me so embarrassed and upset that I dared not come to serve by your side for several days. Since you already know it, I will no longer hide the truth from you. Please allow me to give you a detailed account. You and I are old acquaintances. Without the extreme passion that we reflect to each other we cannot have such a relationship.

Zhao Yuan asked why. She replied sorrowfully, "Could you not blame me? I am indeed not a girl of this world, but I will also not bring you harm. Perhaps it is the hidden fate that caused us meeting like this, and we have an unfinished affair from the past life."

Surprised, Zhao Yuan said, "Tell me more details." She said:

> I was a maidservant of the late Song chancellor Jia Qiuhe. Originally, I was from a decent family.[8] I excelled in playing chess when I was young, so I entered [his residence] to serve him as a chess child at

---

6. This alludes to the poem "Lüyi" 綠衣 in "Odes of Bei" 邶風 from the *Shijing*. Yellow is regarded as one of the five primary colors, and green one of the five secondary colors. Hence, when green is used for upper garment and yellow for lower garment, the order is reversed. The Lady in Green's green top and yellow bottoms thus refers to illegitimate relationships, such as treating a maid servant or a concubine as if she is the wife. The first two stanzas of "Lüyi" in the *Shijing* read: Green is the upper robe, 綠兮衣兮, Green with a yellow lining! 綠衣黃裏。The sorrow of my heart, 心之憂矣, How can it cease? 曷維其已: Green is the upper robe, 綠兮衣兮, Green the upper, and yellow the lower garment! 綠衣黃裳。The sorrow of my heart, 心之憂矣, How can it be forgotten? 曷維其亡。See James Legge, *The Chinese Classics*, Vol. IV, Book of Poetry, p. 41.

7. *Kou* 扣, ask. In Zhou Yi's edition, the character is 叩. In the three other editions I refer to, the character appears to be 扣. I follow Qiao Guanghui's edition here.

8. *Liangjia zi* 良家子, a person from a decent family. Here it refers to a person from a family without criminal records.

the age of fifteen. Each time when Jia Qiuhe returned home from court, he would entertain in Half Leisure Hall[9] and have me serve him during chess games. I was favored greatly. At that time, you were a servant of his family in charge of cooking tea. Since you brought the tea set to Jia Qiuhe, you were often able to reach the inner quarters. You were young and handsome back then, so I admired you at first sight. I once secretly gave you embroidered wallets. In return, you gave me a rouge box made of tortoiseshell. Although we both loved each other, the strict guarding inside and outside of the quarters made it difficult for us to have a chance to be together. Soon, some colleagues discovered our relationship and slandered us to Jia Qiuhe. We were then sentenced to death and were killed under the West Lake's Broken Bridge. You now reincarnated as a human being in this life, but my name remains on the list of ghosts. Isn't it destiny?

Having said that, she sobbed in tears. Zhao Yuan also changed his countenance for her story.

After a while, he said, "If it is true, our union now is a continuation of that in our previous life. We should love each other even more to compensate for our willingness of the past."

Since then, she stayed at Zhao Yuan's place and no longer left. Yuan was not good at playing chess, so she taught him all the tactics and tricks. Since then, all those who were known for their superior skills in the game were no longer Yuan's match.

Every time she talked about stories of the late Jia Qiuhe, she gave detailed descriptions of what she had witnessed.

She once said: One day, Jia Qiuhe was leisurely watching while leaning against the balcony, with the service of all of his maidservants. By chance, two men, dressed in white robes with black kerchief, disembarked from a small boat. One maidservant said, "Such two handsome young men!" Jia Qiuhe asked, "Would you like to serve them? I shall ask them for a bride-price." The maidservant smiled but did not respond. After a while, Jia Qiuhe asked a servant to bring in a box. He called the other maidservants to him and said, "I have just asked them for her bride-price." They opened the box and looked inside, they discovered the maidservant's head. They were all terrified and backed off.

---

9. *Banxian tang* 半閒堂 is located in Jia's residence at Ge Hill.

4. The Tale of the Lady in Green

Another time, Jia Qiuhe commissioned several hundred ships worth of salt to be sold in the city. A scholar from the imperial college wrote a poem about this:

Green waves surged above the river last night,
Fully-loaded ships carried the chancellor's salt.
Though he can use it for cooking soup,[10]
There is no need to use that much!

Jia Qiuhe heard of the poem, and immediately had the scholar thrown in jail for libel.

Once Jia Qiuhe was enforcing the Law of Public Land[11] in west Zhejiang. Civilians suffered from the law, so someone left a poem on the side of the road:

The city of Xiangyang has been besieged [by the Yuan army] for years,
[Jia] rests in the mountains and lakes instead of fighting the enemy,
Not knowing the importance of Xiangyang as key point,
He pushed for the law of public land to persecute the commoners.[12]

After Jia Qiuhe read the poem, he had the poet captured and exiled.

Another time, Jia Qiuhe offered vegetarian meals to a thousand Buddhist monks and Daoist priests. After admitting a thousand, a ragged Daoist priest came and asked for a meal. The people in charge

---

10. The term for cooking soup used here, *tiaogeng* 调羹, can also refer to managing the state as the chancellor. Hence, the phrase is used as a pun to imply Jia's abuse of power for profit.

11. *Gongtian fa* 公田法 was enacted in 1263 by Jia Sidao. Under this law, landowners were compelled to sell one-third of their holdings beyond 200 *mu* to the state. See Richard von Glahn, *An Economic History of China: From Antiquity to the Nineteenth Century* (Cambridge: University of Cambridge, 2016), p. 278.

12. The poem, titled "Ci Jia Sidao" 刺賈似道 (Criticizing Jia Sidao), is a poem by Shi Songzhi 史嵩之 (1189–1257), chancellor of Southern Song dynasty. In 1268, Xiangyang, located in modern-day Hubei province of China, was besieged by the Yuan army. Jia Sidao did not report this to the court nor lead a troop to help out, but stayed at his residence with his concubines at Ge Hill. See *Song shi* 宋史, pp. 474: 13779–13787.

refused because they have reached a thousand. The priest adamantly refused to leave, so they served him at the side of the gate. He departed after the meal, but he left his overturned bowl on the desk. Many people came to lift the bowl but could not remove it. They reported it to Jia Qiuhe, so he went to lift it himself. Underneath the bowl, there was a couplet:

Stop gracefully while you can,
The flowers will go to seed in Zhangzhou.[13]

He then realized a true immortal had descended but nobody had recognized him. However, he still did not understand the connotation of "Zhangzhou." Alas! Who could have known about the disaster [assassination] in the Cotton Tree Nunnery in Zhangzhou![14]

Yet another time, a boatman anchored his boat at the Su Causeway[15] during the height of summer. He lay at the end of the boat but could not fall asleep throughout the night. He saw three men, all shorter than one *cun*,[16] gathered at the shore. One of them said, "Mr. Zhang has arrived. What shall we do?" Another said, "Jia Qiuhe is inhumane. We shouldn't forgive him!" The other said, "My life is about to be over. You guys should wait and see him fail!" They cried and stepped into the river.

13. Zhangzhou 漳州 is located in modern-day Fujian Province. In Zhou Yi's edition, the place in the poem is "Zhangzhou." In the three other editions I refer to, the place appears to be "Mianzhou." I follow Zhou Yi's edition here.
14. Disaster in the Cotton Tree Nunnery 木棉庵之厄, refers to Jia Sidao's death in the Cotton Tree Nunnery, located in modern-day Zhangzhou in Fujian Province. Jia Sidao was exiled to Xunzhou 循州. On his way to Xunzhou, located in modern-day Guangdong Province of China, Zheng Huchen 鄭虎臣 (1219–1276), the court-designated sheriff, accompanied him to the Cotton Tree Nunnery. He stated the following before assassinating Jia, "I will kill Jia Sidao for all under heaven. There is nothing to regret even though I will be punished with death." See *Song shi* 宋史, pp. 474: 13779–13787.
15. *Su di* 蘇堤, located in modern-day West Lake in Hangzhou, Zhejiang Province of China. It was built during Su Shi's 蘇軾 (1037–1101) governance in Hangzhou, thus named after him.
16. *Cun* is a traditional Chinese unit of length. It represented one-tenth of a *chi*. Its traditional measure is the width of a person's thumb at the knuckle.

The next day, a fisherman called Mr. Zhang caught a turtle more than two feet long. He took it back home. In less than three years, the Zhangzhou incident happened. This is because sentient beings know of the future and destiny is inescapable.

Zhao Yuan said, "Isn't the fact that we can meet today also predestined?" The lady said, "That's true!"

Zhao Yuan said, "Can your energy sustain your existence in this world?" She replied, "When my time is up on earth, I will disappear."

Zhao Yuan said, "Then when will it be?" She said, "I only have three years left."

Of course, Zhao Yuan didn't believe her.

In three years, the lady was sick in bed. Zhao Yuan wanted to call the doctor, but she refused. She said, "I told you before, that our predestined relationship as husband and wife will end here."

She seized Zhao Yuan by the arm and bade him farewell:

> I served you as a ghost, but you never disrespected me. I have been here for so long. In the past life, our affection caused both of us great trouble. However, since our regret would last until the sea is dry and the rock is rotten, our love doesn't cease until heaven and earth wear out, we are so lucky to be able to fulfil our promises and continue our love in this life. I am grateful to have spent three years with you here. Please allow me to leave today, and don't miss me anymore!

Having said so, she turned to face the wall, and stopped responding to him.

Zhao Yuan was deeply saddened. He prepared a coffin, but when he was about to bury her, he found that the coffin was extremely light. He opened the coffin and found only her clothes and accessories. He buried her nominally at the foot of the North Mountain. Since he was so touched by her love, he did not marry again. He became a monk at the Lingyin Temple[17] in Hangzhou, where he spent the rest of his life.

---

17. *Lingyin si* 靈隱寺 is a famous Buddhist temple located northwest of modern-day West Lake in Hangzhou, Zhejiang Province.

NOTES AND READING GUIDE

Yunwen Gao

I. The Love Story between Scholar and Ghost

"Lüyi ren zhuan" (The Tale of the Lady in Green) is preserved in *juan* 4 of *Jiandeng xinhua*. Some scholars believe the story was written by Wu Qiuyan 吾邱衍 (1272–1311) and edited by Qu You.[18] Wang Qiancheng states that since Wu passed away before the Yanyou era (1314–1320), the story should not be attributed to him. Further, since the narrator refers to the time of the story as the Yanyou era, the story was most likely written in the Taiding 泰定 era (1324–1328), if not later.[19]

The story depicts the romance between Zhao Yuan, a young scholar, and the Lady in Green, a female ghost who claims to have known the former in their previous life during the end of the Southern Song dynasty. A typical scholar-beauty romance, this story falls into the eight types of oral stories categorized by Luo Ye 羅燁 (thirteenth century) in his *Zuiweng tanlu* 醉翁談錄 (The Talk of an Old Drunkard), namely, *yanfen* 煙粉 (rouge and powder).[20] This type of story, prevalent in the Song and Yuan dynasties, features courtesans or female ghosts who fall in love with a scholar.

Unlike other stories in this collection, such as "Aiqing zhuan" 愛卿傳 (The Tale of Aiqing), "Cuicui zhuan" 翠翠傳 (The Tale of Cuicui) and "Qiuxiang ting ji" 秋香亭記 (The Record of Autumn Fragrance Pavilion), in which the romance between the couples is disrupted by

---

18. He Mingxin 何明新, "'Jiaohong ji' he 'Lüyiren zhuan' de fan fengjian qingxiang" 《嬌紅記》和《綠衣人傳》的反封建傾向, *Chongqing shiyuan xuebao* 重慶師院學報, Vol. 4 (1986): 79.

19. Wang Qiancheng 王前程, "'Hongmei ji' yu *Qiantang yishi*— 'Hongmei ji' zhong Jia Sidao shaqie deng gushi yuanliu kaoshu" 《紅梅記》與《錢塘遺事》—《紅梅記》中賈似道殺妾等故事源流考述, *Huazhong xueshu* 華中學術, Vol. 2 (2015), pp. 116–17.

20. The eight types of oral stories include: *lingguai* 靈怪 (spirits and demons), *yanfen* 煙粉 (rouge and powder), *chuanqi* 傳奇 (marvels), *gong'an* 公案 (court cases), *podao* 朴刀 (broadsword), *ganbang* 桿棒 (staff), *yaoshu* 妖術 (sorcery), and *shenxian* 神仙 (immortals). See Luo Ye, *Zuiweng tanlu* (Shanghai: Gudian wenxue chubanshe, 1957), p. 3.

war, Zhao Yuan and the Lady in Green develop their relationship in a relatively secluded space free from the turmoil of the outside world and moral judgment from relatives and peers. Their unfortunate deaths in the previous life caused by the violence of Jia Sidao and Zhao's reincarnation in the early years of the Yuan dynasty allow the narrator to skip the turbulent years of warfare. Readers can only learn about the besieging of Xiangyang by the Yuan army through a poem recalled from the Lady in Green's memory.

Not much is said about Zhao Yuan's background. We know that his parents passed away when he was young, and he came to Qiantang for study. The imperial exam system had lately been reestablished during Emperor Renzong's reign. Yet throughout the story, Zhao Yuan does not attempt to take the imperial exam nor become an official. After the Lady in Green's demise, he converts to Buddhism and ends his life at the Lingyin Temple. This reflects the "secularization" of tales in terms of the social class of the male protagonist since the Song dynasty tales.[21]

Unlike a typical scholar–beauty romance in which the beauty falls for the scholar's talent, the Lady in Green admires Zhao Yuan because of his appearance. As the Lady in Green explains to Zhao Yuan, she falls in love with him because of their unconsummated relationship in the previous life. Back then, they were both servants at Jia Sidao's residence. The Lady in Green was favored by Jia because of her excellent chess skills. Zhao Yuan, however, was just a servant in charge of cooking tea back then. The Lady in Green admired him because he was "young and handsome." Neither of them was able to resist Jia's cruelty before they were killed. The Lady in Green, not willing to forsake their love, lingers in the world as a ghost to wait for Zhao's reincarnation.

Similarly, Zhao Yuan is also attracted to the Lady in Green's appearance at the beginning. He finds the lady exceptionally beautiful and flirts with her. His frivolous attitude changes only after the Lady in Green reveals her identity. From then on, he pays her due respect and treats her as his wife until she eventually disappears. While their love in this life begins with passion and desire and gradually elevates to a commitment to each other beyond life and death, it is not affected by external forces such as warfare upon the Song-Yuan transition.

---

21. Zhenjun Zhang and Jing Wang, eds., *Song Dynasty Tales: A Guided Reader* (Singapore: World Scientific Publishing, 2017), pp. xix–xxiii.

II. Historical Reference and Song Loyalist Sentiment

If the romance between Zhao Yuan and the Lady in Green does not reflect much about the outside world during the Yuan dynasty, it is the Lady in Green's anecdotes of Jia Sidao that connect their secluded intimacy to a larger historical context of the Southern Song dynasty. A significant portion of the story (more than one third of it) is devoted to the commentary on Jia Sidao. Though the tragedy in the previous life was directly inflicted by Jia Sidao, the Lady in Green goes beyond describing Jia's mistreatment of his servants and sketches out Jia's downfall in retribution for his immorality. A similar narrative can be found in Liu Fu's 劉斧 *Qingsuo gaoyi* 青瑣高議. In *juan* 6 in the *houji* section of *Qingsuo gaoyi*, the tale of Fan Min 范敏 has a similar plot.[22] Fan Min meets a female ghost named Lady Li 李氏 who was a leading flute player at the court of Emperor Zhuangzong 莊宗 of later Tang. She tells Fan the stories of Zhuangzong and her mishap after the emperor's death. The two spend more than ten days together, have a fight with a ghost general of the Qin dynasty named Tian Quan 田權 who kidnapped Lady Li. He wakes from his dream only to find that everything has disappeared.[23]

While both stories depict an intimate relationship developed between a scholar and a ghost, one major difference between the tale of Fan Min and "The Tale of the Lady in Green" lies in the attitudes toward the emperor/master. Lady Li sympathizes with Emperor Zhuangzong and tells his story with great passion and regret. On the contrary, the Lady in Green narrates the incidents of Jia Sidao with contempt and satire. As the persecutor of the couple, Jia Sidao is described as a despotic and selfish master at home, and also an irresponsible and impotent official at the court. The negative portrayal of Jia is further enhanced in the Lady in Green's storytelling since she claims to be an eyewitness to these incidents. Including Jia's persecution of the couple, the Lady in Green shares six anecdotes of Jia with Zhao Yuan, ranging from his cruel treatment of servants, abuse of power for his personal gain, to his failure to defend Xiangyang against the invasion of the Yuan army. Several of

---

22. According to Jing Wang, little is known about Liu Fu's life and career. See Zhenjun Zhang and Jing Wang, eds., *Song Dynasty Tales*, p. 259. Wang Shizhen 王士禎 (1634–1711) commented that "*Qingsuo gaoyi* can be regarded as a predecessor of *Jiandeng xinhua*," indicating the influence of the former on the latter. See Liu Fu, *Qingsuo gaoyi* (Shanghai: gudian wenxue chubanshe, 1958), p. 4.

23. Liu Fu, *Qingsuo gaoyi* (Xi'an: Sanqin chubanshe, 2004), pp. 210–17.

these anecdotes seem likely to happen after the Lady in Green's death. Yet, since she lingers in this world after her death, it renders her eyewitness account plausible to her audience.

Many of these anecdotes can be found in unofficial histories in the Yuan dynasty. Texts produced during the Yuan-Ming transition, *Suiyin manlu* 隨隱漫錄, *Qidong yeyu* 齊東野語, *Guixin zashi* 癸辛雜識, *Shanfang suibi* 山房隨筆, and *Guhang zaji* 古杭雜記, for instance, contain anecdotes of Jia Sidao's misconduct that led to the downfall of the Southern Song dynasty.[24] Heavily tainted by Song loyalist sentiments, these records often bear fabricated materials that falsely accuse Jia Sidao of many crimes.[25] Amongst these unofficial records, Liu Yiqing's 劉一清 *Qiantang yishi* 錢塘遺事, compiled in the early years of Yuan, is an account mixing historical facts with abundant fictional narratives to delineate the life of Jia Sidao. Many of these accounts were later incorporated into the biography of Jia in *Song shi*. Jia Sidao, with Moqi Xie 万俟卨, Han Tuozhou 韓侂冑, and Ding Daquan 丁大全, are listed in *Song shi* as four "treacherous officials" 姦臣 of the Song dynasty.[26]

Similar to these narratives, the Lady in Green also accuses Jia Sidao of these crimes. Poems that appear to be written by Jia's contemporaries are employed as pieces of evidence proving his crimes on the one hand, and as a narratological device enhancing the literariness of the story on the other hand. What brings the accusation of Jia Sidao to connect closely with the main plot are the two anecdotes with supernatural elements. A Daoist priest's warning and the dream of a boatman both serve as foreshadowing of Jia's long-awaited death as a punishment for his crimes. Zhao Yuan, in response to the Lady in Green, claims that Jia's death is pre-destined, just as is the couple's pre-destined reunification in this life. Song loyalist sentiment is thus packaged as retribution and interwoven into a typical scholar–beauty romance.

III. Its Influence

After circulating in China for less than one hundred years, the influence of *Jiandeng xinhua*, as many scholars have discussed, reached Korea and

---

24. Wang Qiancheng, "'Hongmei ji' yu *Qiantang yishi*—'Hongmei ji' zhong Jia Sidao shaqie deng gushi yuanliu kaoshu," p. 118.
25. Ibid., p. 123.
26. *Song shi* 宋史, 474: 13769–13787.

Japan, as well as Vietnam.[27] As a recurring theme, the romance between a scholar and a ghost continued to be popular in Ming and Qing dynasty tales and culminated in Pu Songling's 蒲松齡 (1640–1715) *Liaozhai zhiyi* 聊齋誌異. "The Tale of the Lady in Green," in particular, has inspired literary works such as Zhou Chaojun's 周朝俊 "Hongmei ji" 紅梅記 (The Tale of Red Plum) in late Ming. The story revolves around scholar Pei Yu 裴禹, Lu Zhaorong 盧昭容, and Jia Sidao's concubine Li Huiniang 李慧娘, who becomes a vengeful ghost after being murdered by Jia. Because of its popularity, the tale has been adapted into Kun opera, Peking opera, Yue opera, and Cantonese opera.

Many scholars consider "The Tale of the Lady in Green" as the basis of the story of Li Huiniang.[28] Recent studies postulate that Liu Yiqing's *Qiantang yishi* appeared earlier than "The Tale of the Lady in Green." Moreover, some stories about Jia Sidao from "The Tale of the Red Plum" that did not appear in Qu You's story can also be traced in Liu Yiqing's work. Hence, *Qiantang yishi* should be regarded as the source of inspiration for both authors of the *chuanqi* stories.[29] Nevertheless, as a pioneering work in the *chuanqi* genre that borrows materials about Jia Sidao from Liu's *biji* 筆記, "The Tale of the Lady in Green" adopts the theme of romance between scholar and ghost to enhance the literariness of the tale. Thus, its significance should not be underestimated.

---

27. See William H. Nienhauser, Jr., *The Indiana Companion to Traditional Chinese Literature*. Vol. 1 (Bloomington and Indianapolis: Indiana University Press, 1986), pp. 275–6, and Nguyen Nam, "Writing as Response and as Translation: *Jiandeng xinhua* and the Evolution of Chuanqi Genre in East Asia, Particularly in Vietnam," Ph.D. dissertation, Harvard University, 2005, pp. 1–2.

28. See Guo Yingde 郭英德, *Ming Qing chuanqi shi* 明清傳奇史 (Beijing: Renmin wenxue chubanshe, 2012), p. 316, and Wang Xingqi 王星琦, *Hongmei ji jiaozhu* 紅梅記校注 (Shanghai: Shanghai guji chubanshe, 1985), p. 5.

29. See Wang Ruilai 王瑞來, "Jinggu shufei yinjiancheng – 'Qiantang yishi' kaoshu" 鏡古孰非殷監呈－《錢塘遺事》考述, *Sichuan shifan daxue xuebao* 四川師範大學學報, Vol. 4 (2013): 139–40, and Wang Qiancheng, "'Hongmei ji' yu Qiantang yishi— 'Hongmei ji' Zhong Jia Sidao shaqie deng gushi yuanliu kaoshu," pp. 116–19.

Tale 5

"FENGWEI CAO JI" 鳳尾草記
(THE RECORD OF A PHOENIX-TAIL FERN)

By Li Changqi 李昌祺

Translated by Qian Liu and Joanne Tsao

During the reign of Hongwu (r. 1368–1399), there was a young scholar surnamed Long who was a native of Jiankang.[1] His remote ancestor was a capital official of the Song dynasty, and he followed Empress Dowager Meng 孟 of Longyou (1073–1131) to move to the south.[2] His family remained at Jiangyou[3] where his descendants multiplied and maintained achievements in poetry and literature for generations.

Scholar Long ranked eighth among his siblings. When he was six or seven years old, the elders taught him poetry, and he was able to recite them immediately. At the age of nine, he knew how to compose couplets, and the pentasyllabic and heptasyllabic quatrains he made had great merit, so everyone praised him for his cleverness. Long had a paternal aunt who married into the family of Zu 祖. She particularly favored Long, so he often visited his aunt's house and was very close with the Zu family. His aunt's husband had half brothers, and the families of brothers all lived together but had meals separately. The elder brother passed away

---

This translation is based on the text edited by Li Changqi, *Jiandeng yuhua* 剪燈餘話, in *Jiandeng xinhua, waierzhong* 剪燈新話外二種, edited and annotated by Zhou Yi 周夷 (Shanghai: Zhonghua shuju, 1957), pp. 213–7. We have also consulted the text in *Guben xiaoshuo congkan* 古本小說叢刊, fifth series, volume 1 (Beijing: Zhonghua shuju, 1991), pp. 85–7.

1. Jiankang 建康, located at present-day Nanjing City, Jiangsu.
2. Longyou 隆祐 was the empress of Zhezong 哲宗, named Zhao Xu 趙煦 (r. 1085–1100), an emperor of the Northern Song.
3. *Jiangyou* 江右, the area to the south of the Yangtze River, refers to Jiangxi province.

and his wife, surnamed Lian 練, and their two sons and three daughters survived. Among the daughters, the first two were married, and only the youngest, who was exceedingly beautiful, remained in the household. She was three years older than Scholar Long.

Long was young, yet he was quick-witted, gentle, prudent, not fond of seeking pleasure, and also good at observing other people's thoughts. Therefore, the whole household of Zu was full of joy every time when they heard that the young scholar was coming to visit. The youngest daughter also greeted him in person as her own brother, no longer following the rule of avoidance. Lady Lian really wanted Scholar Long to be her son-in-law after hearing the praise from his aunt that he was ambitious and fond of learning, and her daughter had wholehearted affection for him as well.

In the center courtyard of the Zu household, there was a hundred-year-old phoenix-tail fern.[4] One day, while Long was reciting poetry by the tree, the girl noticed that there was no one else around, so she came out to approach him under the tree and said to him:

> My mother heard about your aunt's praise of your cleverness. She wanted to betroth me to you, and I also would like to be your wife. I will entrust your aunt to make the decision, but I do not know if your parents will agree with it. If we are meant to be together and can become a couple, I will have no regret even if I die! Otherwise, the man I end up marrying will probably either be a son of merchants or that of a farmer. Even if their halls are full of gold and jade, or their lands are connected from east to west, I am not willing to marry them.

Long responded, "If I could have you as my wife, I would be content all my life." Subsequently, they pointed to the phoenix-tail fern and swore, "If our wish succeeds, this tree will blossom and bear seeds. If not, its roots will wither away, and its leaves will die." After the oath, the two separated and left.

Scholar Long stayed on at the Zu household. Everyone from old to young there was fond of him, and the girl particularly respected and admired him. Once, she brought tea to Long herself, and Long

---

4. *Fengwei cao*, also called *jingkoubian cao* 井口边草 in terms of *Bencao shiyi* 本草拾遺. Its leaves spread out like feathers, which looks like the tail of a phoenix, hence the name.

took it and joked, "The tea has been drunk, therefore our plan won't be a failure."[5] The girl's family members heard that but did not inquire about it.

It so happened that later on, Long's aunt was at odds with Lady Lian. Beneath the aunt's ostensible instigating and encouragement of their relationship was her actual intention to prevent it. As a result, Long's parents became hesitant about the marriage proposal, but the girl did not know about this. Thereupon, Long told the girl, "Since for now, you would not accept matrimony, and I also won't send the betrothal gift promptly; I will consult with my mother, and certainly, I will not rest until I make you my wife."

The girl's family was not well-off, and she never had a wardrobe of silk or makeup of powder and rouge. She wore only a hairpin made of a branch and a simple cloth skirt, still, there was not a single stain on her; even her foot wrap was clean as fresh snow. Moreover, her disposition was exceedingly gentle and agreeable, and both her exquisite weaving skills and dexterous tailoring were the best of the whole clan. Her two older brothers' wives were extremely jealous of her, but she did not let it bother her. Long respected her conduct and that further strengthened his determination to marry her. However, because it was difficult to obtain a good matchmaker and Long's aunt did not strongly approve, there was a delay on both sides and time passed by during a prolonged delay.

Once he turned twenty, after the capping ceremony, Long left home to prepare for the imperial examinations, and his visits to the girl's house became rare. The girl, however, missed Long so much that she never dismissed him from her mind. Only her mother understood her affections, so she enlightened her and said, "I again sent someone to Long's house to discuss your marriage. There would be a determining decision sooner or later. Don't be consumed by this, which will merely do harm to your appearance." Sometime later, Long arrived. Although he mainly visited and lodged at his aunt's house, Long's real intention was to see the girl. After Long stayed there for a few days, [one day] both sisters-in-law of the girl went to visit their paternal homes, and the girl was weaving in the attic of a small multistory building by herself. Next to this building was a deep alley, which led to the back garden. In the middle of the alley, there was a path with a stairway built with

---

5. In the old days, both accepting tea (*shoucha* 受茶) and drinking tea (*chicha* 吃茶) represented the figurative ceremony of betrothing a woman to a man.

bricks for ascending the attic. When Long, returning from the back garden, heard the girl weaving, he headed straight to her place. Her face was full of happiness when she saw Long. She stopped weaving to meet Long with courtesy. She then sat face to face with him and started chatting with him while she resumed weaving. She accordingly told Long her birth date and time, asking him to reckon and prognosticate divination to see if their marriage would be harmonious. She also spoke with him in detail about her daily life in the family. Long was moved by her affection, so he composed a poem and presented it to her, which read:

> Deep into the winding fences, one stem of blossom,
> When did this resplendent beauty ever recognize dewy essence?
> Her pure nature is as white as a thousand crystalline petals clustering together,
> Her pink fragrant skin shines on the light silk dress.
>
> Golden bells always intend to protect her,[6]
> The embroidered curtain is so relentless that I suffer from being screened off from her.
> Relying on the Eastern Emperor, she needs to put forth her utmost strength,[7]
> The place where she blooms cannot be done wrong.

---

6. *Jinling* 金鈴 (Golden bells) is from the anecdote about Prince of Ning 宁王 (679-742) of the Tang dynasty recorded in a brief account titled "Hua shang jinling" 花上金鈴 of *Kaiyun Tianbao yishi* 開元天寶遺事 by Wang Renyu 王仁裕 (880-956). According to the story, at the beginning of the Tianbao (742-756) reign, Prince of Ning used bells to disperse birds and protect the flowers: "When spring arrived, in the back garden, people twisted red threads into strings, densely decorated the strings with golden bells, and tied them to the ends of flower branches. Whenever birds came and flocked together, Prince of Ning would order a garden clerk to pull the strings to frighten them, which was for the sake of cherishing flowers." 至春時, 於後園中紉紅絲為繩, 密綴金鈴, 繫於花梢之上, 每有禽鳥翔集, 則令園吏掣鈴索以驚之, 蓋惜花之故也。(See Wang Renyu, *Kaiyuan Tianbao yishi* (Beijing: Zhonghua shuju, 2006), p. 19.

7. Donghuang 東皇, also refers to as Dongjun 東君 (Eastern Lord) or Qingdi 青帝 (Blue Emperor), is the legendary deity who is in charge of spring.

5. The Record of a Phoenix-Tail Fern

The girl did not read much and could only recognize characters, so she said to Long, "You should explain it so that I can hear it." Therefore, Long explained the meanings of the poem to her carefully, sentence by sentence. The girl smiled and said, "If I can serve you at the inner chamber in the future,[8] you must teach me. Although I am ignorant, I will be able to do it after a long time of practice." Long said: "[Some] women and girls are particularly smart. Considering your bright mind, it would be easy for you to learn it." Accordingly, Long wrote a poem in her place as a reply to his poem, which read:

> Deeply thank the beautiful springtime that makes my colors splendid and dense,
> Blowing me open, must be with the aid of the east wind.
> With melancholy and sorrow, night dew condenses into pearl-like tears,
> The most frightening thing is that spring chill might impair my jade-white face.
> When the delicate flower pistil is snapped, dust on the butterfly wings flows in the air,[9]
> There are scarlet spots where the heart of fragrant blossom[10] is broken.[11]
> If I deserve to be offered with golden plates and gorgeous houses,
> I would have already entered the twelve-tiered palace with carved balustrades.

8. The phrase *sifangwei* 伺房帷 (serving at the inner chamber) refers to being one's wife.
9. For *diefen* 蝶粉 (dust on the butterfly wings), see footnote 6 on page 21.
10. *Fangxin* 芳心 (heart of fragrant blossom) refers to the feelings of a young woman.
11. In this couplet, the erotic images such as *nenrui zhe* 嫩蕊折 (delicate flower pistil snapped), *piao diefen* 飄蝶粉 (dust on the butterfly wings flows in the air), *fangxin po* 芳心破 (heart of fragrant blossom is broken), and *dian xinghong* 點猩紅 (scarlet spots) are not only metaphors for a woman losing her virginity after having sexual intercourse with a man, they also indicate the sorrowful feelings of a woman who is betrayed or abandoned by her lover, which echoes "the most frightening thing" in the previous couplet.

Once again, Long explained the meanings of the poem in detail. The girl said, "I often heard that you are talented and quick. After observing you today, I see you are indeed so, which makes me admire you even more!" She looked at Long for a long time and said:

> Your will and spirit show that you are certainly not a mediocre person. You will have noble status and fame. I intend to entrust myself with the texture of rushes and willows[12] to you. There is no other reason, only because my father died early, my mother is aging, first older brother makes copies of official documents in the court for living, while second older brother is buried under clerk labor, and the two sisters-in-law are fierce and shrewd, which you know very well. I only wish to get far away from their fierce and cruel treatment and to entrust myself as hare floss attaches to pine gauze.[13] Even if you have no official position and are not able to make me a wife with an honorary title by imperial mandate, I will still be the wife of a man of worthy. If I ever unfortunately drift about and fall into the hands of a mediocre man, I have no choice but to die! I hope that you will think about this and make plans for me.

---

12. The phrase *puliuzhizhi* 蒲柳之質 (the texture of rushes and willows) is a polite self-denigrating term used to indicate one's physical weakness. It originally comes from *Shishuo xinyu* 世說新語 by Liu Yiqing 劉義慶 (403–444). In the "Yanyu" 言語 chapter, it is recorded: "Ku Yüeh was the same age as Emperor Chien-wen, but his hair had turned white earlier. Chien-wen asked him, 'How is it you've turned white first?'" Ku replied, 'The character of rushes and willows is to drop their leaves as they approach the autumn, while the nature of pines and cypresses is to be still more luxurious amid the ice and frost." 顧悅與簡文同年，而髮蚤白。簡文曰："卿何以先白?"對曰："蒲柳之姿，望秋而落; 松柏之質，經霜彌茂." See the translation in Richard B. Mather, trans., *A New Account of the Tales of the World* (Ann Arbor: The University of Michigan Press, 2002), pp. 60–1.

13. The term *siluo* 絲蘿 (as hare floss attaches to pine gauze) is a metaphor for marriage that first appears in the second couplet of the eighth poem entitled "ranran gusheng zhu" 冉冉孤生竹 in "Gushi shijiu shou" 古詩十九首: "I newly married to you, as hare floss attaches to pine gauze" 與君為新婚，兔絲附女蘿. See Zhang Qingzhong 張清種, ed., *Guoshi shijiu shou huishuo shangxi yu yanjiu* 古詩十九首彙說賞析與研究, pp. 53–4.

At the beginning, Long was pleased with the girl's appearance, but he did not expect her to be as virtuous and insightful as this showed. From then on, he became even more sincere in their discussion of marriage without wasting time.

Soon afterward, the two elder brothers of the girl were dismissed from their official posts as expected, and the family declined financially as well. Long's parents did not want to undertake a marriage agreement with the family, so they made an apology and rejected it. As a result, there was no hope for Long and the girl. Long privately composed a long song and delivered it to the girl, which read:

Back then, I was only a child,[14]
Full of laughter, I rode on my horse made of bamboo by your seat.
Holding blue plums, we played together,[15]
Your body was like a piece of jade and your face was like a lotus flower.
You are fond of my intelligence and obsession with brushes and inkstones,[16]
My phoenix-like writings, and sturdy purple steed.[17]
The wind-touched hair bun, fog-nourished hair on your temples and crimson tinted lips,[18]

---

14. The term *tiaonian* 髫年 originally comes from "Record of the Peach Blossom Spring" 桃花源記 by Tao Qian 陶潛 (also known as Tao Yuanming 陶淵明, 365–427). "Both the old and the children are pleasant and content." 黃髮垂髫, 并怡然自樂. See Li Hua 李華, ed., *Tao Yuanming shiwen shangxi ji* 陶淵明詩文賞析集 (Chengdu: Bashu shushe chubanshe, 1988), p. 233.

15. The two couplets are derived from Li Bai's 李白 (701–762) poem "Changgan xing" 長干行: "You came by on bamboo stilts, playing horse; you walked about my seat, playing with blue plums" 郎騎竹馬來, 繞床弄青梅. See Ezra Pound's translation in Bruce Fogelman, "Pound's 'Cathay': A Structural Model for 'the cantos,'" *Paideuma*, Vol. 16, No. 1/2 (1987): 52.

16. *Biyan* 筆硯 (brushes and inkstones) refers to writing.

17. *Yuezhuo* 鷟鷟 is one of the five legendary phoenixes, which was regarded as an auspicious omen of writing in ancient times.

18. The phrase *fenghuan wubin* 風鬟霧鬢 is used here to describe women's beautiful hair. It is derived from *fenghuan yubin* 風鬟雨鬢 (wind-tossed bun and rain-dampened hair) in Li Chaowei's 李朝威 (ca. 766–820) "Liu Yi zhuan" 柳毅傳, a phrase originally used to describe the fluffy and untidy hair of the Dragon Daughter: "I saw your great majesty's beloved daughter herding sheep in the pastures. Her wind-tossed bun and rain-dampened hair were such that

I saw them so many times beside the phoenix-tail fern.
On the loft tower, in her bower that is deep and secluded,
Her slender fingers[19] reeling out silk strands, thread by thread.
What could I do when the matchmaker[20] did not come?
Who would have thought that our shared heart of silk belts was a disappointing one![21]
Embroidered web and paramount tent, we are separated at the edges of the world,[22]
Not understanding "The story of a detached soul," you cannot follow the example of Zhang Qianniang.[23]

I could not bear to see [them]." 見大王愛女牧羊於野外, 風鬟雨鬢, 所不忍視. See Wang Pijiang 汪辟疆, *Tangren xiaoshuo* 唐人小說 (Hong Kong: Zhonghua shuju, 1985), p. 63. Also see Meghan Cai's translation in William H. Nienhauser, Jr., ed., *Tang Dynasty Tales: A Guided Reader*, Vol. 2 (Singapore: World Scientific Publishing, 2018), p. 6.

19. Translation of *chunxian* 春纖.

20. Translation of Jian Xiu 蹇脩. In "Lisao" 離騷, Jian Xiu was sent out as a messenger to pursue the river goddess Fu Fei 宓妃: "I took off my girdle as a pledge of my suit to her/And ordered Lame Beauty to be the go-between." 解佩纕以結言兮,吾令蹇脩以為理. In later literature, Jian Xiu became the metaphor for matchmaker. See David Hawkes, trans., *The Songs of the South: An Ancient Chinese Anthology of Poems* by Qu Yuan and Other Poets (Westminster, London: Penguin Book, 1985), p. 74.

21. *Luodai tongxin* 羅帶同心 is a metaphor for expressing a love-oath. It originally comes from Lin Pu's 林逋 (ca. 967–1208) romantic lyric titled "Chang Xiangsi" 長相思: "While making love knot by silken belts is still incomplete, the tidewater by the riverside has already brimmed full" 羅帶同心結未成, 江頭潮已平. See Yang Shen 楊慎 (1488–1559), ed., *Cipin* 詞品 (Ming Tianqi 天啓 [1627] edition), p. 3.3b.

22. According to the *Yiwen leiju* 藝文類聚, the *Han Wu gushi* 漢武故事 records: "The Emperor (Emperor Wu of Han, r. 141–87 BCE) mingled azure stones, jewelries, lustrous pearls, and other precious treasures together to make a paramount net." 上以琉璃珠玉, 明月夜光, 雜錯天下珍寶為甲帳. See Ouyang Xun 歐陽詢 (557–641) *Yiwen leiju* (Shanghai: Shanghai guji chubanshe, 1999), p. 1200.

23. Zhang Qianniang 張倩娘 is the heroine in the eighth-century Tang tale "Li hun ji" 離魂記 by Chen Xuanyou 陳玄祐 (ca. 779). See the details of the story in Wang Pijiang, *Tangren xiaoshuo*, pp. 49–51.

Do you know which family you will be betrothed to?
I will have imperial examinations at the Golden Hall.[24]
When I look back towards the Clear River, you are still in my dreams,
My gaze is blocked by Wu Mountain, and my tears are like ice crystals.[25]

One day, when the girl's mother stayed over at her relatives' house, her two sisters-in-law initiated a fight and made a great quarrel with her. Due to her kind and amicable disposition, she hid in her bedroom and dared not to say a word or scold in return, but she really could not endure such unbearable indignation. Moreover, her engagement with Scholar Long was suddenly broken off,[26] which made her feel even more miserable and melancholy. Staying alone with no one to rely on, that night she hanged herself in the attic.

When the mother returned, she cried for the girl with deep sorrow. She washed and buried her daughter by herself. In the process, an embroidered sachet the girl was wearing on her chest was found. Sealed inside was a piece of paper decorated with apricot blossom patterns. The mother took a look at it and found that it was the poem Long sent to her. The mother did not [want to] go against her daughter's wishes, so she placed the embroidered sachet in her coffin. Hearing the news of the girl's death, Long used a visit to his aunt as an excuse and came

24. Originally, *shece* 射策 refers to scholars presenting a set of strategies for governing political affairs in response to an emperor's call for advice. Later, it generally meant taking imperial examinations. *Huangjin dian* 黃金殿 (Golden Hall) is a laudatory phrase for an imperial palace.

25. Wushan 巫山 (Wu Mountain) originally comes from "Gaotang *fu*" 高唐賦 by Song Yü 宋玉 (ca. 298–222 BCE). It became a metaphor for secret dating of lovers in later literature.

26. In the Spring and Autumn Period, the royal families of the Qin 秦 state and the Jin 晉 state made marriage alliances for generations. Therefore, *Qin yue Jin meng* 秦約晉盟 (marriage alliance between the states of Qin and Jin) refers to a marriage engagement here.

to mourn for her. When he arrived there, like a sunken pearl, shattered emerald, perished jade, and blown away flower,[27] the girl was about to be buried in her coffin. Tears streaming down his cheeks like falling rain, Long was so overwhelmed with grief that he could not bear it. He escorted the girl's coffin all the way to the burial site and did not leave until assuring that her grave was covered and completed.

As expected, a few years later, Long passed imperial examinations and held an important position, becoming prominent in his time. Although he married other women as wife and concubine, he still could not forget about the girl in his heart. He often talked about ghosts and deities with the celestial master, the Non-action Perfected Zhang.[28] Occasionally, he brought up what happened to the girl. Master Zhang observed that Long was distressed and grieved, so he drew and burned a Daoist tally to perform the ritual of salvation for the souls in purgatory for the girl. After a few days, Long dreamed of the girl who said:

> It has been more than twenty years since I bid farewell to the human world.[29] The courts of the underworld checked my registration and found out that originally, I should have had three sons and lived to sixty. However, I did not live to the age I should have when I met an untimely end. Because of this, they made me be a woman again and end my sins in previous life. And yesterday, because of Master Zhang's Daoist power, a celestial tally was suddenly sent down, and now I am going to the city of Luoyang county in Henan prefecture to be a man of the Hu family. I am grateful for your profound love. You never forgot about me no matter when I was alive or dead. What I am regretful is that I have nothing to respectfully repay you with. Thereupon you will become wealthy and honorable, reach

---

27. Translation of the phrases *zhuchen bisui*, *yuyun huafei* 珠沉璧碎,玉殞花飛. Both phrases are metaphors for the death of a beautiful woman.

28. This refers to Zhang Yuchu 張宇初 (1361–1410), a famous Daoist of the Orthodox Oneness Tradition (Zhengyi Dao 正一道) and the 43rd Zhang Heavenly Master of Longhu shan 龍虎山 in the Ming dynasty. His studio names are Qishan 耆山 and Wuwei zi 無為子.

29. In the previous text, it is recorded: "He escorted the girl's coffin all the way to the place… a few years later" 送歸葬所……后數年. In the later text, it also explains that the girl "has passed away for three years" 隕三春. However, here it states that more than twenty years have passed since the girl died. This is clearly an error.

the highest official rank to the Emperor. You will possess generous fortune and longevity, and your descendants shall be thriving and prosperous.

After she finished saying that, the girl bowed to bid farewell and left. She walked for a few steps, then turned around and said, "Please take good care of yourself, I am departing forever now." Without warning, she just disappeared. When Long woke up, he assumed that there would be nothing to commemorate the girl, so he sent someone to the girl's residence to check on the phoenix-tail fern, but it had been withered for several years. Thereupon, Scholar Long composed a song of mourning for the phoenix-tail fern ("Ai fengwei ge") which read:

Grass, grass, named phoenix-tail,
Immortals planted it in the Cinnabar Mountain.[30]
Its fragrance casts the other flowers in the world into the shade,
No precious coral tree can be on a par with it.
Luxuriant and flourishing, it looks uniquely like the feathers of a
　　phoenix,
So it is given the same beautiful name as phoenix.
Sailing at sea for a long time to seek it, dampened by pearl-like dew,
Lucid music is played on the bamboo flute, rosy clouds halt for it.
With graceful posture and delicate appearance, it is chaste and gentle,
Its leaves are carved from colored glaze and its stems are made of
　　pearl-like jade.
Like a phoenix with vigorous wings, it bends down frequently,[31]
Brilliantly shines on its extraordinary patterns in five colors.
The luminous sun sprinkles its golden rays in the clear sky,
Midsummer becomes cool and refreshing, the wind fills the forest.
In the bright spring sunshine, it does not act like peaches and plums,

30. Danshan 丹山 (Cinnabar Mountain) is the ancient name of the mountain where phoenixes live. "Ben wei"本味, *Lüshi chunqiu* 呂氏春秋 records: "There are eggs of phoenixes in the western region of the drift land and the southern region of the Cinnabar Mountain. They are used for food by the people of Wo state." 流沙之西, 丹山之南, 有鳳之丸, 沃民所食. See Lü Buwei 呂不韋 (d. 235 BCE), *L*,. 235 *B* 有鳳之, annotated by Chen Qiyou 陳奇猷 (Shanghai: Shanghai guji chubanshe, 2002), p. 741.

31. *Jiubao* 九苞 refers to the nine features of the phoenix. It became an alternative name of phoenix in later literature.

Year-end weather strengthens its mind as strong as pine and cypress.
In the quiet place of a magnificent hall, it swings her verdant green,
I had once met with the fairy maiden beneath its emerald shade.[32]
Not allowed to be close to her, I stole her aroma briefly,[33]
Pointing to the fern, we hoped to become a couple eventually.
But who knew that everything would not come true after all,
Both her delicate fragrance and graceful nature turned to dust.
The divine root preserved in latticed balustrades withered after living for one hundred years,
The beauty in the young lady's chamber has passed away for three years.
Alas! A phoenix occasionally passed by here before,
But the Terrace of Nongyu has collapsed and the phoenix-tail fern has died.[34]

32. Fei Qiong 飛瓊 refers to fairies in general. Originally, the name belonged to one of the maids of the Queen Mother of the West in terms of *Hanwudi neizhuan* 漢武帝內傳.

33. *Touxiang* 偷香 (stealing aroma) is a metaphor from the romance of Han Shou 韓壽 (d. 300) and Jia Wu 賈午 (260–300), the daughter of Jia Chong 賈充 (217–282), referring to a secret love affair between a man and a woman. According to "Huoni" 惑溺, *Shishuo xinyu*, Jia Wu liked Han Shou and sent her maid to express her affections for him, so Han Shou entered her house "by leaping over the wall… After that, Chong became aware that his daughter was being rather lavish in applying make-up, and her elation was far beyond the normal. Later when he called together his aides, he noticed that Shou had about him the aura of an exotic perfume, one which had been sent as tribute from a foreign country. Once it was applied to a person, it lasted for months without fading… Chong kept the matter secret and gave his daughter to Shou in marriage." [壽]踰牆而入……. 自是充覺女盛自拂拭, 說暢有異於常. 後會諸吏, 聞壽有奇香之氣, 是外國所貢, 壹箸人, 則歷月不歇……. 充秘之, 以女妻壽. See the story and translation in Mather, trans., *A New Account of the Tales of the World*, p. 524.

34. Nong Yü 弄玉 was the legendary daughter of Duke Mu of Qin 秦穆公 (r. 659–621 BCE) in the Spring and Autumn period, also known as Qin'e 秦娥 (Beauty of Qin), Qinnü 秦女 (Daughter of Qin), or Qinwang nü 秦王女 (Princess of Qin). She was married to Xiao Shi 簫史, who excelled at playing flute, and learned from him about imitating the cry of phoenixes. Duke Mu built the Phoenix Terrace for the couple and phoenixes often landed on it. At the end of the story, both Xiao Shi and Nong Yu flew away with phoenixes and became immortals. See the story in Liu Xiang 劉向 (77–6 BCE), *Lie xian zhuan* 列仙傳, *Sibu congkan* edition, p. 1.17a.

Mandarin duck-like tiles have fallen down while wild pear trees remain green,
Peacock screens have tilted but unrefined flower blossoms are still as purple as before.
Stirred by the time, recalled in the past, my regret wrenches endlessly,
Like blue feathers and jade flowers, she has gone forever.
On dilapidated stairs, under ruined walls, crickets are mourning for the moon,
In hazy mist, over old trees, birds are crying during the autumn.
Replanted flowers and grasses will bloom again in the spring,
But broken mirrors and fractured hairpins have been eternally scattered.
Thereupon, I sing the song of phoenix-tail to lodge my profound thoughts,
And leave it for sentimental later generations to sigh with feelings.

NOTES AND READING GUIDE

by Jing Wang, Qian Liu, and Joanne Tsao

I. Text and Author

"Fengwei cao ji" (The Record of a Phoenix-Tail Fern) is found in *juan* three of *Jiandeng yuhua*, which has various titles including *Xinkan jiandeng yuhua* 新刊剪燈餘話, *Xin zeng bu xiang jiandeng yuhua Daquan* 新增補相剪燈餘話大全, and *Yunpizi yuhua* 運甓子餘話.[35] This tale was later included in other collections, such as *Qingshi* 情史, *Baijia cuibian* 稗家粹編, and *Yanju biji* 燕居筆記. *Qingshi* changed its title to "Jiankang Longsheng" 建康龍生 (Scholar Long at Jiankang) and collected it under the category of "Qing han" 情憾 (Regrettable love). *Baijia cuibian* adopted the same title of "Fengweicao ji" and organized it under the branch of "Youqi" 幽期 (Clandestine rendezvous).

The authorship of *Jiandeng yuhua* is attributed to Li Zhen 李禎 (1376–1452), better known by his courtesy name Changqi 昌祺, who was a native of Luling 廬陵,[36] and also used studio names Qiao'an 僑庵, Baiyi shanren 白衣山人, and Yunpi jushi 運甓居士. Many scholars point out that the similarities between the life background and experience of the male protagonist Scholar Long in "Fengweicao ji" and that of the attributed author.[37]

A few historical records also show that Li's ancestor was a native of Jiankang (also known as Jinling 金陵) and he moved the whole family to Jiangxi when the remnants of the imperial court moved southward from the capital Bianjing 汴京 (present-day Kaifeng 開封) to Hangzhou 杭州 after the collapse of the Northern Song dynasty. For instance, Yang

---

35. Chen Guojun 陳國軍, *Mingdai zhiguai chuanqi xiaoshuo xulu* 明代志怪傳奇小說敘錄 (Hong Kong: Shangwu yinshuguan, 2016), pp. 31–3.
36. Located at present-day Ji'an 吉安 of Jiangxi province.
37. About this opinion, please refer to Qiao Guanghui 喬光輝, "Li Changqi nianpu" 李昌祺年譜, in *Dongnan daxue xuebao* 東南大學學報 (zhexue shehui kexue ban 哲學社會科學版), Vol. 4, No. 6 (2002): 103–11; Chen Caixun 陳才訓 and Shi Shiping 時世平, "*Jiandeng yuhua*: 'Weihuan gaoyi,' Lun Li Changqi de Shujishi jiaoyu jiqi xiaoshuo chuangzuo de fengjiao yishi" 《剪燈余話》: "薇垣高議"—論李昌祺的庶吉士教育及其小說創作的風教意識, *Zhongguo wenyan xiaoshuo yanjiu* 中國文言小說研究, Vol. 1 (2012): 150–60.

5. The Record of a Phoenix-Tail Fern 77

Rong's 楊榮 "Gu Panzhou Li Chushi muzhiming" 故盤洲李處士墓志銘 is an epitaph for Li Changqi's father, Li Kui 李揆, which states:

> Reclusive Scholar Li, his given name was Kui and his courtesy name was Bocai. His ancestor was a native of Jinling. When the Song imperial court crossed the Yellow River and moved to the south, the head of family who was the Director of the Imperial Secretariat, given name Yi, moved the family to Jishui county of Jiangxi prefecture. Later, the family arrived at present-day Luogang of Luling county after several moves.
>
> 處士諱揆，字伯蔡。其先金陵人，宋南渡時，有尚書郎諱義者，徙家江西之吉水，又數遷至今廬陵之螺岡。[38]

In Qian Xili's 錢習禮 (1373–1461) epitaph for Li Changqi titled "Henan Buzheng shi si Zuo buzheng shi Ligong Zhen mubeiming" 河南布政使司左布政使李公禎墓碑銘 there is a similar depiction:

> [Li Changqi] was from an aristocratic family in Jinling. When the Song imperial court crossed the Yellow River and moved to the south, the head of family whose official position was the Director of the Imperial Secretariat, given name Yi, followed Empress Dowager Meng of Longyou as her retinue to move southward and remain at Wujiang of Jishui.
>
> [李昌祺] 世家金陵，宋南渡有諱義者仕為郎中，扈從隆祐太后，南上留居吉水之烏江。[39]

Moreover, in "The Record of a Phoenix-Tail Fern," Scholar Long came from a family that "maintained achievements in poetry and literature for generations." Long already displayed his talent in poetry and earned many local people's praise in his youth. As expected, Long later passed the *jinshi* examination and became a prominent official scholar. The biographical information on Li Changqi demonstrates that, similar to Scholar Long, Li was also greatly influenced by his family education and obtained the *jinshi* degree. Both Li and his father earned fame

---

38. Yang Rong, *Wenmin ji* 文敏集, *Siku quanshu* edition, 24.15a.
39. See Cheng Minzheng's 程敏政 (1445–1499) *Ming wen heng* 明文衡, in *Siku quanshu huiyao* 四庫全書薈要 (Chizao Tang 摛藻堂, 1777 edition), 82.16b.

through their achievements in poetry and literary works at young ages. The people of Li's hometown also believed that he would certainly be exceptional and prominent. The similarities in the portrayals and comments related to the two scholars, Long and Li, are presented below:

> The ancestors of the Revered Master [Li] passed on the classics for generations. When the lineage passed on to the Revered Master's generation, he became the first person of the family to pass the *jinshi* examination. (Preface to *Yunpi mangao*)

公先世以詩書傳家, 至公乃舉進士。[40]

> The Revered Master Li was endowed with talents when he was born. He was enlightened early to be keen on study. When he was more than eight years old and started composing couplets and poems, his words amazed everyone. ("Henan Buzheng shi si Zuo buzheng shi Ligong Zhen mubeiming")

公生資禀英, 悟早即嗜學, 成童屬對賦詩, 語出驚人。[41]

> Ever since he was young, the Reclusive Scholar [Li] had been quick-witted with marvelous ambition, and gifted with a retentive memory after having casted a running glance over books. He learned *The Book of Odes* with Mao's commentary from Wang Shao who had a *jinshi* degree.

處士自少穎敏, 有奇志, 書過目輒不忘。受毛氏詩於進士王紹。[42]

> When [Li] turned twenty and after the capping ceremony, his writings were overflown with remarkable literary talent and were full of the style of a seasoned writer... The venerable people in the village were also astonished by his literary thoughts, claiming that he would certainly become prominent in his time.

---

40. Quoted from Chen Xun's 陳循 (1385–1464) preface to Li Changqi's *Yunpi mangao* 運甓漫稿, in the Zhengtong 正統 edition of the Ming preserved in the Nanjing 南京 Library. See Qiao Guanghui, "Li Changqi nianpu," pp. 103, 111.
41. Cheng Minzheng, *Ming wen heng*, in *Siku quanshu huiyao*, 82.16b.
42. Yang Rong, *Wenming ji*, 24.15b.

弱冠為文，藻思溢出，蔚有老氣，……．鄉之老成人亦皆駭其文識，謂必顯于世。⁴³

No further evidence shows that "The Record of a Phoenix-Tail Fern" is based on the personal romance of Li Changqi, yet the aforementioned similarities between Long and Li suggest that Li heavily projects his own background and image onto the character of his literary work to create an exceptionally talented protagonist.

II. Emphasis on the Element of "Emotions"

Quite a few modern scholars argue that the compositional purpose of *Jiandeng yuhua* is to accomplish "transformation of customs" (*fenghua* 風化) based on the stories and Li Changqi's preface. The deeds of "chaste widows" (*jiefu* 節婦) are frequently extolled and the identity of virgins are generally hinted in Li's love stories.⁴⁴ Compared with *Jiandeng xinha* that greatly emphasizes "emotion" (*qing* 情), *jiandeng yuhua* pays more particular attention to "chastity" (*jie* 節).⁴⁵ The image of "chaste widow" is based on the unfortunate women who committed suicide after their husbands were killed during wartime, and this image is echoed in many other texts such as "Lianli shu ji" 連理樹記 (A Tree of Intertwining Limbs), "Qiongnu zhuan" 瓊奴傳 (The Account of Qiongnu), "Yueye tanqin ji" 月夜彈琴記, and "Chang'an yexing lu" 長安夜行錄. The following comment on Luanluan's 鸞鸞 death in "Luanluan zhuan" 鸞鸞傳 (The Account of Luanluan) is often quoted by scholars to demonstrate that Li's stories are filled with moral teaching on Confucian principles:

> The gentleman says, "Both chastity and integrity are people's great norms. Gentlemen lectured on them and [people] have already been familiar with them. However, once people are confronting

---

43. Cheng Minzheng, *Ming wen heng*, 82.16b-17a.
44. On this opinion, please refer to Caixun and Shiping, "*Jiandeng yuhua*: 'Weihuan gaoyi,' Lun Li Changqi de Shujishi jiaoyu jiqi xiaoshuo chuangzuo de fengjiao yishi," 155–9.
45. Gao Yuhou 皋于厚 "'Jiandeng er'hua' yu Mingdai chuanqi xiaoshuo de fazhan qushi""剪燈二話"與明代傳奇小說的發展趨勢, *Ming qing xiaoshuo yanjiu* 明清小說研究, Vol. 4, No. 62 (2001): 22.

misfortunes or encountering disasters, very few of them are able to adhere to them. Luan was merely a woman who lived in seclusion, but she was still able to keep her chaste integrity unstained in the turmoil of war. In the end, the husband died for loyalty, and the wife died for integrity, because they were well-educated and steeped in propriety, and their talent and nature were superior. Both heavenly principle and Confucian human relationship must not be extinguished."

君子曰:"節義, 人之大閑也, 士君子講之熟矣。一旦臨利害, 遇患難, 鮮能允蹈之者。鸞幽女婦, 乃能亂離中全節不汙, 卒之夫死於忠, 妻死於義。惟其讀書達禮, 而賦質之良, 天理民彝, 有不可泯。"

However, it is interesting to discover that the image of the female protagonist in "Fengweicao ji" is distinctive, having a much less didactic nature. Those chaste widows in other stories followed "heavenly principle" and died for "integrity," but the woman in "Fengweicao ji" resisted her fate and died for love. In other words, the author lays more stress on the performance of "emotions" (*qing* 情) rather than the admonishment to "chastity" or "integrity" throughout the story.

At the beginning of the tale, the author describes the woman outwardly expressing her adoration for Scholar Long. She, unlike the women pursued by male scholars in other stories, acts as a persistent suitor herself, taking the initiative and planning for the future in their romantic relationship: "My mother heard about your aunt's praise of your cleverness. She wanted to betroth me to you, and I also would like to be your wife. I will entrust your aunt to make the decision, but I do not know if your parents will agree with it."

Although the preference for a talented scholar and the disdain for a "mediocre person" 庸才 are common in love stories, the female protagonist's unwavering determination in the pursuit displayed in "Fengweicao ji" significantly differs from other stories. For instance, in "Luanluan zhuan," after Luanluan was forced to marry a son of the Miao 繆 family, she could do nothing but "gather all the grudges and regrets, and lodge them into poetry and lyrics" 斂茲怨悔, 寓闕詩詞. Penglai 蓬萊, the female protagonist of the story "Lianli shu ji," hoped that her lover would rescue her from an unwanted engagement with the son of the Lin 林 family. The girl's attitude toward untalented men in "Fengweicao ji" was completely different from these other reactions. She repeatedly declared that seeking a talented lover was her ultimate pursuit, and she would not be discouraged even were she to sacrifice her life: "If we are meant to be together and can become a couple, I will have no regret even if I die!" "If I ever unfortunately drift about and fall into the hands of a mediocre man, I have no choice but to die!" Her words turn out to be tragically prophetic. Not only did she sacrifice her young life, but also her soul was detained in the underworld. However, the only thing she regretted was that she had nothing with which to repay Scholar Long, so she blessed him with fortune, longevity, the highest official rank, and prosperous descendants when her ghost set out on a journey to another life. The tragedy reaches its climax at the suicide of the female protagonist. Her mother buried her with the love token, i.e. the poem Scholar Long sent to her, which highlights the unregretted sacrifice and dedication in the pursuit of a talented lover. Undoubtedly, such an eternal fidelity to her talented lover that crosses the boundary between life and death endows the story with strong emotional feelings.

The story utilizes the image of a phoenix-tail fern that lived for one hundred years to symbolize the germination and tragic ending of the protagonists' love. The image might be viewed as an allusion to the poem "Cao Chong" 草蟲 ("Insects in the Grass," Mao no. 14) in the *Shaonan* 召南 (The Odes of Shao and the South) section of *Shinjing* 詩經 (*The Book of Poetry*). In the following second and third stanza of the poem, two ferns, i.e. *jue* 蕨 and *wei* 薇 are used as "stimulus" (*xing* 興).[46]

> I ascended that hill in the south, 陟彼南山
> And gathered the turtle-foot ferns. 言采其蕨
> While I do not see my lord, 未見君子
> My sorrowful heart is very sad. 憂心惙惙
> Let me have seen him, 亦既見止
> Let me have met him, 亦既覯止
> And my heart will then be pleased. 我心則說
> I ascended that hill in the south, 陟彼南山
> And gathered the thorn-ferns. 言采其薇
> While I do not see my lord, 未見君子
> My sorrowful heart is wounded with grief. 我心傷悲
> Let me have seen him, 亦既見止
> Let me have met him, 亦既覯止
> And my heart will then be at peace. 我心則夷

---

46. James Legge, trans., *The Chinese Classics*, Vol. 4, *The She King* (Hong Kong: Lane Crawford Co., 1871), 1.23–24.

There are multiple interpretations for this poem,[47] but it is generally read as a love poem about an ardent woman yearning for her lover or husband. Just as the seedlings of ferns were germinating and growing in the hills in spring, the woman's longing for her beloved one was also stimulated and deepened. The images of ferns are connected with a romantic plaint by the rhetorical device *xing* in the poem. Similar to *jue* and *wei*, *fengwei cao*, which is a common type of fern, is further glamorized by Li Changqi as an embodiment of love in the illustration of a tragic romance.

III. A Glimpse into Common People's Daily Life

Although "Fengwei cao ji" is a far cry from a superior romance, the text's unique value lies in its depiction of the characters' family activities through which readers are allowed to have a glimpse of the daily life of commoners in the Ming dynasty. The female protagonist was neither from an aristocratic clan nor was she an enchanting courtesan with superior talent, identities that are common in traditional scholar-beauty stories. On the contrary, she was the only girl and the youngest child born in an ordinary family. Her father had passed away and she was raised by her widowed mother. Because of her family's lack of means and standing, she was not educated and was unable to read or write. Her illiteracy created a good stage for the male scholar's flaunting of his poetic flair. An unusual and unforgettable point in the story is that Scholar Long wrote a courting poem to the woman and a responding piece in her place.

The woman could never be considered a good match for her literatus lover due to her low-status social background and lack of literary talent, especially when such a relationship was not supported by both families. However, she was not discouraged in her pursuit of love and hope. Rather, unlike aristocratic women growing up in a sheltered boudoir, our female protagonist showed much more

---

47. For instance, in the "Note on the interpretation" Section, James Legge argues that this poem is the expression of a newly married woman's distress about whether she could establish her status as an acknowledged wife. "According to the customs of those days, ladies underwent a probation of 3 months after their 1st reception by their husbands, at the end of which time they might be sent back as 'not approved'" Ibid., 1.24.

independence and proactivity in her interactions with the scholar, without the rigid restraint of propriety. While readers are moved by the female protagonist's bravery in persistently pursuing her ideal love despite their differences in social status and family circumstances, her expectation for marriage eventually becomes an illusion and her pursuit of love is doomed to fail. The love poem buried with her in the embroidered pouch on her chest was probably the last and only comfort she received from this romantic relationship.

With the emotional ups and downs of the female protagonist, the story unfolds in front of modern readers the real-life scenarios of common families at the time. The two-faced go-between who showed herself as a supportive and beloved aunt for the female protagonist tried to ruin the marriage behind the scenes. The young woman's family suffered from financial difficulty due to her father's early death and the dismissal of her elder brother from his official post due to a misdemeanor. Readers cannot help but sympathize with a female protagonist who has had to endure contempt from her fierce sisters-in-law and forced to weave until midnight. The depiction of the sincere affection between the two lovers in a secret rendezvous and details of the woman's simple yet clean clothes such as the snow-white foot wrap intensify the sadness that readers feel at her death. The female protagonist's suicide, ostensibly triggered by a family quarrel and her despair at a hopeless love, is de facto a denouncement of the impassable barrier caused by social disparities and the poisonous family life.

IV. Celestial Master Zhang and Daoist Practice in the Ming Dynasty

At the end of the story, Scholar Long successfully passed imperial examinations and held an important position, but he still could not forget the woman and talked about her with Celestial Master Zhang occasionally. "Celestial Master Zhang observed that Long was distressed and grieved, so he drew and burned a Daoist tally to perform the ritual of salvation for the souls in purgatory for the woman." The ritual of salvation performance worked and Scholar Long met the woman a few days later in his dream. She was rescued from her destiny to be reborn as a woman to end her sins from her previous life. She told him, "Because of Master Zhang's Daoist power, a celestial tally was suddenly sent down, and now I am going to the city of Luoyang county in Henan prefecture to be a man of the Hu family."

Celestial Master Zhang in this story must be referred to Zhang Yuchu 張宇初 (1361–1410), who was a contemporary of Li Changqi. Zhang Yuchu, Daoist title Wuwei zi 無為子 (Master of Non-Action), succeeded his father Zhang Zhengchang 張正常 (1335–1378) to become the forty-third Celestial Master and "is remembered not only for his role as an influential leader of the Zhengyi 正一 school but also as a renowned scholar with a substantial literary legacy to his name."[48] It is mentioned in the *Daozang* 道藏 that because of his intelligence and erudition, he served in the imperial court and was esteemed by nobles and high officials.[49] Scholar Long's interaction with him as seen in this story echos the record in the Daoist canon. Celestial Master Zhang was especially renowned for his highly instructive sermons (*pushuo* 普說) on universal salvation rituals.[50] This was the ritual that he performed for the female protagonist of the story that eventually changed her destiny.

The description of the ritual of salvation in the story opens a window for readers to peek into the Daoist practice in the Ming dynasty. Besides a large number of followers, Daoism during the Ming dynasty was marked by "the participation of the various cultural, political, economic, or even religious elites."[51] Evidence of widespread Daoist influence can be found in several other stories in *Jiandeng yuhua*. In the story "Qiuxi fang Pipating ji" 秋夕訪琵琶亭記 (The Record of Visiting the Pipa Pavilion in the Autumn), the male protagonist Shen Shao 沈韶

---

48. See Judith M. Boltz's entry on Zhang Yuchu in Fabrizio Pregadio, ed., *The Encyclopedia of Taoism II* (London and New York: Routledge, 2008), pp. 1239–40.

49. See *Zhengtong Daozang* 正統道藏, CT/DZ 1311, p. 2a. Vincent Goossaert in his article "The Four Lives of Zhang Yuchu (1361–1410), 43rd Heavenly Master" comments that "no scholar in central Jiangxi could stay outside his networks of master-disciple and friendship bonds." (Cahiers D'Extrême-Asie 25 [2016]: 9, 27.)

50. Ibid. Three long instructive sermons have preserved in Zhang's *Xianquan ji* 峴泉集 including "Sanyuan chuandu pushu" 三元傳度普說 (The Instructive Sermon on Three Origins Salvation Ritual of Ordination), "Shoufa pushuo" 受法普說 (The Instructive Sermon on Initiation of Exorcistic), and "Lingbao liandu pushuo" 靈寶煉度普說 (The Instructive Sermon on Lingbao Salvation Ritual of Sublimation), 27–8.

51. Mark Meulenbeld, "Chinese Religion in the Ming and Qing Dynasties" in *The Wiley-Blackwell Companion to Chinese Religions*, edited by Randall L. Nadeau (Hoboken, NJ: John Wiley & Sons, Inc.), p. 132.

also helped his lover successfully receive salvation through the Lingbao ritual performed by a Daoist practitioner named Zhou Xuanchu 周玄初[52]:

> Shen Shao installed an altar in a quiet place at Huqiu and requested the Daoist priest Helin Master Zhou Xuanchu to perform the Lingbo salvation ritual of sublimation for three days and nights. On the night of performing the Daoist liturgy for his deceased wife, Shen took the opportunity when all the Daoist practitioners had paid their respects and retreated; he wrote a personal eulogy and secretly incinerated it in the censer to seek good fortune in the netherworld for the beautiful women. After the liturgy, Xuanchu dreamed that two women, one surnamed Zhang, the other surnamed Zheng followed by two young maids, came to thank him: "All of your humble servants have accepted the benevolent outcomes, and have been granted the post of Attendant of the Queen Mother of the West at the Jade Terrace." After saying these, they rode auspicious clouds to head west.

> [沈韶] 於虎丘靜處建壇, 請道士鶴林周玄初設靈寶煉度三晝夜。薦妻正齋之夕, 伺道士行朝皆退, 親寫心詞一封, 潛於香爐焚之, 以資麗人冥福。醮罷, 玄初夢二婦人, 一姓張, 一姓鄭, 從二小娃來謝曰:"妾輩俱承善果, 已授瑤臺金母侍宸矣。" 言訖, 駕祥雲向西而去。

A record of another Celestial Master can be found in the story of "Hu Meiniang zhuan" 胡媚娘傳 (The Biography of Hu Meiniang) in which the female protagonist Hu Meiniang, a fox succubus, was brutally killed by Daoist exorcistic rituals:

> [Yin Danran] then built an altar on the back hall of the prefectural office. At noon the next day, Danran pressed the sword in his hand and wrote a talisman to summon the divine generals. After a while, three marshals, Deng, Xin, and Zhang, stood sternly in front of the altar. Danran burned incense to report to the deities: "The Administrative Assistant of Prefecture Xiao Yu is bewitched by a demon fox.

---

52. It refers to Zhou Xuanzhen 周玄真 (1328–?; or Zhou Yuanzhen 周元真), a Daoist priest from Shenxiao 神霄 school during the late Yuan Dynasty and early Ming dynasty. His studio name is Helin xiansheng 鶴林先生.

I have to trouble all of you to exterminate her immediately." He then raised a brush to write an official denouncement and gave it to the marshals who took it and left… A moment later, black clouds surged out like ink, and white rain started pouring down. After the sound of a thunderclap, it turned out that Meiniang had been killed in the market by thunder."

[尹澹然]乃就州衙後堂結壇。次日午, 澹然按劍書符, 立召神將, 須臾鄧、辛、張三帥,　森立壇前。澹然焚香誓神曰:"州判蕭裕, 為妖狐所惑, 煩公等即為剿除。"乃舉筆書檄, 付帥持去……. 俄而黑雲瀚墨, 白雨翻盆, 霹靂一聲, 媚娘已震死闤闠矣。

In order to release the official from the fox demon's spirit-possession, the Celestial Master Yin Danran in this anecdote performed the Thunder Ritual (*leifa* 雷法), requesting the three Celestial Lords of Thunderclap to execute the female antagonist.[53]

Descriptions of Daoist rituals and records of celestial masters in the stories in *Jiandeng yuhua* not only present a vivid picture of local religious practice at the time, but also provide material from a literary perspective for the study of Daoism in the Ming dynasty.

---

53. For further information on thunder ritual and the three thunder marshals, please refer to Mark Meulenbeld, "Civilized Demons: Ming Thunder Gods in Literature," PhD diss., Princeton University, 2007.

Tale 6

"FURONG PING JI" 芙蓉屏記
(THE RECORD OF THE LOTUS SCREEN)

By Li Changqi
Translated by Weiguo Cao

In the *xinmao* year of Zhizheng reign period (1351),[1] in Zhenzhou[2] there was a gentleman whose name was Cui Ying. His family was extremely rich. He was appointed as a district defender of Yongjia County of Wenzhou Prefecture in Zhejiang by virtue of his father's protection privilege.[3] He went to assume his post with his wife Madam Wang. On the way, when they passed by Chuishan in Suzhou,[4] they moored the boat to take a short break. They bought paper money, sacrificial meat, and wine to offer sacrifice in the temple of the god.[5] When it was completed, Ying had a few drinks with his wife in the boat. When the boatman saw that all his drinking vessels were made of gold and silver, he suddenly was struck with evil thoughts. That night, he drowned Ying in the water, and killed his maidservant and manservant.

---

1. Zhizheng (1341–1368) was the reign period of Huizong 惠宗 of Yuan, who was the last ruler of the Yuan dynasty.
2. In modern Yizheng 儀徵 County, Jiangsu province.
3. As Hucker pointed out, appointment by protection (*yinbu* 蔭補) was a process whereby an official in service was entitled to nominate one or more sons or other relatives for official status. See Charles O. Hucker, ed., *A Dictionary of Official Titles in Imperial China* (Stanford University Press, 1985), p. 582.
4. The statement here seems puzzling. Chuishan 圌山 is east of modern Zhenjiang and near the Yangtze River. However, it was very far away from Suzhou. Furthermore, Suzhou is not near the Yangtze River. Thus, if Cui Ying wanted to travel by boat along the Yangtze River, Suzhou would not be on his way. Ling Mengchu (1580–1644), in his adapted version of the story, simply omitted "Chuishan" and just indicated they arrived at Suzhou.
5. In Ling Mengchu's version of the story, the boatman wanted to offer sacrifice to the god of rivers and lakes so that they might have a safe trip.

He told Madam Wang, "Do you know why you are not dead? My second son still does not have a wife.[6] Now he is helping others row a boat to Hangzhou. When he comes back in one or two months, he will marry you. You are my family now, so just rest assured and don't worry." Having said this, he took away all their belongings, and called Madam Wang the new bride. Madam Wang pretended to agree. She tried hard to manage the household chores and did everything to please the boatman. The boatman chuckled to himself that he obtained a good wife for his son. As they gradually got familiar with each other, he no longer kept her under guard.

Over a month later, it came to be time of Mid-Autumn Festival. The boatman held a great feast, started binge drinking and became completely drunk. Madam Wang seized the opportunity when he was sound asleep and went ashore by herself. She walked for two or three *li* and then all of a sudden got lost. She was surrounded by water and a boundless stretch of reed, wild rice, and bulrush. Furthermore, since she was born into a good family, her bound feet were thin and slender, and thus she was unable to endure the hardship of walking. But she was afraid that her pursuer might arrive, so she did all she could to flee, running around wildly.

After a long while, the east sky gradually turned bright. Looking into the distance, she could see that there was a building in the woods. She hurried there to seek refuge. When she arrived, the door was still not open, but she could hear the faint sound of the striking of a bell and the chanting of Sanskrit sutras. After a short while, the door was opened. It was indeed a nunnery. Madam Wang went directly in. When the head of the nunnery asked the reason why she came, Madam Wang dared not tell her the truth, thus she lied to her, saying:

> Your servant is from Zhenzhou. My father-in-law[7] travelled to the region of Jiangzhe 江浙[8] to be an official and brought the entire family

---

6. In the movie version of the story, his son is mute, and he was in the boat with his father. Part of the reason for the murder is that his son was enchanted by the beauty of Madam Wang.

7. Although in modern times *jiu* 舅 means "brother of the mother," it makes no sense for her to move around with her uncle. In the old days the word *jiu* could also mean "father-in-law," which fits better into the context.

8. During the Yuan dynasty, the Jiangzhe province included the area south of modern Jiangsu, Anhui, and the entire Zhejiang province.

with him. When he reached his post, my husband passed away. I lived as a widow for several years, until my father-in-law married me to the district defender of Yongjia as his secondary wife. His primary wife was fierce and malicious, thus it was difficult to serve her. She beat me and reviled me on all kinds of occasions. Recently my husband was relieved from office, and [on our way back home] we moored our boat here. Because it is the time of the Mid-Autumn Festival, an occasion when people enjoy the full moon, she asked me to fetch the golden cup to pour wine in. I accidently dropped the cup in the river. Because of this, she wanted to put me to death. Consequently I fled for my life and came here.

The nun said, "Young lady, you dare not return to the boat and, furthermore, your hometown is far away. If you want to seek another match, you cannot find a good matchmaker in haste.[9] As a lonely and miserable person, whom can you rely upon?" Wang said nothing but kept on weeping. The nun again said, "I, as an old woman, have a piece of advice for you, but I don't know what your esteemed opinion is." Wang said, "If my master can enlighten me with some insights, I won't feel regretful even if I die!" The nun said:

This place is located in a remote and desolate riverside. It is a field without human traces. Aquatic grass and turnip are our neighbors, and gulls and egrets are our friends. Fortunately, I have one or two companions. They are all over fifty years old. Moreover, I have several attendants who are all honest and sincere. Lady, although you are young and beautiful, you have met with ill fortune and had a bad time. You had better abandon worldly love, stay away from delusion,[10] be aware that your human body is nothing but an illusion, put on black garments, cut off your hair, and become a nun from now on. With a Zen couch, Buddha's light, morning meal and evening gruel, you live a simple life by abiding by your destiny. Won't it be better than serving as some other's favorite concubine, suffering the torment of this life, and contracting an enemy for your next life?

Wang bowed to show her gratitude, saying, "This is my intention." Subsequently the nun had her hair cut off in front of the Buddha, and she was given a Dharma name, Huiyuan 慧圓.

9. *Zu* 卒 here is a loan word for *cu* 猝 (in haste).
10. *Chi* 癡. According to Buddhist teaching, *chi* (delusion), *tan* 貪 (greed), and *chen* 瞋 (aversion) are the "three poisons" which cause human sufferings.

Wang was literate and was well versed in both writing and painting. In less than a month, she thoroughly mastered all the Buddhist scriptures and was treated with great courtesy by the head of the nunnery. No one dared to do anything, large or small, without consulting Wang's opinion. Furthermore, she was generous, gentle, and kind. Everyone loved her. Every day she performed a ritual of kowtowing over one hundred times in front of the "White-robed Great Lady,"[11] secretly confessing her inner feelings. She did not abandon this practice even at the time of harsh winter or high summer. As soon as she finished the ritual, she went to stay in an inner room. People seldom saw her face.

Over a year later, someone suddenly paid a visit to the nunnery. He stayed for a vegetarian meal and then left. The next day, he came again, carrying a rolled painting of a lotus flower to donate as alms. The old nun hung it on a white screen. When Wang passed by, she saw it, and recognized that the painting was by Ying. Accordingly she inquired where it came from. The head of the nunnery said, "Recently an almsgiver donated this." Wang asked, "What is the name of the almsgiver? At what place is he living now? What does he do to make a living?" The old nun replied, "He is Gu Axiu 顧阿秀 from our same county. He and his brother work as boatmen. In the past year he has been doing very well. People often say he robs his passengers among the rivers and lakes.[12] I don't know whether it is true." Wang further asked, "Does he often have dealings with this place?" The old nun said, "He seldom comes." At this Wang memorized the information by heart. Then she held a brush to write the following poem on the screen:

The romanticism at the time of youth can be found in the brush of Zhang Chang.[13]

---

11. This refers to bodhisattva Guanyin 觀音, who was also called the Goddess of Mercy.
12. The term *jianghu* 江湖 usually refers to a society of outlaws or outsiders who observed their own rules, especially the code of brotherhood, in traditional China. The literal meaning of *jianghu* is "rivers and lakes." It was possibly so named because many bandits were active among the rivers and lakes. To a certain extent it is similar to the usage of the English word "greenwood," which means a wood or forest, but which was also used to refer to the scene of medieval outlaw life.
13. Zhang Chang 張敞 (d. 48 BCE) was a literatus during the Han dynasty. There was a famous anecdote about him: he loved his wife so much that he often painted her eyebrows.

In drawing living things, do not count Huang Quan.[14]
The drawing of lotus flower brings out its brilliance.
Who would know that such a charming image,
could endure the injustice related to life and death.
The colorful painting of desolation makes one wonder about the illusory nature of life.
Wandering about, bereft, who would take pity on me.
A white screen and loneliness accompany Zen meditation.
The marital tie in this life is cut off.
May the tie in the next life be formed!

The tune of this poem is Linjiangxian 臨江仙 (Immortals Reaching the River). None of the nuns understood its meaning.

One day, a man named Guo Qingchun from the city suddenly visited the nunnery due to some other business. When he saw the painting and the poem, he admired its refinement, so he bought it back, treating it as a curio. It just so happened that at this time Lord Gao Nalin, the Grand Master of Imperial Scribes,[15] retired and stayed in Suzhou. He liked to collect paintings and calligraphy works extensively. Qingchun presented the screen to him. The lord put it in his inner chamber but did not have the leisure to ask about its details. By coincidence, there was a man outside his house selling four rolls of cursive style writing. The lord obtained and examined these. The writing style was similar to that of Huaisu (737–799).[16] It was elegant and out of the ordinary. The lord asked, "Who wrote this?" The person replied, "It was written by myself, who is learning calligraphy."[17] The lord, by examining his appearance,

---

14. Huang Quan 黄荃 (903–965) was a famous painter during the Five Dynasties period. He was especially good at bird-and-flower painting, including the painting of lotus flowers. It is noteworthy that the pronunciation of his name, "Huang Quan," is exactly the same as another Chinese word, *huangquan* 黄泉 (Yellow Springs), which refers to the realm of the dead in Chinese mythology. Thus, by stating "do not count Huang Quan," this line might imply that her husband was dead and therefore could not be counted.

15. This is a historical figure. See his biography in *Yuan shi* 元史, 142.3406-8.

16. Huaisu 懷素 was a famous monk and calligrapher during the Tang dynasty. He was famous for his cursive-style calligraphy.

17. This is a self-deprecating expression.

thought he was not a mediocre person, so he inquired about his name and hometown. The man then began to snivel[18] and replied:

> I am Ying. My surname is Cui and my style name is Junchen 俊臣. For generations my family resided in Zhenzhou. I was appointed as a district defender of Yongjia by virtue of my father's protection privilege. I took my family with me to go to the post. Because I am not cautious myself, I was entrapped by the boatman, who sank me in the water. Thus I can no longer take care of my family property, my wife and concubine.[19] Fortunately I am good at swimming since childhood. I swam under the waves. When I reckoned that the boatman had gone far way, I climbed ashore and went to a common family's house for refuge. My whole body was soaked. I didn't have a single coin with me. Relying on the kindness of the host, I was able to change clothes, and was treated with wine and food. He gave me some money and sent me off, saying, 'Since you were robbed by the bandits, you ought to report it to the government officials. I dare not let you stay in my place, for fear that I might be implicated.' Thereupon I asked the direction to go to the city,[20] and filed a lawsuit at Pingjiang 平江 Route.[21] Up to now I have been waiting for a year,

18. *Cu e* 蹙頞 was usually interpreted as "to knit one's brows." However, "to knit one's brows" is usually used to express one's dissatisfaction or anger, whereas in his speech, Cui Ying told his story in a more sorrowful manner. It is noteworthy that the meaning of *e* is "bridge of the nose," and *cu* means "to shrink." *Cu e* is possibly similar to the modern expression *ku bizi* 哭鼻子 (literally, "a crying nose"), which means "to snivel, to sniff." Ling Mengchu most likely understood the meaning of the word in this way. In his parallel account, he wrote: "That person shed tears…"

19. This is the first time his concubine is mentioned in the story. The role of concubine was further developed in the Ming drama of later ages. (See the "Reading Guide.")

20. *Chu cheng* 出城 normally means "to go out of the city," but here it makes no sense to say "Cui Ying asked the direction to go out of the city," because Cui Ying at that time was in the countryside, and he needed to go to the city to report his case to the government officials. *Chu* in classical Chinese may mean "to come," as the expression *chuxi* 出席 (to come to a meeting) shows. The parallel account in Ling Mengchu's version read 英便問路進城 (thus Ying asked the direction to enter the city).

21. The Pingjiang Route was an administrative area located in modern Suzhou. As Hucker (p. 322) pointed out, during the Yuan dynasty, *lu* 路 (route) was a stably defined territory administered by a Route Command.

but there is no news about my case at all. I just have to rely on selling my writing to eke out an existence, but I dare not say I am good at calligraphy. I didn't expect that this ugly piece of mine would be brought to you for your sagacious viewing."

When the lord heard his words, he took great pity on him, saying, "Since you have come to such a state, you can do nothing about that. For the time being you can stay at my place as a tutor, teaching my grandsons to write Chinese characters. Doesn't that sound good to you?" Ying felt he was very fortunate. The lord invited him to his inner chamber and drank with him. Suddenly Ying saw the painting of the lotus flower on the screen and started to weep passionately. The lord felt surprised and asked him, who replied, "This is one of the lost items in the boat. The painting comes from my own hand and brush. How can it be here?" He further read aloud the poem, and said, "This was written by my wife." The lord asked, "How could you tell?" He replied, "I can recognize her handwriting and painting. Moreover, judging from the content of the poem, it was undoubtedly written by my wife." The lord said, "If so, I shall take the responsibility to catch the bandits for you. For now, please keep it a secret." Thus he let Ying stay under his roof.

The next day, the lord secretly summoned Qingchun to question him, who said, "I bought it from the nunnery." The lord then dispatched him to politely interrogate the nun, "Whom did you get the painting from? Who wrote the poem on the painting?" Several days later, he reported, "Gu Axiu, from the same county, donated this painting. Huiyuan, a nun from the nunnery, wrote the poem." The lord sent a messenger to give a persuasive speech to the head of the nunnery, saying, "Our lady[22] likes to read aloud the Buddhist sutras, but she has no one as her companion. We have heard that Huiyuan has a deep understanding of the Buddhist teaching. Now we respectfully invite her to be our teacher. We hope you would not decline." The head of the nunnery did not consent to this. However, when Huiyuan heard about it, she was very willing to go there, thinking that she could probably use this opportunity to revenge herself. The nun could not turn down her request. The lord had her brought to his residence by a palanquin. He asked his wife to live and sleep together with her. Once, when they were spending some leisure time together, the wife asked her the details of her family background. Wang wept bitterly, told her the truth, and further informed her of the matter of her writing a poem on the lotus screen, saying, "The bandits

---

22. Referring to Gao's wife.

are not far away. I hope you, milady, could pass on my words to the lord. If the culprits are caught, my past humiliation can be wiped out, and I can repay my husband in the underworld. The lord will indeed do me a great favor!" However, she did not know that her husband was still alive. The wife told all this to the lord, and further said that Wang was well educated, faithful, and kind, and that she was definitely not a woman from a petty family. The lord knew she was undoubtedly Ying's wife. He told his wife to take good care of her, but he did not speak to Ying about this at all. Through investigation, the lord obtained the address of Gu's residence and the track of his movements. However, he dared not take action rashly. He just asked his wife to secretly persuade Wang to grow her hair and to return to her previous mode of dress.

In another half a year, Xuelipuhua 薛理溥化,[23] a *jinshi* degree holder, was appointed as an Investigating Censor[24] and came to the region to assume his investigative duties. Puhua was a subordinate official of Lord Gao in the old days. The lord knew that he was nimble in his action, so he told all the details to him, who, seizing an opportunity when the culprit was off guard, caught him. The document of Ying's official appointment, as well as his family property, were still there; the only thing missing was the whereabouts of Madam Wang. After being thoroughly interrogated, the culprit said, "I truly intended to retain her to marry my second son, so I no longer took any precautious steps against her. Unexpectedly she ran away during the Mid-Autumn Festival of that year. I did not know where she went." Thereupon Puhua sentenced him[25] to receive capital punishment, and he returned the looted goods to their original owner, Ying.

Ying was about to bid farewell to the lord and go to assume his post. The lord said, "Please wait, for I will act as a matchmaker for you. It will not be too late to go to your post after you marry the girl." Ying declined, saying:

---

23. This seems to be a Mongolian name. In Ling Mengchu's version, the name became Xue Puhua 薛溥化, which sounds more like a Han Chinese name.

24. *Jiancha yushi* 監察御史. According to Hucker (p. 145), they were "the most concentrated, broad-ranging investigative and impeaching officials."

25. In this story it is unclear whether the "culprit" refers only to Gu Axiu, the chief criminal, or his entire band. In the parallel account in Ling Mengchu's version of the story, it was indicated that all the bandits who were involved in the boat robbery were immediately beheaded.

My wife and I have shared the hard lot of being poor and humble for a long time.[26] Unfortunately she is wandering about in an unknown place now, and I actually don't know whether she has survived or perished. However, I will go to my post alone and wait for a while. If Heaven and Earth take pity on us, maybe she is still alive, and hopefully we, husband and wife, could be reunited. I am grateful for your favor and kindness, and I shall not forget about it till I die, but it is against my will to talk about marrying another woman.

The lord sadly said, "You, sir, uphold such a high moral standard. Heaven will surely do something to assist you. How dare I force you to do something against your own wish! Just allow me to hold a farewell dinner for you. Then you can set off on your journey."

On the next day, the lord gave a banquet, at which the officials of the Pingjiang Route district as well as the celebrities of the region all gathered. The lord raised the cup and announced to everyone, "Today, I, an old fellow, will settle the marital tie for District Defender Cui!" None of the guests understood what he said. The lord sent someone to make Huiyuan come out. She was none other than Ying's former wife. The husband and wife embraced each other, bursting into tears. They had not expected that they could meet each other again at such an occasion. The lord told the whole story, from beginning to end, and further took out the lotus screen to show it to the guests. Only then did they understand that "settle the marital tie," which the lord spoke of, was a reference to the lines in the poem written by Ying's wife;[27] and that Huiyuan was the name of Ying's wife after she changed her name. All those who were present wept with hands covering their faces, and sighed with admiration, claiming that the high moral character of the lord was unsurpassable. The lord gave Ying two servants, one male and one female, and also gave him money to send him off on his journey.

When Ying's term of office expired, he again visited Suzhou. However, the lord had passed away. The couple (Ying and his wife) wailed, just as if they had lost their parents. They performed the Buddhist Ritual of

---

26. This seems contradictory to the description of Cui Ying at the beginning of the story, which indicated that he was from an extremely wealthy family and that his father was also an official.

27. The lord's words echoed the last two lines of the poem Madam Wang wrote on the lotus screen: "The marital tie in this life is cut off. May the tie in the next life be formed!"

Water and Land[28] at his tomb for three days and nights to repay his kindness, and then left. Because of this, Madam Wang abstained from eating meat and fish permanently, and she never stopped praying to Bodhisattva Guanyin.

Lu Zhongyang,[29] a gifted scholar of Zhenzhou, composed "a song of lotus painting on the screen" to record this event. Accordingly, the song is recorded here, to caution the people of the world. It reads as follows:

> Seeing the painting of the lotus flower on the screen, I, a humble woman,[30] wrote a poem on it with suppressed pain.
> The blood and tears on the screen are like the red color of a flower.[31]
> Withered leaves, dead twigs, both looking desolate.
> Fragmentary painting, inkwork left behind by the deceased, both looking decayed.
> The current of water flows away rapidly,[32] separating the living and dead.
> A lone soul, and a solitary shadow, drift aimlessly.
> While drifting aimlessly, to whom could one entrust the remains of the body?
> The loitering spirit beneath the Yellow Springs[33] eventually will not return.
> The beautiful appearance in the painting is just like something yesterday.

28. The ritual was thus named because its purpose was to expiate the sins of the dead on both land and water. Normally the ritual lasted for seven days at least, and forty-seven days at most.

29. Some editions read Zhongyan 仲巚 for Zhongyang 仲旸.

30. Although the author was a male, he spoke in the female voice of Madam Wang in this poem.

31. In reality, the painting only depicted the red lotus flower in the water, not "blood and tears." This line might imply that the poet, in an extreme stage of agony, hallucinated and thereby mistakenly perceived the red flower and water as blood and tears.

32. Qushui 去水 might be a term in Chinese geomancy, referring to the water flowing away from one's tomb. However, the image of "current of water flowing away" might also be employed to refer to the passage of time, which, like the current of water, would never come back once it was gone. Thus, in this line the poet seems to express her sadness that she would never be able to go back to the bygone time to meet her deceased lover.

33. The Yellow Springs refers to the realm of the dead in Chinese mythology.

Although it is just like something yesterday, I, a humble woman, am heart-broken.[34]
How can I endure the harshness of the autumn rain and the autumn frost!
I would rather pursue the boatman[35] among the rivers and lakes.
And I am willing to pay respect to the King of the Doctors from the treasure land.[36]
The King of the Doctors is naturally merciful and shows mercy on all living creatures.
To the soul which already passed away, I want to remind you:
This widow relies on your guidance.
The image of the lotus flower is charming,
My husband drew it with his own hands.
The flower withered, because its stem was broken.
The flower dried up, because its seedling was damaged.[37]
Though its pistil is dried up, its heart still has the feeling of bitterness.
Though its root is decayed, its feeling of hatred cannot be wiped out.
People only talk about crying for Han Hong[38] at the Illustrious Terrace Palace,

34. It seems that these two lines imply that on one hand, even though all those beautiful things occurred long ago, it seems to the poet that it just happened yesterday; on the other hand, all those beautiful things are gone today, and they will never come back. Thus, the poet felt heartbroken.

35. Referring to the boatman who murdered her husband.

36. "The King of the Doctors" refers to the Buddha; "the treasure land" refers to the Buddha's land or temple.

37. It might seem puzzling that, in the poet's eyes, the lotus flower is both "charming" and "withered." Again, the poet tried to show the contrast between her beautiful memory of the past and her miserable state at present. Thus, although the poet was looking at a still picture, by adding a dimension of time, it became more dynamic, which allows the poet to "fly" freely back and forth between the past and present. In other words, rather than looking at the picture of a lotus flower at a certain moment, the poet was narrating something more like a history of the lotus flower through the passage of time.

38. Han Hong 韓翃 (719–788) was a poet during the Tang dynasty. He and his wife were forced into separation due to the turmoil caused by the military rebellion. His wife cut her hair, ruined her appearance and took refuge in a Buddhist temple. Later, Han sent a poem, titled "The Willow at the Illustrious Terrace Palace," to his wife to express his sorrowful feeling. After his wife read the poem, she sobbed bitterly and wrote a poem in response. The couple was eventually reunited.

Who would expect to encounter Wenxiao at the Primary Tent?[39]
The lotus flower indeed has profound meaning.
The lotus flower cannot be discarded.
Fortunately, the reunion of husband and wife was accomplished under the bright moon.[40]
Be kind to each other, love each other, and never abandon each other.
Who will listen to my verse of lotus flower?
Married couples in the human world, do not quarrel.
Look at this lotus flower: it is really pitiful.

39. According to a Tang tale, when Wenxiao 文蕭, a young scholar, went sightseeing in a Taoist temple in a mountain during the Mid-Autumn Festival, he encountered a beautiful fairy, who invited him to go to the fairyland, where there was the Primary Tent. The two of them eventually got married and became immortals. The Primary Tent was first made by Emperor Wu 武 of Han (r. 141–87 BCE), who used jade, pearl, colored glaze, and various other gemstones to decorate the tent.

40. *Bao yue* 寶月 means "bright moon." However, the term might also have a Buddhist meaning, related to the concept of the reunion of the couple. The first two lines of Lu Zhaolin's 盧照鄰 (ca. 634–684) poem "Shijing si" 石鏡寺 (Temple of Stone Mirror) read, 銖衣千古佛,寶月兩重圓 (Wearing the clothes of the immortals, the Buddha of eternal ages. The bright moon bears double roundness). *Chong yuan* 重圓 literally means "double roundness." Here it might refer to the shape of the moon and its halo both being round. But the term has another meaning: "to become round again," which is usually used to refer to the reunion of family members, especially husband and wife.

NOTES AND READING GUIDE

Weiguo Cao

I. Historical Figures in the Story

Although the story of the lotus screen is basically a fictional account, some of the characters were based on real people in history. In the *Yuan shi* 元史, there is a biography of Gao Nalin (1281–1359). In the story, Gao Nalin was a retired official who helped Cui Ying revenge himself and reunite with his wife. According to the historical biography, Gao Nalin was appointed as the Grand Master of Imperial Scribes in 1347. The next year he was impeached by another official and forced into retirement in Suzhou. According to the story, Cui Ying was attacked by the ferryman in 1351, and one year later he met Gao Nalin, who was a retired Grand Master of Imperial Scribes residing in Suzhou. Thus, the date, official title, and residing place narrated in the story correspond to the historical accounts of Gao Nalin very well. But why did the author, Li Changqi, make Gao Nalin, a historical figure, one of the main characters in his story?

It is possible that the story has some historical basis. Li Changqi might have heard about Gao Nalin and created a story based on that. It is noteworthy that the *Yuan shi* gave a very positive account of Gao Nalin. He was an ideal, *qingguan* 清官 (an honest and upright official) type of official. It was recorded that, when he served as the Route Commander of Hangzhou 杭州 in 1328, he got rid of those evil forces in the region so that his subordinate officials were in awe and his people were pleased. The next year he was transferred to be the Surveillance Commissioner of Jiangxi. At that time there was a great famine in the area, but the local administration would not provide aid to the common people. Gao Nalin donated his own grain and saved a lot of people's lives. There was a poem "Shang Gao Jiansi" 上高監司" (A poem submitted to the Surveillance Commissioner Gao) composed at that time in praise of Gao Nalin's charity and altruistic action. The poem extoled him to such an extent that at the end of the poem it suggested that a shrine should be built so that people could worship him, and that a stele should be erected so that his virtuous deeds could be recorded. Thus, it is not hard to imagine that besides this poem, there were other poems or stories circulated at that time in praise of Gao Nalin's virtue. Li Changqi might have created this story based on one of these stories.

It should be pointed out that this story, to a certain extent, can be viewed as a *gong'an xiaoshuo* 公案小說 (stories about judicial cases), which usually describes how an incorruptible official maintained the justice by punishing the evildoers and righting the wrongs. In this story, Gao Nalin played a crucial role in catching the murderers and bringing Cui Ying and his wife to reunite. Thus, at the end of the story, when Gao Nalin gave a banquet and told everyone what had happened to Cui Ying and his wife, the author wrote, "all those who were present wept with hands covering their faces, and sighed with admiration, claiming that the high moral character of the lord was unsurpassable." The story also indicated that Gao Nalin gave Cui Ying money and servants when he sent him off on his journey to the post. At the end of the story, it was indicated that when Cui Ying returned to Suzhou after his office term expired, Gao Nalin had already passed away. Cui Ying and his wife wailed bitterly as if they had lost their parents. This episode is not historically true, because according to the biography in *Yuan shi* Gao Nalin died in the capital. The author clearly tried to employ this episode to reinforce the positive image of Gao Nalin. In Chinese there is an expression *fumu guan* 父母官, which means a truly good official should be just like one's parents.

It should also be pointed out that the author Li Changqi's official career was similar to that of Gao Nalin. According to his official biography in the *Ming shi* 明史, when Li served as an official, he endeavored to get rid of those local despots and to provide aid to poor commoners. As Gao Nalin was once impeached and forced into retirement, Li Changqi likewise was once banished and sent into exile. It is very likely that Li Changqi might have composed the story in his exile. In his preface to his story collection *Jiangdeng yuhua* (which included this story), Li Changqi indicated that he composed the stories while he was traveling around, and that he was feeling frustrated about his official career at that time. The story of the lotus screen can be interpreted as a veiled criticism of the government. Cui Ying was robbed by the ferryman. He reported it to the government, but more than one year passed and still no one could help him. In the end, it was through a retired official, Gao Nalin, that the case was finally solved. Through this story, Li Changqi might have tried to express his sentiment that good officials like Gao Nalin and himself were often treated wrongly by the government. Thus, the purpose of his writing of this story might be twofold: on the one hand, he wanted to praise Gao Nalin for his great virtue; on the other hand, he wanted to criticize those corrupted officials who did nothing to save people from their sufferings, and to lament for the misfortunes good officials such as Gao Nalin and he endured in their careers. Li Changqi might have deliberately changed the ending of Gao Nalin's life to illustrate this point. According to the official biography, four years after Gao Nalin retired, peasant rebellion broke out in the country, and he was summoned to become an official again, in charge of putting down the rebellion. He successfully accomplished this mission and resumed his official position as the Grand Master of Imperial Scribe. He received great honor from the imperial court, his official position reached as high as the Grand Commandant, and finally, he died in the capital when he paid a visit to the court. In the story, none of those glorious deeds were mentioned; instead, it was simply stated that, after Cui Ying completed his official term, he visited Gao Nalin in Suzhou, and found out that he had already passed away. It seems likely that Li Changqi altered the historical fact in the story in order to express his personal frustration against the government and society at that time.

Xuelipuhua 薛理溥化, a minor character in this story, might also be a real person in history. There was a person named Xielipuhua 燮理溥化 (1295–1360). The pronunciation of *xue* and *xie* is very similar. Xielipuhua is a Mongolian name; this is why in the story *Xie* was changed to *Xue*, because the latter is a typical Han Chinese name. Later, in the Ling Mengchu version and the dramatic version of the story, the name was changed into Xue Puhua, making it sound more like a Han Chinese name. In the story we are told that Xuelipuhua, a *jinshi* degree holder, became the Investigating Censor in the region. He was formerly a subordinate of Gao Nalin, who asked him to arrest the bandits. Historically, there is only scanty information of Xielipuhua. We do know that he obtained the *jinshi* degree in 1327. In terms of the time frame, it fits into the account of the story. Xielipuhua was fourteen years younger than Gao Nalin, who started his official career in 1302, twenty-five years earlier than Xielipuhua. Xielipuhua once served as an official in Jiangxi 江西. As discussed above, Gao Nalin served as Surveillance Commissioner in 1329, thus it is possible that Xielipuhua became a subordinate of Gao Nalin at that time. Besides, Li Changqi was a native of Jiangxi, and he might have heard stories about both of them in his hometown. It is also noteworthy that Xielipuhua had a garden called Xie Garden (Xie Yuan 燮園). Inside the garden there was a lake called Xie Family Lake. All over the lake were planted lotus flowers. In the story, the painting of lotus flower played an important role in reuniting Cui Ying and his wife, thus the story was named "The Record of the Lotus Screen." The image of the lotus flower is associated with the feeling of love in two ways. First, the pronunciation of the Chinese word *lian* 蓮 (lotus flower) is same as *lian* 憐 (love); secondly, the image of *bingdilian* 並蒂蓮 (two lotus flowers growing on one step) was usually employed to refer to the harmonious union of husband and wife. The inclusion of the painting of the lotus flower in the story might have something to do with Xielipuhua and his love of the lotus flower.

Cui Ying, the main character in this story, might also have some historical basis. In the *biji* 筆記 (miscellaneous writings) collection *Lei shuo* 類說 compiled by Zeng Zao 曾慥 (fl. 1126), there is an account of an anecdote of a man with the same name. According to that account, Du You 杜佑 (735–812), a famous historian and official during the Tang dynasty, had two marriages. After his first wife (née Liang) died, he established his favorite concubine née Li as his primary wife, and she also received the honorific title "Lady of the State." Cui Ying, however, tried to persuade Du to give the title to his deceased wife. He argued that it was not appropriate to establish a concubine as wife. Furthermore, he pointed out that Du's deceased wife had shared the hardships of life with him when he was in a humble position. On the other hand, when Du became prominent in his official career, it was his concubine who enjoyed the honor. This was unfair. Du accepted Cui's advice, and in the end both women received the honorific titles. Because of this, Du's second wife harbored resentment against Cui Ying, and eventually killed him by putting poison in his food. Although we cannot say for sure that the author, Li Changqi, had read this account, it seems his story reflected a similar theme. In the story, when Gao Nalin suggested that Cui Ying marry another woman, Cui rejected this proposal and stated, "my wife and I have shared the hard lot of being poor and humble for a long time." It seems both Li Changqi' story and the account in *Lei shuo* emphasized the traditional Chinese virtue "a wife who shared her husband's hard lot must never be cast aside" 糟糠之妻不下堂.

II. The Source of the Story and Stories of Murderous Ferrymen in the Early Period

In the famous Chinese song "My Homeland," there is a line: "I am accustomed to listening to the song of ferrymen, and I am accustomed to looking at the white sails on the boats." Although this line depicts a poetic river scene, in real life in ancient China traveling on the river could be dangerous, as attested by the many stories of murderous ferrymen in traditional Chinese literature. It is very likely that Li Changqi had read or heard some of these stories when he created the story of the lotus screen. Although he might have a story prototype (one is associated with Gao Nalin, as discussed above), he might have also combined elements from other stories, then added his own creative thoughts, and finally wove them together and completed his story. It is interesting to note that in the Western tradition there are many stories about pirates in the ocean, but there are scarcely any stories of murderous ferrymen in the river. The situation is just the opposite in Chinese tradition: there is virtually no story about pirates, but stories of murderous ferrymen are abundant.

Quite a few elements commonly appear in the Chinese stories of murderous ferryman: (1) a husband and wife try to cross a river; (2) the murder occurs while crossing a river; (3) the murderer is the ferryman who was hired to carry the victims across a river; (4) the murder was not planned beforehand, but usually occurs when the ferryman notices the beauty of wife and/or the victim's wealth; (5) the murder of the husband; (6) sex with the wife (usually in the form of rape); (7) the separation of husband and wife; (8) an important object that serves as a medium to enable the reunion of the separated parties. (In the story of the lotus screen, it was the lotus screen that enabled the reunion of Cui Ying and his wife.) (9) a supernatural power; and (10) the final reunion and revenge. The reunion can be either reunion of husband and wife, or (if the husband is dead) the reunion of mother (the wife) and her son.

The earliest example of a murderous ferryman in a Chinese text is probably from the "Hereditary House of Chancellor Chen" in the *Shiji*, or *Grand Scribe's Records*. When Chen Ping 陳平 was on his way to join Liu Bang's 劉邦 army, he asked a ferryman to help him cross the Yellow River. The ferryman, seeing that Chen Ping was a handsome man, suspected that he had gold and jade hidden inside his clothes, so he frequently looked at him, intending to kill him. When Chen Ping realized what the ferryman was about to do, he took off his clothes, and, naked, helped the ferryman to pole the boat. In this way, the ferryman realized that Chen Ping had nothing valuable with him, thus he abandoned his plan. The story contained an important element of Chinese stories of murderous ferryman: the robbery of wealth. Although sex was not explicitly mentioned, the account of the ferryman frequently looking at Chen Ping, a handsome man, as well as Chen Ping's act of taking off his clothes, are quite suggestive and thus may imply sex was also involved.

III. The Stories of the Murderous Ferryman from the Tang to the Yuan Period

There are at least nine stories in this period that share certain elements with the story of the lotus screen. They are as follows:

1. "Xie Xiao'e zhuan 謝小娥傳" (Biography of Xie Xiao'e) by Li Gongzuo 李公佐 (fl. 813) of the Tang dynasty.
2. "Chen Yilang 陳義郎" by Wen Tingyun 溫庭筠 (812–866) in the Tang dynasty.
3. "Cui wei zi 崔尉子" (The son of District Defender Cui) in *Yuan hua ji* 原化記 (Investigation of the Origin of Transformation) of the Tang dynasty.
4. "Li Wenmin 李文敏" in *Wen qi lu* 聞奇錄 (Records of Strange Tales), a story collection at the end of the Tang dynasty.
5. "Pei Du 裴度" in *Yutang xianhua* 玉堂閒話 (Casual Talks at the Jade Hall), a story collection of the Five Dynasties.
6. "Bu Qi zhuan" 卜起傳 (Biography of Bu Qi) by Liu Fu 劉斧 in his story collection *Qing suo gao yi* 青瑣高議 (Enlightened Discussion in the Fancy Mansion) of the Song dynasty.
7. "Wang congshi qi" 王從事妻 (The Wife of Retainer Wang) by Hong Mai 洪邁 (1123–1202) in his story collection *Yi Jian zhi* 夷堅志 (Accounts of an Ancient Erudite Scholar) of the Song dynasty.
8. "Wu Jiqian gaizhi" 吳季謙改秩 (The Promotion of Wu Jiqian) by Zhou Mi 周密 (1232–1298) in his story collection *Qidong yeyu* 齊東野語 (Wild Talks from the Countryside) of the Song dynasty.
9. "Mu zi chong jian" 母子重見 (The Reunion of Mother and Son) in *Yi Jian xu zhi* 夷堅續志 (Sequel to Accounts of an Ancient Erudite Scholar) of the Yuan dynasty.

The common elements shared by these stories can be summarized as follows:

1. Identities of the victims: in all of these stories, the victims involve husband and wife. This is the same as the story of the lotus screen, in which the victims were Cui Ying and his wife. In two stories, the victims are identified as rich people. In the majority of the stories (six), the male victims are identified as officials who had just received official appointments and were on their way to the official post with their wives. In two stories (#3 & #6), the victims were

appointed to the same position as Cui Ying in the story of the lotus screen: the District Defender.
2. Identities of the murderer: in six of the stories, the murderers were simply identified as bandits; in two of the stories, the murders were identified as friends or relatives of the husband; in one story, the murderer was identified as a ferryman (#3), which is exactly the same as in the story of the lotus screen.
3. The location of the murderous action: in six of these stories, the murderous action occurred while the victims were trying to cross a river or were near a river. This is same as the story of the lotus screen.
4. The crime against the husband: in five of these stories, the husbands were murdered and their bodies were dumped into the river. In one story, the husband ran away. This is similar to the story of the lotus screen, in which Cui Ying was dumped into the river, but he escaped because he was good at swimming.
5. The crime against the wife: in six of these stories, the murderer forced the wife to marry him. In one story (#1), the wife ran away. In the story of the lotus screen, the murderer tried to force the wife to marry his son, but the wife managed to run away.
6. The hiding place of the runaway victim: in one story (#1), after the wife ran away, she hid herself in a nunnery. This is same as the story of the lotus screen.
7. The reunion of the family members: in six of these stories, the couple already had an infant son (in one story the wife was pregnant) at the time of the murder. The murderer loved the son and took him as his own son. When the son grew up, he had a reunion with the mother of his father and thus realized his true identity. In two stories (#5 & #7), the husband and wife had a reunion through the help of a worthy official. This is similar to the story of the lotus screen, in which Cui Ying and his wife reunited through the help of Gao Nalin, a retired official.
8. An object that played an important role in enabling the reunion and catching the murderers: in story #2, that object is a shirt with blood stain. In other stories, objects such as a shirt with a burned hole, a black box, a cooked turtle, a painting, and a character riddle play an important role. The important object is sometimes related to certain skill or art (such as writing, painting, or cooking). In the story of the lotus screen, the important object is the painting of the lotus screen. When Cui Ying read the poem in the painting, he immediately said the poem came from his wife's

hand because he recognized her calligraphy and style. In story #7, the husband immediately thought of his wife when he ate a cooked turtle, because he recognized her style of cooking turtle. In story #1, the official helped the wife to find the names of the murderers through his skill at solving character riddles.

9. The revenge: in one of the stories (#1), several years after the wife ran away, she disguised herself as a servant to work for the family of the murderers. At an occasion when the murderer and his company had a feast and all got drunk, she availed herself of the opportunity to kill the murderers and then reported to the officials. This episode is to a certain extent similar to the story of the lotus screen, in which Cui Ying's wife pretended she was willing to serve the murderers, and during the Mid-Autumn Festival she took the opportunity when they all got drunk and ran away. In the majority of the other stories, the revenge took place when the victim's son grew up and realized his true identity, he reported to the officials, who captured those murderers. In the story of the lotus screen, Gao Nalin gathered information about the criminals and asked the official to arrest them.

10. The supernatural and religious theme: in story #1, the murdered husband and father appeared in a dream of the victim and told her the clue to catch the bandits. The victim lived in a nunnery for a while and, after she accomplished her mission of revenge, she eventually became a nun herself. In several other stories, it was described that it was Heaven's will that led to the reunion of the family members through certain miraculous incidents. For example, in story #3, when the victim's son grew up and was on his way to the capital, he lost his way at night. There was a fire leading his way. He followed the fire and reached a house, where he found his father's mother. In the story of the lotus screen, after Cui Ying's wife ran away, she took refuge in a nunnery, and it was described in the story that she prayed to the Bodhisattva Guanyin over one hundred times every day. Toward the end of the story, it was again mentioned that she never ceased praying to the Bodhisattva Guanyin for the remainder of her life. Furthermore, after Cui Ying and his wife were separated, it was a series of miraculous coincidences that led to their final reunion.

11. The role of worthy officials in solving the case: in three stories (#1, #5, #7), officials played an important role in solving the case, either through their intelligence or through their kindness and magnanimity. In the story of the lotus screen, Gao Nalin, the retired official, played the same type of role.

12. The issue of morality and legality: in story #1, the surviving wife was praised for her high morality because she was able to keep her chastity. However, in seven stories (#1, #3, #4, #6, #7, #8, #9), the moral principle of chastity was compromised because the surviving wife actually was married to the murderer, albeit in a forced manner. In two stories (#3, #6), the surviving wife was actually charged with a crime for not reporting to the official promptly. Only after her son begged the official for mercy was she pardoned. In the story of the lotus screen, such a dilemma was avoided through changing the plot: instead of marrying the murderer, the wife ran away.

By the time Li Changqi created the story of the lotus screen, he might very well have read some of the stories listed above. It should also be pointed out that there might have been a large number of similar stories circulated in oral tradition at that time. The stories transmitted through written form might be just like the tip of an iceberg compared with the stories in the oral tradition. Li Changqi played a role in preserving the past heritage and in the meantime opening up a new path for the story tellers of future generations. In other words, his story absorbed various elements from the previous generations and in the meantime it also has tremendous influence on similar stories in the future. Comparing this tale with the previous stories, we see that Li Changqi's story was much longer. In subsequent generations, the story appeared in even longer versions, such as Ling Mengchu's adaptation of the story in his *Slapping the Table in Amazement* and Bian Sangang's adaptation of the story in his drama. Li Changqi's story also made the story much more refined and art-oriented. Li Changqi was good at writing poetry and painting. Thus, he might want to use this story to show off his literary talent. This is why poetry, painting and calligraphy were introduced into the story. The element of painting had already appeared in story #9, but poetry and calligraphy were both introduced to the story for the first time.

In terms of themes, Li Changqi's story reflected Buddhist ideas as well as the ideal of the morality of virtuous officials, which can already be seen in some of the stories in the previous generation. Li Changqi further developed the love theme of the story by describing how Cui Ying and his wife loved each other. For example, after the murderers were caught, Gao Nalin, who had done a great favor to Cui Ying, pretended to act as a matchmaker and suggested to him that he marry another woman. Cui Ying firmly rejected this proposal. This episode is certainly designed to show that Cui Ying was faithful and loyal to his love. Li Changqi also changed the plot of the previous stories to make it more "clean." In almost all of the previous stories, the wife lost her chastity because she was forced to marry the murderer. Li Changqi made the wife escape from the clutches of the murderer so that she could keep a clean body and reputation.

IV. The Adaptations of the Story in Later Ages

1. Ling Mengchu's 凌濛初 (1580–1644) adaptation of the story in his *Slapping the Table in Amazement*.

In the opening part of the story of lotus screen, the description of Cui Ying and his wife was scanty. The author just stated that Cui's family was extremely rich, but he did not give any comments on Cui's wife. On the other hand, Ling Mengchu version gave a more detailed account of the couple: Cui Ying was a talented scholar and his skills in the art of painting and calligraphy were peerless at the time; Madam Wang was young and beautiful, and she was also well versed in painting and writing. Then the author made such a comment: the couple can really be called "a gifted scholar (matched with) a beautiful lady." During the late Ming and early Qing period the so-called *caizi jiaren xiaoshuo* 才子佳人小說 (stories about gifted scholars and beautiful ladies) became a very popular genre. Although the story of the lotus screen can be viewed as a type of *gong'an xiaoshuo* 公案小說 (stories about judicial cases), as discussed above, it contains certain romantic elements and thereby can also be viewed as a type of "stories about gifted scholars and beautiful ladies." Ling Mengchu's adaption further developed the romantic love theme in the story.

In terms of characterization, Ling Mengchu also attempted to give a more detailed portrayal of the characters. In his version, the character of Cui Ying is more complicated: although he was a gifted scholar, he was also naive and knew nothing about the dangers involved while traveling on a river. When he had a feast with his wife in the boat, he felt so excited that he took out the gold and silver wine cups. This reckless action directly led to the disaster—the ferryman decided to murder him after he discovered how wealthy he was.

Madam Wang, on the other hand, was smarter and more careful than her husband. When the ferryman suggested to move the boat to a remote area under the pretext that he wanted to find a cool spot, she immediately responded, "Is it safe at night?" Cui Ying, on the other hand, felt there was no need to worry and let the ferryman move the boat to the ideal spot for the murder.

In Li Changqi's story of the lotus screen, there was an episode showing Cui Ying's loyalty to love: when Gao Nalin suggested to him to marry another woman, he rejected this proposal. Ling Mengchu added another episode to show Madam Wang's loyalty to love. After Madam Wang came to live in Gao Nalin's house. Gao asked his wife to persuade Madam Wang to grow her hair and return to her previous dress (so that she would no longer dress like a nun). Gao's wife even offered to adopt her as her stepdaughter. However, Madam Wang adamantly rejected this proposal, stating that a widow like herself has no desire to arrange hair or put on powder and rouge. In Li Changqi's story, there was only one short sentence: "he (Gao Nalin) just asked his wife to secretly persuade Wang to grow her hair and to return to her previous dress." Ling Mengchu developed this sentence into a long paragraph, detailing the hot debate between Madam Wang and Gao's wife. In this way, he further developed the love theme of the story by emphasizing that both the husband and his wife are devoted to their love.

2. Bian Sangang's 邊三崗 adaptation of the story in his drama "The Record of the Lotus Screen."

Although Li Changqi's story was adapted in drama versions numerous times during the Ming and Qing era, only two versions are extant today: Jiang Ji's (fl. 1573) 江楫 "Furong ji" 芙蓉記 (The Record of the Lotus Flower) and Bian Sangang's "Furong ping ji" 芙蓉屏記, which was probably produced around 1576.

Compared with Li Changqi's story, Bian's drama made several significant changes. First of all, the drama depicted Cui Ying not only as a loving husband, but also a filial son. Bian created a new character: Cui Ying's father, a prominent official who was fond of the lotus flower. Cui Ying drew the painting of lotus flower in order to express his longing for his father.

In the story of the lotus screen, the author simply mentioned that the ferryman murdered Cui Ying's maidservant and manservant. In the drama version, the author added more new information. The name of his concubine is Zhen Ji 貞姬, which means "a loyal concubine." She ran away together with Madam Wang, and on their way, she sacrificed her life in order to save Madam Wang. The name of his servant is Cui Yi 崔義 (Cui the righteous), who also sacrificed his life for the sake of his master. By adding these two characters, the author tried to advocate the traditional Chinese value of *yipu* 義僕 (loyal servant) and the idea of *she shen qu yi* 捨身取義 (to sacrifice one's own life for a good cause).

In the story of lotus screen, the murderous ferryman committed his crime with his brother, but in the drama version, he worked for a large bandit group that occupied a stronghold in a mountain.

The character of Cui Ying also underwent significant changes in the drama version. In the story, Cui Ying was basically a weak scholar, but in the drama, Cui Ying was described in part as a mighty hero who eventually led troops to attack and destroy the bandit stronghold.

The author also changed the ending of the story. In the original story, when Cui Ying's term of office ended, he and his wife visited Gao Nalin, and learned that Gao had passed away. The couple performed a religious sacrifice to mourn for him. As discussed above, the author of the story, Li Changqi, described the death of Gao Nalin at the end of the story probably in order to imply hidden criticism against the government and society at that time. Bian Sangang, the author of drama, deleted this episode and put a happy ending instead. Cui Ying was promoted to be a higher ranking official. His wife received the honorific title of "Lady of the Commandery." Gao Nalin insisted on living in retirement and was thereby granted the title of Duke. The two deceased servants also received posthumous honorific titles. The change of the ending reflects the tradition of *da tuanyuan* 大團圓 (the grand finale) ending prevalent in the novels and fictions at that time, on the other hand, it weakened the sad tone and the critical spirit implied in the original story.

The drama also developed the religious theme of the story. In the story, it was indicated that, after Madam Wang became a nun, every day she performed the ritual of kowtowing over one hundred times in front of bodhisattva Guanyin. At the end of the story, it was again indicated that Madam Wang abstained from eating meat and fish permanently, and never stopped praying to the bodhisattva. However, the religious theme of the story is not very strong because the story didn't explicitly indicate whether the bodhisattva gave help to Madam Wang. On the other hand, the drama version clearly indicated that supernatural power played an important role. Cui Ying and Madam Wang were "gold boy and jade maiden" of Heaven in their previous lives. The Jade Emperor in heaven felt unhappy about the chaotic relationship between husband and wife in the human world: sometimes a husband abandoned his wife, sometimes a wife betrayed her husband. Therefore, the Jade Emperor sent them down to establish a model of the proper way of marital relationship. The drama also tried to use the Buddhist idea of karmic retribution to explain why Cui Ying encountered this disaster in his life. Cui Ying's father previously helped the Mongol empire invade China. Thus, Cui Ying suffered in his life so that his father's previous sin could be redeemed.

In addition, there are at least seven stories in the Ming and Qing era that share certain elements with the story of the lotus screen. They are as follows:

1. Chapter 9 in *Xiyou ji* 西遊記 (Journey to the West)
2. Chapter 65 in *Shuihu zhuan* 水滸傳 (Water Margin)
3. Chapter 36 in *Xingshi hengyan* 醒世恆言 (Stories to Awaken the World)
4. Chapter 11 in *Jingshi tongyan* 警世通言 (Stories to Caution the World)
5. Chapter 23 in *Yushi mingyan* 喻世明言 (Stories to Instruct the World)
6. "Geng niang" 庚娘 in *Liaozhai zhiyi* 聊齋誌異 (Strange Stories from a Chinese Studio)
7. Chapter 71 in *Qixia wuyi* 七俠五義 (The Seven Heroes and Five Gallants)

Throughout the centuries, the story of the lotus screen has been adapted into various forms of literature and art. The story of the murderous ferryman has also been retold again and again in numerous versions. It seems the story is so fascinating because it contains different layers of meaning. It is a story about separation, reunion, joy, and sorrow in life, love and loyalty between husband and wife, filial piety between father and son; it is also a story about revenge, justice, robbery, rape, competent and incompetent officials. Different authors can look at the story in different angles and explore different meanings of the story.

Tale 7

"QIUQIAN HUI JI" 鞦韆會記
(THE TALE OF THE SWING-PLAY GATHERING)

By Li Changqi
Translated by Jing Wang

On the Wuxu[1] day in the second year of the Dade Reign (1297–1307) in the Yuan dynasty (1271–1368), Boluo 孛罗[2], son of the former Prime Minister the duke of Qi, was appointed Palace Provisions

---

This story, written by Li Zhen 李禎 (1376–1452), style name Changqi, was preserved in his collection of tales titled *Jiandeng yuhua* 剪燈餘話. This translation is based on the original Chinese text from Li's collection attached to Qu You et al., *Jiandeng xinhua* (Shanghai: Gudian wenxue chubanshe, 1957), pp. 267–71. The collection was collated by Zhou Yi. This story was included by Ling Mengchu (1580–1644) in his collection *Chuke pai'an jingqi* 初刻拍案驚奇 (Slapping the Table in Amazement) with the title "In the Director's Garden, Young Ladies Enjoy a Swing-Set Party, at Pure and Peaceful Temple, Husband and Wife Laugh and Cry at Their Reunion." Ling's version was longer—it included creative details and imagined dialogues and was written with colloquial language in a storytelling style; however, the story's basic plot remained the same. Ling's version of the story was translated into English by Shuhui Yang and Yunqin Yang in their *Slapping the Table in Amazement: A Ming Dynasty Story Collection* (Seattle and London: University of Washington Press, 2018), pp. 178–92. Their rendering was used as reference for the current translation.

1. The date in ancient China was indicated by using a combination of the ten heavenly stems and the twelve earthly branches. The year was indicated in the same way. *Wu* 戊 is a heavenly stem and *Xu* 戌 is an earthly branch. Every sixty days is a cycle, and the combination of heavenly stems and earthly branches restarts after each cycle.

2. Among the officials who appear in this story, some—such as Boluo, Baizhu, and Kuokuochu—are historical figures whose biographies were preserved in *History of Yuan*, while others—such as Yandula—are fictional

Commissioner; Yandula 奄都剌 was appointed Administrative Assistant; and Rongfu,[3] Prince of Dongping, was appointed Registrar. These three families lived next to one another to the west of Haizi[4] Bridge. The Commissioner was born in the family of a prime minister and thus lived an extremely extravagant life. His residence was unparalleled in its grandeur and magnificence. Because the Commissioner was a scholar with literary talent and respected worthy men, he enjoyed a good reputation among his contemporaries.

personae whose names cannot be found in the dynastic history. However, it should be noted that the experiences of the historical figures as told in the story do not align with the historical records. For example, in the case of Boluo, there is record of his appointment as Vice Military Affairs Commissioner and Palace Provisions Commissioner in the fourteenth year of Emperor Shizu's 元世祖 reign (*History of Yuan*, 9.188–189). However, none of the four officials who were given the title "Duke of Qi" in the beginning of the Yuan Dynasty served as Prime Minister, nor did they have children named Boluo. It appears that the author borrowed names to create verisimilitude and thus set the story in a more specific historical background.

3. The only mention of Rongfu 榮甫 in *History of Yuan* is in "The Memoirs of Good Officials." Tian Zi 田滋, style name Rongfu, served in the court of Emperor Shizu of Yuan. He did not hold the title "Prince of Dongping" and died during the Zhiyuan 至元 reign (1264–1294). Therefore, the Prince of Dongping in this story is a fictional figure. Zhu Yangdong 朱仰東 interpreted "wang" as a surname instead of "prince." He argued that Wang Rongfu was a member of the prestigious Wang family in Dongping. Rongfu could be a different name used by Wang Shixi 王士熙, son of the *Hanlin* Academy scholar Wang Gou 王構. See Zhu Yangdong, "Li Zhen *Qiuqian huiji*: yi xiaoshuo xingshi zaixian yuandai mingzu ronghe jingxiang de dianfan" 李禎《鞦韆會記》:以小說形式再現元代民族融合鏡像的典範 (*Zhongguo gudai xiaoshuo xiju yanjiu* 中國古代小說戲劇研究, 2018 (00): 64). However, there is no historical evidence that this is the case.

4. *Haizi* 海子 is a colloquial term that means a big pond or lake. According to the records in *History of Yuan*, Haizi, originally named Jishuitan 積水潭 (Pond of Accumulated Water), was located to the north of the Imperial Palace and to the south of Wanshou Mountain 萬壽山. It was referred to by the people in the capital as a "sea" due to its large size. Water from the springs in the northwest coursed through the capital city into this lake (*History of Yuan*, 58.1347 and 64.1592).

7. The Tale of the Swing-Play Gathering 115

At the back of his private residence there was an apricot garden, which was named in celebration of the couplet "The spring beauty in the whole garden could not be contained, a branch of red apricot blossoms stretched out of the wall."[5] Because of its rare plants and fine pavilions, this garden was the best of those of all the noble families. Every spring, sisters and daughters of the Commissioner would invite the female family members of the Administrative Assistant and the Registrar to come over. They set up a swing set in the garden for amusement, laid out a lavish feast with wine, and basked in joyous laughter for the entire day. The other two families would take turns hosting a feast [to reciprocate] two days later. The gathering began at the end of the second month and lasted until after the Tomb Sweeping Festival. It came to be called the swing-play gathering.

It so happened that [one day,] Baizhu,[6] son of the Assistant of the Bureau of Military Affairs Tiemuer Buhua

---

5. This is the second couplet from Ye Shaoweng's 葉紹翁 (fl. 1115) cut-off verse "Youyuan buzhi" 遊園不值 (On Visiting a Garden When Its Master Is Absent). This couplet has a sexual connotation which was obvious to readers as early as the Ming-Qing dynasties. See Kathryn A. Lowry, *The Tapestry of Popular Songs in 16th- and 17th century China: Reading, Imitation, and Desire* (Leiden: Brill Academic Pub, 2005), p. 280. The interpretation of sexual innuendo works well in the context of this story. "The spring beauty in the garden" alludes to the women at the swing-set party who attracted the attention of the young man outside of the wall and the "branch of red apricot" is a metaphor for the female protagonist. The following is a translation of Ye's poem by A. R. Davis, *A Book of Chinese Verse* (Hong Kong: Hong Kong University Press, 1990), p. 185:

應憐屐齒印蒼台，
It is proper to hate the marks of shoes on the green moss;
十叩柴扉久不開。
Of ten that knock at this brushwood gate, nine cannot have it opened.
春色滿園關不住，
Spring's colors fill the garden but cannot all be contained,
一枝紅杏出墻來。
For one spray of red almond-blossom peeps out from the wall.

6. Various arguments have been made as to the identity of Baizhu 拜住. Luo Jintang 羅錦堂 claimed that Baizhu was Prime Minister during the reign of Emperor Yingzong 英宗 (r. 1320–1323) and that Baizhu's biography was preserved in *juan* 136 in *History of Yuan*. Luo's opinion was challenged by Hu Shi 胡適 (1891–1962) who believed that Baizhu's father and grandfather

帖木而不花,[7] passed by the garden. Upon hearing the laughter, he rose slightly from his horse and gazed into the garden. He saw how the swings swung high as if in competition with one another and heard laughter and happy shrieks. He hid himself in the shadow of the willow trees and spied on them. Finding that all the women were exceptionally beautiful, he stayed for quite a while until he was discovered by the gatekeeper. The gatekeeper ran to report to the Commissioner, who ordered him to apprehend the man, but the man had already fled. When Baizhu returned home, he told his mother everything. His mother understood his intention and sent a matchmaker to the Commissioner's house to seek a marriage alliance. The Commissioner said, "Isn't he the lad who peered from outside of the wall? I am selecting a son-in-law so you may send him over so that I can take a look. If indeed he is an excellent young man, then I will give my consent." His father, the Assistant, made Baizhu dress in fine clothing and go for a visit. When the Commissioner found out that he was a handsome young man, he was rather pleased. However, he had no insight into the young man's talent and learning, so he tested him by saying, "You enjoyed watching the swing-play; can you compose a southern style lyric on that topic

were both famous officials and that Baizhu had nothing to do with this story. The fact that Prime Minister Baizhu was born in 1298 when the story took place makes it impossible for him to be the protagonist. There were two other historical figures with the name Baizhu during the Yuan Dynasty who were considered by scholars to be the protagonist of this story. One was a loyal official who committed suicide upon the demise of the Yuan Dynasty, and the other was a scholar who passed the *Jinshi* Imperial Examination in 1342 but later surrendered to Korea after being defeated in a battle. Zhu Yangdong argued that neither of them could be identified as the protagonist in this story due to the time periods during which they lived. See Zhu Yangdong, "Li Zhen 'Qiuqian hui ji' Baizhu benshi bianyi" 李禎《鞦韆會記》拜住本事辨疑, *Neijiang shifan xueyuan xuebao* 內江師範學院學報, Vol. 34, No. 4 (2019): 9–12.

7. There are two references to Timur Buhua in *History of Yuan*. In "Tables of Genealogy," the record shows that he was a great-grandson of the founding emperor of Yuan Dynasty and a royal prince. However, Buhua did not have a son named Baizhu (107.2705). In "The Basic Annals of Emperor Chengzong," the emperor bestowed upon him gifts of gold, silver, silk, etc., and appointed him as Manager of Affairs of the Secretariat (18.384).

7. The Tale of the Swing-Play Gathering 117

to the tune of 'Bodhisattva Barbarian'?" Baizhu wielded his brush and wrote a poem in the national character,[8] which read:

> Red ropes, decorated boards, and fingers like the blades of the young white-grass,
> In the east wind, swallows fly high in pairs.
> Flaunting their handsomeness and striving to swing the highest,
> They tied their skirts all the more tightly.
> On elegant beds, exhausted, they fell asleep,
> Not bothered by their gold hairpins falling down.
> Pushing aside the pillows, they got up late.
> When the moon climbed up and shone through the screen window.[9]

Although the Commissioner loved the young man's quick wit, he was worried that Baizhu had prepared in advance or had asked other people to help him. Therefore, he treated Baizhu to a grand feast, during which he again asked Baizhu to compose a poem on an oriole to the tune of "Red Filling the River." Baizhu smoothed out a piece of paper made with vines in the Shan creek,[10] wrote a poem in Chinese characters, and presented it to the Commissioner. The commissioner was pleased and said, "I have obtained a son-in-law." Thus he promised on the spot to marry Sugeshili 速哥失里,[11] the daughter of his third wife, to Baizhu. Furthermore, he summoned his wife and asked his daughter to come out to meet Baizhu. His other daughters had peeked at Baizhu through

---

8. *Guozi* 國字 (the National Alphabet) refers to Phags-pa Script, a Mongolian alphabet designed by Preceptor of State and Leader of the Tibetan Buddhism Phagpa (1235–1280) for Kublai Khan. It was mainly used as a romanization tool for Chinese characters and was abandoned when the Ming dynasty overthrew the Mongolian rule. See Bai Shouyi 白壽彝, *Zhongguo tongshi* 中國通史 (Shanghai: Shanghai renmin chubanshe, 2015), pp. 8.1:43–44.

9. Luo Zongqiang 羅宗強 examined *Jiandeng Yuhua* and concluded that most poems that were included in the collection were composed by the author Li Zhen himself. It is highly possible that the two *Ci*-lyrics in this story were also Li Zhen's work. See Luo Zongqiang, *Mingdai wenxue sixiang shi* 明代文學思想史 (Beijing: Zhonghua shuju, 2013), p. 173.

10. Shanxi 剡溪 (the Shan creek) is located in modern Sheng 嵊 county in Zhejiang province. It was famous for the production of white, thin, yet strong writing paper made from the region's vines.

11. One of Emperor Wuzong's 武宗 (r. 1307–1311) empresses had the same name of Sugeshili (*Yuan shi*, 114.2874).

the crack between the windows and they privately congratulated Sugeshili, saying: "It can be said that 'There is much happiness in the household, and the son-in-law is about to ride a dragon.'"[12] Baizhu picked an [auspicious] day and sent his betrothal gifts. The gifts were in such abundance and his lyrics were so elegant that people in the capital city, Duxia 都下, were all talking about them and considered the upcoming wedding a grand event. Baizhu's lyric on the oriole is appended below:

The sweet day is nice and sunny,
The springtime is gorgeous,
And the blue sky just cleared up after rain.
It is the time that the peach trees are half-blooming,[13]

12. This couplet is from the first poem in a two-poem series titled "Li Jian Zhai" 李監宅 (On Director Li's Residence) by Du Fu 杜甫 (712–770). See Qiu Zhao'ao 仇兆鰲, *Dushi xiang zhu* 杜詩詳註 (Beijing: Zhonghua shuju, 2007), Vol. 1, p. 30. The original Chinese text depicted the man as "riding a dragon" *chenglong* 乘龍, which was a metaphor for a son-in-law with a bright future. The *locus classicus* of this metaphor comes from an anecdote about Nongyu 弄玉 and her husband Xiaoshi 蕭史 in Liu Xiang's (77–6 BCE), *Lie xian zhuan* 列仙傳. Xiaoshi was skilled at playing the flute and he married Nongyu, daughter of Emperor Mu of the Qin State. He taught her to play the flute and her tunes resembled the sound of a phoenix. The emperor built a high terrace for her named after the mythical animal. The couple later ascended to Heaven from the terrace riding phoenixes. See Wang Shumin 王叔岷, *Liexian zhuan jiaojian* 列仙傳校箋 (Beijing: Zhonghua shuju, 2007), p. 80. Wang quoted *Liexian zhuan shiyi* 列仙傳拾遺 in his commentary that Xiao rode a dragon and Nongyu rode a phoenix (Wang, p. 82). Qiu Zhao'ao's note in *Dushi xiangzhu* quoted an anecdote from *Chuguo xianxian zhuan* 楚國先賢傳. When the two daughters of Defender-in-chief Huan Yan 桓焉 married, people commented that "Both his daughters rode a dragon" which means that his sons-in-law were like dragons (Qiu Zhao'ao, p. 31).

13. Peach blossoms are a well-known metaphor for the beauty of a young lady who is at marriageable age. See "Taoyao" 桃夭 in the *Shijing* (Mao #6):
逃之夭夭, The peach tree is young and elegant,
灼灼其華。 Brilliant are its flowers
之子於歸, This young lady is going to her future home,
宜其室家。 And will order well her chamber and house.
See Cheng Junying 程俊英, *Shijing yizhu* 詩經譯釋 (Shanghai: Shanghai guji chubanshe, 1997), pp. 11–12. The translation is from James Legge (1815–1897), *Chinese Classics*, Vol. IV, *The She King* (Taipei: SMC Publishing Inc., 1994), p. 12.

7. The Tale of the Swing-Play Gathering   119

And the orioles began to try their singing.
By my lonely pillow, low notes from strings suddenly reached my ears.
By my folding screen, I sometimes heard the slight sound from pipes.
The lovely chirping[14] from the delicate tongue echoing the east wind,
Became even more lovely and charming.

Awakened from a sad dream,
it sank into unexplained sorrow.
The withered apricot blossoms faded,
And the doors were closed.
Ingenious tune and graceful rhyme,
Are quite enchanting.
It flits through the willow trees and flowers, back and forth,
Intending to seek a good companion,[15] but truly in vain.
Gazing into the imperial garden,[16] it wondered when it could perch with a mate.
Its thoughts roamed far, far away.

Shortly after, [Baizhu's father,] the Assistant of the Bureau of Military Affairs was reckless in his behavior. He was eventually accused of corruption for breaking the rule[17] and was thrown into prison at

---

14. The original Chinese word *mianman* 綿蠻 refers to the chirping of an oriole. It comes from the *Shijing* (*The Book of Songs*) poem "Mianman" (Mao#230) in which the opening line of each of the three stanzas read "chirping is the oriole," 綿蠻黃鳥 (Junying, *Shijing yizhu*, p. 479).

15. The image of the bird looking for a companion alludes to the following couplet in the *Shijing* poem "Cutting the Tree" 伐木 (Mao#165). The translation is taken from James Legge, *Chinese Classics*, Vol. IV, *The She King*, p. 253.
  While *ying* goes its cry, 嚶其鳴矣,
  Seeking with its voice its companion. 求其友聲。

16. The Shanglin 上林 Imperial Garden was first built during the Qin Dynasty and was renovated and expanded during the reign of Emperor Wu 武 (r. 141–87 BCE) of the Han Dynasty. Sima Xianru (ca. 179–118 BCE) described and exaggerated the grandeur of this imperial resort in his famous "Rhapsody on Shanglin Park" 上林賦.

17. The original Chinese *fugui buchi* 簠簋不飭 means the sacrificial utensils were not properly arranged. It is a metaphor for the corruption of an official. *Fu* and *gui* were both containers for grains, made of either clay or bronze. In the entry on *sheren* 舍人, a position that was in charge of the use of grains in the imperial palace, in the "Diguan" 地官 chapter of *Zhou li* 周禮 (*Rituals of Zhou*), the text

the Censorate. He fell ill while in detention. According to regulations, because he was a high-ranking official he was allowed the privilege of being temporarily released to go home for medical treatment. In less than ten days, his condition deteriorated, and he ultimately did not recover. The entire household became infected and was completely wiped out while Baizhu alone remained alive. The family collapsed like melted ice and broken tiles, its wealth dispersed and its people dead.

The Commissioner planned to ask Baizhu to move into his home, to educate and provide for Baizhu; however, his third wife resolutely opposed this plan. Although there were many women in the Commissoner's harem, his third wife had power over the household and was the most favored. When she saw that the daughters of other concubines had all married into wealthy and noble families, while only her own son-in-law's family became destitute in such a way, she made up her mind to break off the engagement. Sugeshili admonished her mother, saying:

> Making a marital alliance is like making an oath of fraternity. Once an alliance is made with someone, it should not be altered at all. It is not that I do not see the prosperity of my sisters' families. I envy them as well, but receiving just an inch of silk constitutes a betrothal agreement, and ghosts and spirits are not easily deceived. How can we abandon him because he is in dire straits?

Her parents did not listen and made other arrangements to marry her to Sengjianu 僧家奴, the son of Kuokuochu,[18] Administrator of the

---

reads, "Whenever there is a sacrifice, *fu* and *gui* are provided. They are filled with grains and are displayed." In his commentary, Zheng Xuan 鄭玄 explained that the square-shaped vessel was called *fu* and the round-shaped one was called *gui*. There are different opinions about the shapes of these utensils and some of the excavated *gui* items are both round and square in shape. See Sun Yirang 孫詒讓, *Zhouli Zhengyi* 周禮正義 (Beijing: Zhonghua shuju, 1987), Vol. 4, p. 1229.

18. Kuokuochu 闊闊出 (d. 1314) was the eighth son of Kublai Khan (r. 1260–1294). He was enfeoffed as Prince of Ningyuan 寧遠 in 1289 and was in charge of military affairs during the reign of Emperor Chengzong 成宗 (r. 1294–1307). He was accused of conspiracy against Emperor Wuzong (r. 1307–1311), and was therefore imprisoned, deprived of his fief, and banished to Korea; his wife was killed. He was exempted and summoned back in 1313, but died in the following year. See records about him in the "Basic Annals of Emperor Wuzong" (23.523) and "Biography of Tiege 鐵哥" (125.3077) in *History of Yuan*.

Secretariat. The ceremony of presenting betrothal gifts was even more lavish than the previous one. [On the day] they were to be married, on her way to her fiancé's home, Sugeshili secretly untied her foot wraps and hung herself in her sedan chair. Upon arrival to her fiancé's, she had already died. The Commissioner's third wife asked that her beloved daughter be carried back on her sedan chair. Her body was put into a coffin along with her dowry and the betrothal gifts from the groom's family, and her coffin was placed at the Pure and Peaceful Buddhist Monastery for the time being.

When Baizhu heard what had happened, he privately went to mourn her. He knelt down, knocked on her coffin, and said, "Baizhu is here." A voice responded from inside the coffin, saying, "You may open the casket. I have come back to life!" He looked at the four corners of the coffin, which was painted and nailed tightly shut. There was no way to open it. He then sought help from the monk, saying: "Could you lend me a hand? I will take full responsibility for the offense of opening the coffin, and you will not be implicated. We will share what is inside." The monk knew that there were many valuables in the coffin, and he felt the stirrings of greed. He thus smashed the lid of the coffin with an axe. The woman indeed had come back to life. Both of them were extremely happy. She then took off a pair of gold bracelets and half of her jewelry and offered them to the monk in gratitude. What remained was still worth tens of thousands of strings of coins. They entrusted the monk to buy paint to fix the coffin so that nothing would leak out about the incident.

Baizhu then went to Kaiping,[19] the secondary capital, with Sugeshili. They lived there for a year without anybody's knowledge. In addition to bringing a large amount of money with them, Baizhu also tutored several Mongolian students and received a monthly income, which allowed them to live an affluent life. The Commissioner was unexpectedly dispatched to serve as Prefect of Kaiping. As soon as he alighted from his carriage, he began seeking a guest retainer. However, there were very few educated men in the secondary capital. Someone

---

19. *Shangdu* 上都, the secondary capital, refers to Kaiping 開平 prefecture, which was located northeast of modern Dushikou 獨石口 in Hebei province (Tai Qixiang 譚其驤, *Zhongguo lishi ditu ji* 中國歷史地圖集 [Beijing: Zhongguo ditu chubanshe, 1982]).

said, "Recently there was a scholar who moved from the capital[20] to take up residence here with his family. He is also a *Semu*[21] man. He set up a private school in the neighborhood and is truly knowledgeable. Sir, if you want to find a guest retainer, this man would be the only suitable person." The Commissioner immediately summoned him, and it turned out that the man was Baizhu. The Commissioner had assumed that Baizhu had likely wandered away and died, so he was surprised to find that he looked quite well. He asked: "How come you are here? Whom did you marry?" Baizhu told him the truth. The Commissioner did not believe him and ordered Baizhu's wife to be brought over on a sedan chair. It was indeed Sugeshili. The entire family was astonished. They were both happy and sorrowful. However, the Commissioner was still afraid that she was a ghost who disguised itself in the form of a human being to delude and seduce young men. He secretly sent a messenger to visit the Pure and Peaceful Monastery to inquire after the monk, and his story was exactly the same as Baizhu's. The messenger then dug up the tomb and found only an empty coffin. He returned and reported to the Commissioner. The Commissioner and his wife were ashamed and sighed. They treated Baizhu with even more kindness and took him as a live-in son-in-law. Baizhu spent the rest of his life in their household.

Baizhu had three sons: Jiaohua 教化, the eldest, served in the court with the highest position as Assistant Director of the Left of the Branch Secretariat in several places including Liaoyang, but he died young. Monggudai 忙古歹, the middle son, and Heisi 黑厮, the youngest son, both became members of the palace guard and were permitted to carry weapons. Manggudai died before Heisi, who had advanced to

---

20. *Dadu* 大都, the capital city of Yuan Dynasty, was located in modern-day Beijing.

21. *Semu* 色目 refers to non-Mongol foreigners from west and Central Asia such as Uyghurs, Tanguts, Tibetans, etc. It was one of the four ranks into which people were divided during the Yuan dynasty. The other three ranks were Mongols who enjoyed the highest status, *Han*, which included all subjects of the former Jin Dynasty such as Khitans and Jurchens, and Southerners, who were people from the Southern Song Dynasty. The latter two ranks were lower in status than *Semu*. This four-tiered status system was imposed on the entire population of the Yuan dynasty by Khubilai Khan. As Mote pointed out, "The four tiers described certain kinds of legally and institutionally differentiated degrees of privilege, not economic status or social power." (Frederick W. Mote, *Imperial China: 900–1800* [Cambridge: Harvard University Press, 1999], p. 492).

7. The Tale of the Swing-Play Gathering 123

the post of Military Affairs Commissioner. When the heavenly army of the Ming reached the Yan region, Emperor Shun (r. 1333–1370)[22] ruled from the Pure and Serene Hall in the palace. He gathered the imperial consorts in his harem and the Crown Prince to discuss how to elude the troops. Heisi and the Prime Minister Shiliemen[23] remonstrated in tears, saying, "The world under Heaven is an empire from Emperor Shizu.[24] We should defend it to death." The Emperor would not listen. In the middle of the night, the Emperor ordered the Jiande Gate to be opened and took flight. Heisi followed the Emperor into the desert and nothing was ever heard of him again.

22. Shun 順 (Obedience) was the posthumous title bestowed upon Emperor Huizong 惠宗 of the Yuan Dynasty by the founding emperor of the Ming dynasty, who thought that Emperor Huizong was able to be obedient to Heaven's Mandate, withdraw the Mogolian troops and flee the capital (*History of Yuan*, 47.986).

23. Shiliemen 失列門 served as Prime Minister of the Left during the reign of Emperor Shun. The description of his and Heisi's remonstrating with the emperor not to abandon but to firmly defend the capital was based on the record in "The Basic Annals of Emperor Shun" in *History of Yuan* (47.986). The difference between this passage and the historical record was that the heart-felt remonstration was actually not made by Shiliemen, but by a eunuch, and the incident of the emperor's flight was narrated in more detail.

24. Emperor Shizu was Kublai Khan (1215–1294).

NOTES AND READING GUIDE

Jing Wang

"The Tale of the Swing-Play Gathering" by Li Changqi is a miracle romance story from the fourteenth century. The male protagonist Baizhu happens to see beautiful girls at a playful gathering in the Commissioner's private garden. He is enchanted and seeks a marriage alliance. The commissioner is impressed by Baizhu's handsome appearance and poetic talent and agrees to marry his daughter Sugeshili to Baizhu. But "unfortunately, the road to happiness never runs smooth,"[25] just as the statement in a more detailed version of the story appearing in the Ming dynasty collection *Slapping the Table in Amazement* warns. Baizhu's father is accused of corruption and dies after being infected by an epidemic disease, which eventually wipes out the entire family, except for Baizhu. Despite Sugeshili's opposition, her parents decide to break off the engagement and marry her off to another powerful family. Sugeshili commits suicide on her wedding day and her coffin is placed temporarily in a Buddhist monastery. When Baizhu goes to mourn her, a miracle occurs: the young woman comes back to life! The couple runs away to the secondary capital with the dowry and betrothal gifts that had been placed in the coffin and lives a comfortable life there. Later, when the Commissioner is appointed as the governor of the secondary capital, he discovers the truth. The story ends happily: parents feel ashamed of their previous behavior, and the family lives happily together. While the story includes twists and turns that keep it amusing, it falls into various clichés and character simplifications, which disqualify it from being considered a masterpiece.

I. The Motif of Resurrection

The plot point of the female protagonist coming back to life after she commits suicide is a key element and turning point in this story. Resurrection as a motif can be traced to the genre of *zhiguai* (Records of the Anomalies) in Chinese literary history. There are several anecdotes with such a motif in Gan Bao's 干寶 (fl. early fourth century) *Soushen ji* 搜神記 (*In Search of the Supernatural: The Written Record*). Among

---

25. *Slapping the Table in Amazement*, p. 186.

them, the records of "Wang Daoping's Wife" 王道平妻 and "The Girl from Hejian" 河間女 bear much similarity to "The Tale of the Swing-play Gathering." In both anecdotes, the young couple that loved each other is separated because the man enlists in the army. The woman's family forces her to remarry, and she dies from depression and illness. When the man comes back and finds out about the death of his lover, he goes to mourn and cry at her tomb. The woman comes back to life, and the couple's reunion is granted legitimacy by the endorsement of local government at the secular level and by the recognition of their "sincerity of spirit" (*jingcheng* 精誠) that "is capable of moving Heaven and Earth" at the transcendent level.[26] The core plot of resurrection in "The Tale of the Swing-play Gathering" does not have any development or embellishment compared to its predecessors from over a thousand years ago. Later in the Ming dynasty, the motif of resurrection was elaborated on by Tang Xianzu 湯顯祖 (1550–1616) in his master play "The Peony Pavillion," and emotion (*qing* 情) was invested with the extraordinary therapeutic function "for which the living could die" 生者可以死 and "the dead could be resurrected" 死者可以生.[27]

II. In Search of the "Original Events"

Studies on this tale either focus on discovering the story's *benshi* 本事 (original events) or on the non-Han ethnic identity of the story's characters. Since the ninth century, it has been a popular practice to examine the circumstances surrounding the writing of poetic compositions. Meng Qi's 孟棨 *Benshi shi* 本事詩 and Fan Shu's 范攄 *Yunxi youyi* 雲溪友議, which include many anecdotes related to the circumstances of the writing of certain poems, are two good examples. To apply such an approach to the study of tales, scholars attempt to identify the plot's prototype in the story. In other words, scholars are in search of literary texts or historical records that can be identified as the origin of the tale in question. In his study of Yuan Dynasty Drama, Luo Jintang 羅錦堂 considered "The Tale of the Swing-play Gathering" as one of the sources, i.e. "original events," of

26. See Kenneth J. DeWoskin and J. I. Crump, Jr., trans., *In Search of the Supernatural: The Written Record* (Stanford: Stanford University Press, 1996), pp. 170–2.
27. See Tang Xianzu, "Mudanting ji tici" 牡丹亭记题词 in *Tang Xianzu quanji* 湯顯祖全集 (Beijing: Beijing guji chubanshe, 1999), Vol. 2, p. 1153.

Bai Pu's 白樸 (1226–ca.1295) play "Qiangtou mashang" 墙頭馬上 (On Horseback and Over the Garden Wall).[28] In both the drama and the tale, young lovers were "thwarted by unyielding parents and ritual, social prescriptions,"[29] and the garden served as a critical space that gave birth to the romantic encounter.

The following couplet by Ye Shaoweng was quoted in the beginning of "The Tale of the Swing-play Gathering" to explain the origin of the name of the garden in Boluo's backyard.

The spring beauty in the garden could not be contained,
a branch of red apricot blossoms stretched out of the wall.

The strong and obvious sexual connotation of the couplet foreshadows the romantic relationship between the male and female protagonist. However, the encounter was not elaborated upon in the tale due to its simplified plot and was reduced to only a short statement: "[Boluo] asked his daughter to come out to meet Baizhu." There was not an obliging maid acting as go-between and no poetic exchange between the young couple as was seen in the drama. The two poems in the tale that Baizhu used to win the favor of his future father-in-law served a practical function to move the plot forward and provided a chance for the author to show off his own literary talent. In the second poem, about orioles, there is an explicit message of a strong desire to pursue a mate at the end of the poem and an implicit comparison of the young woman to a peach blossom, which alluded to the *Shijing* poem "Taoyao." It is certainly not a coincidence that the apricot imagery is also repeated in the poem on orioles:

The withered apricot blossoms faded,
And the doors were closed.

The images of withered flowers and closed doors can be considered a prophecy predicting the misfortune that befalls the lovers and the ruthless abandonment that the male protagonist will soon face from his future parents-in-law. Both the tale and the drama have a

---

28. Luo Jintang, *Yuan zaju benshi kao* 元杂剧本事考 (Xi'an: Shanxi shifan daxue chubanshe, 2017).

29. C. T. Hsia, Wai-yee Li, and George Kao, eds., *The Columbia Anthology of Yuan Drama* (New York: Columbia University Press, 2014), p. 334.

happy ending; however, the illicit sexual reunion in the tale was not "legitimized through the young men's eventual success in the civil service examination and the discovery of a prior arrangement for marriage made by the parents,"[30] as in the drama, but rather through the miracle of the young lady's resurrection and the parent's own sense of shame upon seeing their daughter had come back to life.

Although there are some similarities between the plot of the tale and of the drama, the divergence in characterization and plot development raises doubt about Luo Jintang's hypothesis that the tale provided the "original events" for the Yuan drama. Furthermore, as Zhu Yangdong pointed out, Luo was mistaken in saying that the tale was composed during the early Ming dynasty, as the tale actually was written during the Yuan period. How could Bai Pu, a Yuan drama writer, have based his work on something that was to be written a hundred years later?[31]

III. Confucian Morality in a Non-Han Context

As opposed to subjecting this story to literary analysis, previous written interpretations of this tale have praised the unique value of its depiction of "love affairs between a young man and a young woman from minority ethnic groups"[32] and its symbolic representation of "integration among ethnic groups during the Yuan Dynasty."[33] It is true that the main characters in the tale are non-Han and non-Mongolian *Semu* people, a term that refers to people from west and Central Asia, such as Uyghurs, Tanguts, and Tibetans. *Semu* people enjoyed the second highest rank in the four-tier hierarchical structure of the Yuan dynasty. The fact that Baizhu was skilled in composing southern-style lyrics, was celebrated for his poetic flair, and was able to make a decent living as a tutor for Mongolian students, also illustrated to some extent the "ethnic integration" and subtle influence of Han culture.

---

30. Ibid.
31. See Zhu Yangdong, "Li Zhen *Qiuqian huiji* Baizhu benshi bianyi," p. 9.
32. See Qi Yukun 齊裕焜, *Zhongguo gudai xiaoshuo yanbian shi* 中國古代小說演變史 (Beijing: Renmin wenxue chubanshe, 2015), p. 108.
33. See Zhu Yangdong, "Li Zhen *Qiuqian huiji*: yi xiaoshuo xingshi zaixian yuandai mingzu ronghe jingxiang de dianfan," pp. 63–9.

When it comes to cultural transformation, the female protagonist Sugeshili, daughter of a prestigious family, actually deserves the reader's attention more than her male counterpart. When her mother decides to break off the engagement between Sugeshili and Baizhu because Baizhu's family has fallen into destitution, Sugeshili admonishes her mother, saying:

> Making a marital alliance is like making an oath of fraternity. Once an alliance is made with someone, it should not be altered at all. It is not that I do not see the prosperity of my sisters' families. I envy them as well, but receiving just an inch of silk constitutes a betrothal agreement, and ghosts and spirits are not easily deceived. How can we abandon him because he is in dire straits?

The key terms in her speech, such as *jieyi* 結義 (to make an oath of fraternity), which literally means "be connected through righteousness" and *pinjian* 貧賤 (poverty and lowly status), carry a strong Confucian connotation. Furthermore, instead of using "talk," "persuade" or other more reasonable words applicable to a conversation between mother and daughter, the author used *jian* 諫 (to admonish, to remonstrate) which is typically used when a loyal minister tries to advise the sovereign against doing something wrong. It echoes the second appearance of this character *jian* at the end of the story when Sugeshili's son entreats the emperor to guard the capital against the Ming army. In addition, marital engagement in her speech is defined in terms of righteousness and is considered as an alliance that should not be infringed. This reminds the reader of Sima Qian's 司馬遷 (ca. 145–90 BCE) comments on the moral principle of wandering knights in the *Shiji* 史記 (*The Grand Scribe's Records*). Sima Qian states that this group of people remains "true to their word and invariably fulfill what they undertake. What they have promised they invariably carry out." 言必信, 行必果, 已諾必誠.[34]

Sugeshili explains that she certainly admires her sisters who married into wealthy and prosperous families, yet she questions the legitimacy of her mother's decision to abandon Baizhu because he became "poor and lowly." Her stance on wealth and status fits remarkably well with Confucius' teaching regarding this topic:

---

34. Sima Qian, *Shiji* (Beijing: Zhonghua shuju, 1999), 124.3181.

The Master said, "Wealth and high station are what men desire but unless I got them in the right way I would not remain in them. Poverty and low station are what men dislike, but even if I did not get them in the right way, I would not try to escape from them."

富與貴, 是人之所欲也；不以其道得之, 不處也。貧與賤, 是人之所惡也；不以其道得之, 不去也。"[35]

These references and allusions to Confucian concepts in Sugeshili's speech make her sound more like a Confucian scholar than an unmarried young woman talking to her mother in her boudoir.

It is not rare for female figures to speak in the tone of a Confucian scholar in tales. A precedent for this can be found in the Song Dynasty text, "The Tale of Lady Sun," written by Qiu Jun 丘濬 in the eleventh century. The female protagonist in this story is depicted as a virtuous woman who holds fast to her moral principles and righteousness. In her writing and speaking to a seductive suitor, she often alludes to Confucian classics. Her virtue is not limited to the integrity and chastity of a woman in terms of marriage or a relationship with a man but is elevated to the Confucian value of benevolence and righteousness.[36] We witness a similar approach in the depiction of Sugeshili who was rewarded by the ghosts and spirits "who are not easily deceived" with a miraculous resurrection, which eventually leads to the story's happy ending. The author shares his understanding of Confucian values through the mouth of the female protagonist in this text.

The minority ethnic identity of Sugeshili adds another layer to the reader's understanding of the tale's moral teaching. Does the author intend to tell his readers that the Confucian moral principle was well received by non-Han people, and that it even found its way into the female quarters, during the Yuan Dynasty? Zhang Yangdong quotes examples from *History of Yuan*, which speak of the Mongol court establishing local schools and the imperial university, and of the poetic exchanges among scholars from different ethnic groups, that provides some evidence in favor of such a hypothesis.

---

35. Yang Bojun 楊伯峻, *Lunyu yizhu* 論語譯注 (Beijing: Zhonghua shuju, 2000), p. 36. Translation is from D.C. Lau, *The Analects* (Westminster, London: Penguin Books, 1979), p. 72.

36. See Zhenjun Zhang and Jing Wang, *Song Dynasty Tales: A Guided Reader* (Singapore: World Scientific Publishing, 2017), pp. 249–50.

As Yu Yingshi 余英時 pointed out, "Moral principles and values are always unclear and uncertain in meaning; they require constant interpretation and reinterpretation on our part, particularly in a time of crisis."[37] "The Tale of the Swing-play Gathering," and especially the speech of the female protagonist, reflects the author's personal interpretation of the Confucian values prevalent in everyday life during the non-Han Mongolian reign of China.

37. Yu Yingshi, "The Radicalization of China in the Twentieth Century," *Daedalus, Journal of the American Academy of Arts and Sciences*, Vol. 122, No. 2 (Spring 1993): 126.

Tale 8

"YAO GONGZI ZHUAN" 姚公子傳 (THE TALE OF YOUNG MASTER YAO)

By Shao Jingzhan 邵景詹
Translated by Chen Wu

There once was a young master Yao from Zhedong,[1] whose native place we don't need to identify. His father was appointed as the Minister. His wife also came from a family of officials. Yao's family accumulated a huge fortune [over the years]. All the farms and gardens, pools and ponds, mountains and forests, and rivers and swamps within a 100-*li* radius were the Yao family's property. Taking advantage of his inherited wealth and power, the young master did not engage in earning a living. Instead, he enthusiastically engaged in hunting and associated himself with evil friends. Whenever Yao met with guests who discussed Confucian classics or were studying for the presented-scholar examination, his face would turn red, and he became drowsy, not knowing where to put his hands or feet. As for those who tracked their estate's profit and loss, or sought to accumulate goods, he would laugh at them, regarding them as unsuccessful, small-minded people, not even worth his notice. Only those folks who were robust and bold, amusing and agile, and men who were amusing and comical, fierce and sly, would he associate with, unleashing the hounds, releasing the falcons, hunting foxes, and hitting rabbits. Those young rogues from the marketplace whom Yao summoned and attracted to his gates numbered in dozens or even a hundred.

The family of these dozens or a hundred people all depended on the young master for their livelihood and young master was never stingy

---

1. Zhedong 浙東 refers to the east part (covering the area of Ningbo Prefecture 寧波府 and Taizhou Prefecture 台州府) of the Ming dynasty Zhejiang, the full name of which was Zhejiang Chengxuan Buzhengshi Si 浙江承宣佈政使司 (Zhejiang Provincial Administration Commission).

with them. On occasion, he would squander a thousand pieces of gold for them to purchase fine horses; other times he poured out a hundred *hu*[2] of grains, allowing them to buy good bows. Sometimes he and his men would gallop along different routes to meet at an appointed time and place, and those who arrived late would be punished. Sometimes he would organize his men into competing hunting teams, measuring these teams' respective merits by the quantity of their trophies and awarding those teams that captured more prey in the hunt; sometimes they lit candles and hunted in the night, though never getting tired of doing so; sometimes they spent ten days or so on a long hunting trip and forgot to return home.

As for the cases in which [Yao and his men] trampled on people's crops or damaged their firewood, the young master would estimate the total cost and double the compensation to the owners. Yao observed: "One lives a life simply to enjoy its pleasure. Why should one ever be stingy?" Occasionally, someone would remonstrate with him concerning the skills with which his father, the late Minister, amassed great personal wealth by exploiting other people. Before the young master could open his mouth, those young men interjected: "That man [who just remonstrated] is an old ploughman and has a very shallow and ignorant mind. How does he deserve to be mentioned by you?" The young master nodded.

One day, Yao and his men went a bit too far from the hunting grounds, and the grain transport could not keep up with them. Although they had money in their bags, there was no inn or store in the open country. While they were hungry and distressed, several local folks suddenly greeted them, bowing on the left-hand side of the road, and said: "We humble people rarely see you, the young master, come here, so we respectfully prepared some fruit, wine, and meat to present to your followers." The young master and the young men clapped their hands and loudly laughed, believing that god was making a gift to them. Therefore, they dismounted from their horses, walked all the way into those people's house and indulged themselves in extravagant eating and drinking. [Finishing their feast], the young men declared: "These folks must be repaid." The young master thereupon tripled their compensation [for this meal]. These folks received more than they had wished, so they prostrated themselves before the young master's horses as Yao and his men rode off. The young master was again highly pleased

---

2. Hu 斛 was a dry measure equal to 10 *dou* 斗 in the Tang dynasty (since the Song, it has equaled 5 *dou*), which was approximately 100 liters.

and said: "These folks are not only considerate, but they also know proper etiquette." He immediately ordered the horsemen following him to give all that was left in their saddle bags to these folks, thus expressing their appreciation.

After this incident, the climate had been fostered and everybody followed the example. When the young master rode to the east, [even those] people in the west were already preparing food for him; when he was hunting in the south, [even those] people in the north already sent orders for his food down to the kitchen. Thus, the young master's men had surplus grains, and their hunting animals also had excess food. Even if the hunting party was out for as long as ten days, they no longer needed to bother with the grain transport. When the young master gave a single call, a hundred people would respond to him. When he looked around, his eyes were brimming with radiance. As he was just seen off from here, he was already welcomed there. The honor and glory he received were incomparable. The young master was greatly pleased and even though he tried his utmost to repay people, still he felt regretful [about not paying enough] in his heart. All those young men wanted to step in and make a profit [from Yao], so in collaboration they loudly applauded the young master's practice and suggested: "These folks were humble people, and now without our supervision or urging, our food supplies are fully sufficient. The way they serve and honor you, the young master, is better than how they treat the lord. Should you not handsomely reward them? How could you better comfort them?" The young master thought this suggestion was correct.

Within a few years, however, the young master squandered all the money in his pockets and food in his sacks with only the family estate remaining. His young men all advised him: "You, the young master, have vast and boundless farmland that covers more than half the area of our prefecture. One cannot measure how much land you have never stepped on. Yet, by and large, the common people either presented this land to you as a tribute or the government deeded this land to you as a gift when you had power. [In any case], you yourself did not purchase it with your own money. Even the land you did purchase was just the repayment of debt by the poor and desperate sellers who had no other choice but to let you take away their sandy and barren farmland. How much could it now be worth? Most of the land is now desolate with only a little being under cultivation. Even so, you still have to trouble yourself to supervise the collection of the meager land taxes, which in your eyes are worth no more than dirt and mud. But if you use the dirt and mud from this desolate land to reward the common people, after they obtain it, every inch of this land would become as valuable as gold. Hence, the mud and sand would be used as pure gold. How could this be infeasible?

The young master wholeheartedly believed that he had a sound strategy. Consequently, wherever he traveled, he signed the necessary title deeds as their rewards [to commoners]. People pretended to be reluctant to accept this land; then the young men would try to persuade them to do so with good words. The young master looked embarrassed and humble, fearing that the common people would refuse to accept these title deeds. Whenever treacherous villains plotted to obtain certain fertile farmland from the young master, they would always first bribe his young men who would then deliberately ask the young master to accept the villains' food and wine. Some of them employed singing girls to dress up to appear to be their wives and daughters and then flirt with the young master. Sometimes the young master saw through this trick, but still he would not question them. Before the villains left, one of the young men held the brush to write, one counted [the land holdings] with his fingers, and one checked the record [of land ownership]. After the title deeds were drafted, the young men would ask the young master just to sign them. As for the quantity and quality of the land, the young master had no control at all. Soon after [the signing], the young master exclaimed: "I'm tired! How can I always hold the brush to sign the deeds and also work so laboriously as a scholar?" His young men then had the title deeds carved on woodblocks and printed out with all the relevant information such as the reason of selling the land, its location, age, and so forth. At the bottom [of the title] a seven-character poem of eight lines was attached, written by the young master, which read:

> While the farmland lasts for a thousand years, a man's life is no more than 800 years;
> Why should one haggle over success or failure?
> Of those noble and wealthy, in the past and today, who is still alive?
> The mountains and rivers of the Tang and Song dynasties turn out to be nothingness.
> The time of going is as easy as the time of coming;
> Not having something is the same as having it.
> If people laugh at me for losing my ancestors' inheritance,
> I'd laugh at them living in a dream.

Every morning when the young master went out, he would print out several dozen of the deeds to bring with him, and when needed on the spot, he would just fill in some specific numbers.

8. The Tale of Young Master Yao

However, since the young master went hunting to excess and gave out rewards lavishly, and moreover, his young men were always embezzling his money while he maintained an extravagant life style, within just a few years, he had squandered the entire family fortune. He could not even afford to preserve his ancestors' tombs or keep his wife and children's living rooms. His former young followers, on the other hand, were wearing fine clothes, dining on delicacies, and riding on sturdy horses and in imposing carriages. As they continually went out in this fashion and encountered the young master, gradually they alienated him. Those who once prostrated themselves in welcoming the young master by the road now behaved even more arrogantly toward him than the young men. When these people observed the young master suffering from hunger and cold, they turned around and walked away. Looking at one another, their eyes all filled with scorn.

The young master was unable to find a way out [of his financial troubles], so he began to think of selling his wife. Yet, he dreaded his father-in-law and dared not open his mouth. His father-in-law was invariably an understanding man and had clear insight into his son-in-law's mind. He first asked a man to accept the divorce [on his behalf], and soon thereafter, he secretly took his daughter home and provided for her in another house. He then asked another man, pretending to come from a wealthy clan, to take generous betrothal gifts to the young master and make a deal with him. This man then told the young master: "Your wife isn't actually worth so much, but I heard she is virtuous and capable, so I am sparing no expense to marry her. However, once she is married into our prominent family, you should not see each other again for the rest of your lives." The young master was overjoyed and willing to sell his wife to this man.

Just a few months after the young master's wife left, he had spent all the betrothal money. He looked around and found himself quite alone and helpless, so he was about to sell himself, only being troubled that he had no prospective buyer. Again, his former father-in-law asked one of his yard hands to disguise himself and make a deal to purchase the young master, stating: "You were originally a noble man, so I highly regard your value. Nonetheless, after we sign this contract, you will have to follow all my dictates—and not disobey." The young master thought to himself: "When I myself was rich and prosperous, I had hundreds of retainers. All of them just wandered around, well fed and well clad, and that's it, and nobody suffered from anything at all." He then made his promise and followed the man home. Upon their arrival, his new master ordered him to gather firewood every morning and urged him to pound millet every evening. The young master's body was tired and his strength was exhausted. He could not bear this ordeal a moment longer. After several days, therefore, he escaped and joined some beggars. He wrote a long song to beg for food in the market. Its lyrics read:

> People all say time flies like a shuttle,
> While I feel time goes at two different speeds.
> In the past when I was prosperous and people envied me,
> One year elapsed so quickly that it was easy to be idled away.
> It's a pity that I have no money today,
> And one moment passes like a long year!
> I used to also wear a light fur coat, ride sturdy horses and imposing carriages;
> I had commanded the multitude to rush to the mountain springs [in the hunting field].
> Upon hearing the order "encircle," even mountain spirits and devils would have been startled.
> Common people used to invite and welcome me as a deity.
> But today! All the gold has gone and who would still have compassion for me?
> My former friends have broken our alliance and my hunting dogs have been cooked!
> I do not have porridge during the day and cannot fall asleep in the night.
> I have learned to sing the Lotus Rhyme to beg in the street.
> Who could bear the two contrasting halves in one life?
> I shall blame neither my parents nor Heaven!
> If I knew earlier that I would encounter these frustrations at this point,
> I would have refused to be associated with the demons in those years!
> Now I am helpless and unable to do anything,
> But only earnestly exhort people to not follow my example!

His former father-in-law knew that the young master was in the market, so he asked the beggars to humiliate him in every possible way. If he were not completely submissive, they would threaten him: "We will tell your master." The young master would then cover his head and scurry away like a rat, not daring to look back. Because of this ill treatment, he drifted from place to place, having nowhere to live. Cold, starved, worried, and depressed, he had undergone all kinds of hardships. His former father-in-law then asked his daughter to build a narrow cabin by the side of their main gate and prepare some simple daily necessities and bedding. Afterward, he again asked someone to advise the young master:

> You originally came from a noble family, but are now humiliated by the beggars. You are not afraid of the beggars, but your master. He is searching for you day and night. You are lucky to have not run into him, but if you do, then you will be locked up in jail and will soon die. Your former wife is now the Mistress of a prominent family, and her eminent social status is no different than before. Why not let me tell you, you should seek to be her gatekeeper, then you need only to do the labor of opening and closing gates, but not to be tortured by wood gathering, or millet pounding. You will finally enjoy an easy and comfortable life without the concern of being hungry or cold again. Isn't this better than dying at any time soon in ditches?

With tears and snot running down his face, the young master begged this man for pity. He prostrated himself in the muddy road and said: "If we can make this arrangement work, then you will be my second parent." Thereupon, the young master was led into his former wife's other house. The young master saw a quiet and clean room with utensils and clothes neatly placed, so he was beside himself with joy, as if he had entered fairyland. The man [who led him here] warned the young master:

> Your Mistress is wealthy, so she treats all her servants in a solemn and serious way, yet because of her great prestige and reputation, she will be embarrassed to see your face. You must swear not to sneak into the central hall room. Also, you'd better not go out even for a short time. If you are caught by your old master, we will be in big trouble!

Therefore, the young master strictly adhered to this prohibition. When he was eating his fill and dressing warmly, the young master could not help but think about his earlier hunting. Yet, out of deep concern from inside and dread from outside, he was very strict about the clear and strict boundaries of going in and out of the house. Till the very end he had no idea that his former wife was not married again. He did not dare to meet her even once for the rest of his life and eventually died in his small cabin.

NOTES AND READING GUIDE

By Xin Zou

"The Tale of Young Master Yao" is the dramatic life-story of a young man, Master Yao, from a prominent family. In his youth, he led an profligate life, engaged in hunting and associated himself with evil friends. He soon squandered his entire inheritance; his followers even carved up his family estate. Having nothing left to his name, the young master first sold his wife and then himself. His father-in-law secretly sent people to bring his daughter back home where he provided her with a separate house. He further had people purchase the young master as a laborer. Yet the young man could not bear the bondage of physical labor, so he escaped and joined a gang of beggars. He thereafter drifted from place to place and endured all kinds of hardships. Only then did the father-in-law send people to advise the young man to seek to serve as his daughter's gatekeeper. From then on, the young master led an extremely simple life in a tiny cabin. Yet to the end of his life, he had no idea that his former wife hadn't remarried, nor did he dare to ever meet her.

I. Background Information

This story is found in Shao Jingzhan's (fl.1560) *Mideng yinhua*, a collection of classical tales published during the Wanli reign (1573–1620) of the Ming dynasty. Shao's collection was modeled on Qu You's *Jiandeng xinhua*, a highly acclaimed collection in this genre and hugely popular in the fifteenth and sixteenth centuries. Shao Jingzhan notes in the preface to *Mideng yinhua* how his collection came about: reportedly, a friend of Shao once visited him and discovered a copy of Qu You's *Xinhua* lying on Shao's desk. The friend quickly became engrossed in these stories and could not tear himself away from them until midnight. When the two men relaxed together, the friend went on to relate to Shao the marvelous stories he had heard or events he himself witnessed. The two men became so excited that they got up, relit a lamp and inscribed these stories.

It is noteworthy that in his preface the compiler Shao Jingzhan not only cited Qu You's collection as his source of inspiration, but he also inherited the literary trope of authors exchanging stories by lamplight, assuming the stance of literati whose stories were part of their own social lives. The preface further highlights some significant features Shao Jinzhan displays in his stories: these stories concern either retribution of the netherworld, or the ultimate Way or truth. They can be strange, but not deceptive; they can be serious, but not banal. The beautiful stories can move and those unsavory can provoke readers. 非幽冥果報之事，則至道名理之談；怪而不欺，正而不腐；妍足以感，醜可以思. The "Tale of Young Master Yao" as translated here demonstrates these ideas above—it is an intriguing story with many twists and turns yet conveying a clear didactic message.

The Ming writer Ling Mengchu (1580–1644) later transformed the "The Tale of Young Master Yao" into a vernacular story in his *Erke Paian jingqi* [*Slapping the Table in Amazement, Second Collection*] (1632). The story also inspired a theatrical adaptation of the story, "Not to be Traded for Gold" 金不換, which comes from the ancient saying, "The return of a prodigal son is not to be traded for gold" 浪子回頭金不換. This textual history of "The Tale of Young Master Yao" confirms what Tina Lu calls an "ecology of narratives" in the Ming dynasty, that is, a wide variety of storytelling, both fictional and dramatic, sharing "the same pool of source material, a shared stratum of narrative." As Tina Lu explains, a classical tale can be converted into a vernacular story doesn't necessarily mean the classical tale has a higher status in the hierarchy of literature. Rather, it simply stood at a higher end of "the food chain of transmission" (*Cambridge History of Chinese Literature*, Vol. 2, 116–27).

II. Trope and Originality in Shao Jingzhan's Story

The "Young Master Yao" is a standard prodigal son story readily found in both the Chinese and Western literatures a wayward son inherited and then squandered his family's fortune and became destitute. Only at that point did he become fully aware of his wrongdoings. He came back home after countless hardships, and in the end, he was forgiven and welcomed back into his family. A closer examination of this current story, however, shows how Shao Jingzhan, as a skillful writer, brought novelty to this old story plot with his unique storytelling technique and fresh insights.

What's most intriguing and entertaining about this story is the plot of "deception": how, in the first half, the young rouges defrauded the young master of his great wealth and far-flung landholdings step by step; how, then in the second part, the young master Yao's father-in-law led the young man back on track through a series of stratagems. These twists demonstrate Shao Jingzhan's skill as a storyteller to craft an absorbing story out of a formulaic plot.

Shao's adroit handling of the "deception" plot also warrants our close reading. The young master learned about the first deception the hard way. After the young man became destitute, he fully recognized the fickleness of human relationships and came to repent his dissipated youth among those wastrels. The second "deception," however, is never unveiled to the protagonist in the story. The young master remained in the dark to the end of his life that he was actually living under the same roof with his ex-wife as his father-in-law had arranged. Ling Mengchu later significantly revised this second part. He gave the story a happy ending, believing, perhaps, that "the return of a prodigal son" would be incomplete and imperfect without a "rebirth" of the young master. That is, the young master, after experiencing many of the hardships of life, eventually became a diligent and thrifty man who won back not only his father-in-law's trust, his wife, but also regained his own family fortune. This "rebirth" motif requires an unveiling of the deceptions to the protagonist in the story. But for readers who know the fact long before the protagonist does, such a retelling as we see here in Ling Mengchu's version renders the entire story relatively repetitive and uneconomical at the narrative level.

III. The Question of Human Nature

While most "prodigal son stories" end with the return and rebirth of the son, this current story is unique in that such a fundamental change never happens to the young master. This point becomes even clearer when we compare this current story, a classical tale, with Ling Mengchu's re-writing in vernacular language. Many of the differences between the two narratives correlate to two very different literary genres—classical tale and vernacular story. Yet, the sharply contrasting ways Shao and Ling end their stories also reflect their distinct responses to the question at the core of this story: can basic human nature be changed? The happy ending in Ling Mengchu's story indicates his optimistic attitude to this question, which is clearly demonstrated in his comment below:

> It is thus evident that his [young master Yao] nature as seen in his early behavior is simply because he had never experienced any hardships in life. For those descendants of rich and noble families,

it is better to know something about the difficulties of sowing and reaping (i.e. farm work).

可見前日心性，只是不曾吃得苦楚過。世間富貴子弟，還是等他曉得些稼穡艱難爲妙

Shao Jingzhan, on the other hand, manifestly doubts human nature can be changed at all. Toward the end of this current story, Shao tells readers that the young master eventually settled in a small cabin where he spent the rest of his life in isolation:

> When he was eating his fill and dressing warmly, the young master could not help but think about his earlier hunting. Yet, out of deep concern from inside and dread from outside, he was very strict about the clear and strict boundaries of going in and out of the house.

雖飽食暖衣, 不無弋獵之想;而內憂外懼, 甚嚴出入之防.

In other words, the young master Yao never became a "new" man. Rather, the father-in-law's machinations were able to *contain* or *control* those "dangerous" impulses in this young man's nature, but were unable to *eliminate* them. One may recall that the young man's father-in-law, when first entering the story, was described as "broad-minded, understanding, and had a clear insight into his son-in-law's mind." 乃翁固達者,深識其情. A fine writer of classical tales, Shao Jingzhan himself also exemplifies such a profound understanding of human nature.

Tale 9

"FUQING NONG ZHUAN" 負情儂傳
(THE FAITHLESS LOVER)

By Song Maocheng 宋懋澄
Translated by Zhenjun Zhang

During the Wanli reign period (1573–1620),[1] Scholar Li of Eastern Zhe 浙, the son of a regional governor,[2] became a visiting student through donation at the Northern Imperial Academy,[3] where he fell in love with Du Shiniang, a girl from a brothel.[4]

They associated intimately for years, until Li's wealth was depleted. The girl's mother became fairly tired of his frequent visits, but the girl and the young man's affections for each other grew even deeper.

The girl's beauty was without compare in all the brothels,[5] and she was also famous for her skills in playing musical instruments, singing,

---

This translation is based on the text in Song Maocheng's (1569–1620) *Jiuyueji* 九籥集. I have also consulted Huang Min 黃敏, ed., *Mingdai wenyan xiaoshuo xuanyi* 明代文言小説選譯 (Nanjing: Fenghuang chunmei chuban jituan, 2011), pp. 199–219.

1. The only reign period under 神宗 of the Ming, Zhu Yijun 朱翊鈞 (r. 1573–1620).
2. Fannie 藩臬, *fansi*藩司 and *niesi*臬司, refer to Buzhengshi布政使 (provincial governor) and Anchashi按察使(judicial commissioner) during the Ming and Qing dynasties.
3. After the capital of the Ming Empire was moved from Nanjing to Beijing in the eighteenth year of Yongle's reign (1420), the Imperial Academy was divided into two. The one in Beijing was called Beiyong 北雍, the Northern Imperial Academy. According to the governmental policy, a scholar could be eligible to study at the Imperial Academy by donating money or grain to the government.
4. Jiaofang教坊, institute of music, also refers to brothels during and after the Song and Yuan dynasties.
5. Pingkang平康[Ward] in the capital Chang'an of the Tang dynasty was filled with brothels. In later times Pingkang became another name for brothels.

and dancing. Thus, the youth of the capital all regarded her as the symbol of amorous affairs and a life of gaiety.

Vexed by Li's affection for her daughter, the mother started provoking him with bad words, but the young man was as polite as before. Later, the mother became harsh in tone and severe in her expressions. Unable to bear her mother's behavior, the girl pledged to marry Scholar Li.

The mother thought to herself: This girl was not given birth by me, and, based on the regulation, expunging her name from the list of brothels requires at least several hundred *liang* of gold. Furthermore, I know very well that the young man is now penniless. If I find a way to stump him, making him feel embarrassed, he will probably run away himself. Thus she smacked her palms and told the girl, "If you can urge your man to raise three hundred *liang* of gold for me, I'll let you go anywhere you want."

The girl replied frankly, "Although Mr. Li lives at the inn in poverty, it is still possible for him to raise three hundred *liang* of gold. Considering that it is not easy to collect the gold, if the gold is ready but you break your promise, what can we do?"

Intending to drive Scholar Li into a dead end, the mother insulted him by pointing at the candle wick and saying with a laugh, "As long as Mr. Li is able to enter with the gold in his hand, you can go with your man right away. The candle producing a charred wick predicts that Mr. Li will obtain a girl."

Thereupon, they made their promises to each other and parted.

At midnight, the girl wept in grief. She said to Li, "The cash you have on hand is of course not enough to ransom me. But are you willing to borrow money from your friends and relatives for this urgent situation?"

Pleasantly surprised, Li replied, "Yes, of course! It is not that I was unwilling to do so previously. I just dared not tell you."

The next day, Li intentionally bundled himself up, bidding farewell to his relatives and friends and begging for loans from everyone he visited. His relatives and friends all knew that he had indulged in visiting prostitutes for quite a long time. Now he suddenly wanted to journey southward [to his home], which seemed dubious and unlikely. Moreover, Li's father, angered at his wandering, had sent letters to cut off his returning. Thus, if anyone made a loan to him, they would neither please his father, nor be able to collect the debt. Therefore, everyone prevaricated with excuses. Li continued to beg loans for a month, but finally came to Shiniang with empty hands.

At midnight, the girl sighed, saying, "You could not raise any money? Inside my cotton-padded mattress there are one hundred and fifty *liang* of gold. They are wrapped in the cotton toward the edge. Tomorrow let's ask the servant to secretly take them and give them to my mother respectfully. Beyond this, I cannot raise any more money. What should we do?"

Pleasantly startled, the scholar cautiously took the [cotton cloth from inside the] mattress and left. He took out the gold from the mattress and talked with his relatives and friends. Taking pity on the girl who had set her mind on marrying Li, his relatives and friends resolutely raised gold and gave it to the scholar. However, it was only one hundred *liang*.

The scholar told the girl while weeping, "I have exhausted all my resources. Where can I find the remaining fifty *liang* of gold?"

The girl jumped with joy, saying, "Don't worry! Tomorrow morning I'll get it from my sisters next door."

At the appointed time, she truly obtained fifty *liang* of gold. She put all the gold together and delivered it to her mother.

When she realized that her mother intended to break her pledge, the girl wept with grief, saying, "Previously you ordered my lover to raise three hundred *liang* of gold. Now the gold is ready, yet you broke your promise. I'll let the man leave with the gold, and I will kill myself right now!"

Afraid of losing both the girl and the gold, her mother said, "I'll do whatever I promised; however, from your head to your heel, neither an inch of earring nor a foot of silk belongs to you." The girl happily accepted her mother's request.

The next morning, following the young scholar, Shiniang walked out of the door of the brothel in commoner's clothes, with her hair unpinned.

Touched by her situation, all her sisters wept tears, saying, "Shiniang has been the head of us courtesans, but now with her lover she leaves our courtyard in rags. Isn't this a shame upon us?"

Each of them then gave Shiniang whatever they brought with them. After a moment, she was bedecked in all-new accoutrements: hairpins, rings, clothes, and shoes.

The sisters said to each other, "Our older sister and her lover will travel for thousands of *li*, yet they have little luggage." So they jointly gifted them a suitcase. Neither the scholar nor the girl knew what was in it.

At sunset, each of her sisters bid her farewell and parted in tears.

The girl reached the inn where the scholar stayed, but within the four walls it was empty. Being at a loss, the scholar merely stared at his tablet. The girl took off the raw silk fabric from her left arm and tossed him twenty *liang* of *Zhuti* silver,[6] saying, "Take this as compensation for the boat and cart."

Next day, the scholar hired a carriage. They left the town through the Chongwen Gate, reached the Lu River,[7] and paid for the boat. They spent all the silver when the boat arrived. Again, the girl exposed the raw silk fabric on her right arm, took out thirty *liang* of silver and said, "This can be used for food."

The scholar had experienced frequent mishaps, but he was delighted by his encounter with Shiniang. It was late autumn. He laughed at the flying wild geese for not being coupled and belittled the swimming fish for lacking companionship. As white dews became frost, they pledged to be together until their hair turned gray; they pointed to flaming red maples and likened them to their sincere hearts. How happy they were!

When they reached Guazhou,[8] they left the big ship, rented a small boat, and would cross the Yangtze River the next day. That night, the whole river glowed with moonlight, like fluttering white silk reflected in a bright mirror.

The scholar told the girl, "Since we walked out of the gate of the capital, you have never shown your face to the outside world. Tonight we are in our own boat; what do you worry about? Moreover, how can the wind and smoke north of the fortress compare with the river and moon south of the Yangtze River? Why do you keep silent?"

The girl had long covered herself. Now, touched by the interflowing of the river and moon, she felt sad for being distant. Hand in hand, she and the scholar sat at the head of the boat in the moonlight.

The scholar became excited. Raising a wine cup, he asked the girl to sing a song to toast the moon on the river. The girl gently chanted with her sweet and soft voice, and suddenly started singing. Even the caw of a crow and the cry of an ape could not be more sorrowful than her song.

In a neighboring boat, there was a young man who was accumulating salt at Weiyang and would be back in Xin'an by the end of the year.[9] He

---

6. Zhuti 朱提 was a place located in modern Zhaotong of Yunnan that produced high quality silver.

7. Lu 潞 River refers to the northern canal flowing through east suburb of Beijing.

8. On the north bank of the Yangtze River, south of Modern Yangzhou in Jiangsu.

9. Weiyang 維揚, part of Modern Yangzhou. Xin'an 新安, modern She County 歙县 in Anhui.

was only about twenty years old, and he was esteemed as the leader of the frivolous brothel-gang youth. Drunk, he heard the song. He felt that he could fly, but the song stopped suddenly, and he could not sleep all the rest of night.

At dawn, strong winds and heavy snow blocked the ferry. The man of Xin'an saw the scholar's boat, knowing that inside was the beautiful woman. Thus he donned a mink cap and a down jacket, acted flirtatiously and admired his own reflection. Upon seeing any movement, he would knock on the side of the boat and sing.

When the scholar lifted the canopy to look around, he saw the thick snowfall. The man from Xin'an suggested to the scholar that he take precautions, and then invited him ashore to have a heart-to-heart talk in a restaurant.

When they drank to their hearts' content, the man of Xin'an asked the young master, "Who sang last night?"

The scholar told him the truth. Then the man asked further, "After crossing the river, are you going to go home?"

The scholar looked sad, and he told the man why it was hard for him to return home. Lingering over the wine cup, he disclosed all the truth without reason: "The beauty invited me to wander around the mountains and rivers in the Wu and Yue."

The man of Xin'an sternly said to the young master:

What you are doing is like traveling through fragrant grasses while carrying peaches and plums. Yet didn't you hear that when bright pearls fall upon the ground, men of strength will vie with each other for them? Besides, men south of the Yangtze River are extremely good with romantic affairs: whenever one loves a woman, he dares not begrudge his life. Even in my own mind, this idea emerges from time to time. Furthermore, while the beauty is talented, her conduct is unpredictable. How do you know that she is not merely using you like a ladder to secretly make some upcoming appointment? In that case, the mist-covered waves of Zhenze,[10] the wind and waves of Qiantang,[11] and fish bellies and shark teeth, would all form your tomb. I have also heard the reasoning: who is dearer between your

---

10. Zhenze震澤, the Lake Tai, lies between Jiangsu and Zhejiang.
11. Qiantang River springs from the borders of Anhui and Jiangxi and passes Hangzhou before flowing into the East Sea.

father and a beauty? What is more urgent between pursuing pleasure and avoiding calamity? I hope you will think about these questions carefully.

With a worried frown, the scholar asked, "Then what can I do?" The man of Xin'an said, "I have a perfect plan, which fits your case extremely well. But I'm afraid that you won't be able to do it." The young master asked, "What is the plan?"

The man replied:

> If you can really part with your lover, of whom you are now tired, I would willingly offer a thousand *liang* of gold for your birthday, though I'm not smart and capable. After obtaining a thousand *liang* of gold, you can return home to report to your respected father; you would have no worries on your way by getting rid of the beauty. I hope you will seriously consider this proposition!

The scholar had been wandering alone for years. Though the companionship of lovers should last until death, his situation resembled a swallow nesting on a curtain, and it pushed him into a dilemma. Like a goat whose hooves are hitched in a fence, or a fox whose tail dipped into the water before crossing a river, he doubted what he was doing. Thinking of the Flying Swallow, Empress Zhao of Han, who killed numerous princes with her sister,[12] and the Baosi, Consort of Emperor You of Zhou, who was said to be born of dragon saliva and ruined the Zhou dynasty, he felt as if he was a forlorn soul, crying in a dream. Thus he lowered his head, contemplated for a while, and then

---

12. Empress Zhao refers to the second empress of Emperor Cheng 成 of Han 漢 (r. 32–7 BCE). Zhao was known for her beauty and skilled dancing, and she was so slim that she could walk in small steps, shivering like a soft, weak branch in one's hand. The biography of Empress Zhao states that both Empress Zhao and her sister were childless even though they had monopolized the favor of the emperor for over ten years. Both history and legend have a long record detailing her and her sister Zhao Hede's 趙合德 (d. 7 BC) persecution of palace women pregnant by the emperor and of the babies born to them. See *Han shu*, 97b.3988–99; "Zhao Feiyan biezhuan" (Supplementary Biography of Empress Zhao). An English translation of this tale by me can be found in Zhenjun Zhang and Jing Wang, *Song Dynasty Tales: A Guided Reader* (Singapore: World Scientific Publishing, 2017), pp. 1–31.

declined the suggestion by saying that he would go back to talk with the woman. Hand in hand, he disembarked with the man of Xin'an and both returned to their own boats.

Having trimmed the wick, the girl was waiting for the scholar to have a few drinks. Turning away his eyes several times, the scholar intended to talk to her but kept silence instead. They slept together, sharing the same quilt. At midnight, the scholar cried sadly.

The girl sat up urgently, held him in her arms, and said:

> I have lived together with you for nearly three years. We have traveled several thousand *li* yet have never been sad. Now we are crossing the Yangtze River and we should be happy for our long-lasting harmonious union. I don't understand why you suddenly show me a face like this. Perhaps this means that you are going to part with me, but why?

The scholar poured out his words together with his tears, and he became saddened by his deep feelings for her. Having poured out everything that was on his mind, the scholar cried and shed tears as before.

The girl released the scholar and asked:

> Who made such a plan for you? This person is a great hero! You get a thousand *liang* of gold and can see your parents; I would follow a man and not be a burden upon you. An affair derives from feelings and yet stops within [the bounds of] ritual and righteousness.[13] This is great! Both of us would get what we want. But where is the gold?

The scholar replied, "Since I did not know what you would think, the gold is still in that man's possession."

The girl said, "Tomorrow, please go quickly to promise him that you agree to the arrangement. But transferring a thousand *liang* of gold is a big event. I won't go into that man's boat until the gold is in your box."

---

13. *Fahu qing, zhihu liyi* 發乎情, 止乎禮義, "derives from feelings and yet stops within [the bounds of] ritual and righteousness," is from an anonymous author's comment on the *bianfeng* 變風, "Changed Airs," of the *Shijing* (The Classic of Odes) in his Shi daxu 詩大序 (The Great Preface), a work of the late Western Han dynasty. It became a Confucian moral code for people later on. The translation here is from Victor H. Mair, ed., *The Columbia Anthology of Traditional Chinese Literature* (New York: Columbia University Press, 1994), p. 122.

Midnight had just passed but she arose to apply formal makeup, saying, "Today's makeup is for seeing off the old and welcoming the new, it cannot be informal." When her makeup was done, it was almost dawn.

The man of Xin'an had already moved his boat next to the scholar's. Hearing of the message from the girl, he was greatly pleased and said, "Please show me your box as a proof."

The girl delightedly said to scholar Li, "Give it to him." Then she asked the man of Xin'an to transfer the betrothal fee to Li's boat and weigh it to make sure it is the exact amount.

Thereupon the girl walked out from the middle of the boat. Standing by the side of the boat, she told the man of Xin'an, "In the box you previously took there is Scholar Li's passport. Please bring it back and return it to him immediately."

The man of Xin'an followed her order.

The girl asked Scholar Li to pull out a box which was filled with colorful jade phoenixes worth several hundred *liang* of gold. The girl threw them all into the river. Scholar Li, the frivolous man from Xin'an, and the people on both boats, all started yelling loudly at her.

The girl asked the scholar to pull out another box, filled with jade bird feathers, bright earrings, jade flutes, and gold pipes worth several thousand *liang* of gold. Again she cast them into the river.

Then she asked Scholar Li to take out a leather bag, filled with antiques of old jade and purple gold, all invaluable rare treasures. She also cast them into the river.

Finally, she asked the scholar to pull out a flat case filled with a handful of luminous pearls. At this moment everyone in both boats was terrified, and the sounds of yelling disturbed and attracted people of the city.

When the girl was about to cast away the pearls, Scholar Li felt great regret. He embraced the legs of Shiniang and tried to stop her while weeping. Even the man of Xin'an came to persuade her.

The girl pushed the scholar away and spat in the face of the man of Xin'an, cursing: "The song you heard stirred your lust, and then you wagged your tongue like a warbler. Despite the spirits and Heaven, you made the bottle drop into the well by cutting the rope, causing me to die unjustly.[14] I hate that I am merely a weak woman and cannot draw my knife to fight you, you crude man.

---

14. Guyinxuebi 骨殷血碧 (dark red bone and blue blood) indicates a wrongful death.

9. *The Faithless Lover*

"However, by coveting money, you came to hold me by force. How can your behavior be differentiated from a dog vying for bones after foolishly following others? After I die, if my soul is numinous, I'll sue you before the spirits and deprive you of your mortal life in no time.

"Moreover, by hiding my own tracks and trusting my sisters to store rare treasures, I intended to help Scholar Li return to see his parents. Now he is unable to be with me until the end.[15] I now expose everything publicly because I want everyone to know that Scholar Li has eyes, yet fails to see.

"For the sake of Scholar Li, I had shed tears until my eyes were dry, and my united souls were scattered numerous times.[16] Luckily, we achieved preliminary success. Unexpectedly, however, he quickly forgot our joining hands[17] and neglected the harmony between us and suddenly succumbed to the glib tongue.[18] Like being afraid of walking because of too much dew on the road,[19] he suddenly abandoned me, as if I was nothing but leftovers. Seeing that he covets the remnant [jewelry] and intends to gather the water that has been poured out, how can I not help feeling ashamed if I allow him again to lead me by the nose?

"My life is over! The brightness of the East Sea coast comes from the gathering of sands, and the height of Huashan, the West Sacred Mountain,[20] owes itself to the accumulation of tiny particles of earth and stone. What a pity [that our accumulated love stopped in such a way]! When will it end if I am tangled in it?"

15. *Xuwobuzu* 畜 (慉) 我不卒 is from "Riyue" 日月 of "Beifeng" 邶風 in the *Shijing* (Classic of Odes), meaning "loving me not to the end."

16. Chinese believe that there are three souls in one's body and that they will scattered when their host is startled.

17. *Xieshou* 携手, "join hands," is from "Beifeng 北風" of "Beifeng 邶風" in *Shijing*: "Ye who love and regard me, let's join hands and go together" 惠而好我, 携手同行. See James Legg, ed., *The Chinese Classics* (Hong Kong: Hong Kong University Press, 1960), p. 67.

18. Shenghuang 笙簧, "reeds of a panpipe," refers to a "glib tongue" or "cunning talk." "Qiaoyan 巧言" of "Xiaoya 小雅" in *Shijing*: "Their artful words, like organ-tongues, / Show how unblushing are their faces" 巧言如簧, 顏之厚矣 (see Legg, ed., *The Chinese Classics*, p. 342).

19. Wei xingduolu 畏行多露, "being afraid of walking because of too much dew on the road," is from "Xing lu" 行露 of "Zhaonan" 昭南 in *Shijing*: "Might I not [have walked there] in the early dawn? But I said there was [too] much dew on the path" 豈不夙夜, 謂行多露 (see Legg, ed., *The Chinese Classics*, p. 27).

20. One hundred and twenty kilometers west of Xi'an, Shanxi province.

Thereupon, the spectators on the boats and the riverbank all shed tears, cursing Scholar Li as an ingrate. The girl, holding the bright pearls, threw herself into the water and died.

At that time, all the witnesses intended to beat the man of Xin'an and Scholar Li. Both Scholar Li and the man of Xin'an hoisted their sails and fled. Nobody knew where they had gone.

Alas! This young lady deserves to be called an unyielding woman by Zizheng.[21] Even a virgin deep inside the boudoir could not be more chaste than she was!

---

21. Zizheng 子政 is the nickname of Liu Xiang (77–6 BCE), a Han dynasty scholar and the author of the *Lienü zhuan* 列女傳 (Biographies of Exemplary Women).

NOTES AND READING GUIDE

Zhenjun Zhang

I. Text and Author

This tale is from volume 5 of Song Maocheng's (1569–1622) *Jiuyue ji*, a collection of his works widely transmitted during the late period of the Ming dynasty. Many scholars, such as Chen Zilong 陳子龍 (1608–1647; *Chen Wozi xiansheng Anyatang gao* 陳臥子先生安雅堂稿 *juan* 10), Wu Weiye 吳偉業 (*Meicun Jiacang gao* 梅村家藏稿 *juan* 47 *Wenji* 文集), Wang Shizhen 王士禛 (1634–1711; *Daijingji* 帶經集 *juan* 81, *Chibei outan* 池北偶談 *juan* 23), GuoTingbi 郭廷弼 (*Songjiang fuzhi* 松江府志 *juan* 44 and 50), all recorded this collection in their works.[22] Feng Menglong's 馮夢龍 *Qingshi leilue* 情史類略 includes a story titled "Du Shiniang" 杜十娘, which says at the end "[This is the] 'Faithless Lover' by a man of Zhe" 浙人作《负情侬传》, though he didn't mention the *Jiuyue ji*.

Since it was banned during the years under Emperor Qianlong 乾隆 (r. 1736–1795) of the Qing dynasty, however, the *Jiuyue ji* was rarely seen for a long time afterward. The story included in Feng Menglong's *Qingshi leilue* became the only work related to this tale, but it was hard to know if it is a complete version of the tale without comparing it with the one in Song Maocheng's anthology.

It took modern scholars quite some time to find the original source of this tale. In 1932, Sun Kaidi 孫楷第 found a Korean copy in *Shanbu wenyuan zhaju* 刪補文苑楂橘 (see《日本東京所見中國小說書目提要》Vol. 6). In 1980, Hu Shiying 胡士瑩 found this tale in a Ming dynasty edition of *Jiuyue ji* and included it in his *Huaben xiaoshuo gailun* 話本小説概論.[23] It is the same story found in Feng Menglong's *Qingshi leilue*. In 1984, Wang Liqi 王利器 published a hand-copied version of *Jiuyue ji* from his family library.[24] For the first time, this collection became available for scholars and the public. When the edition of *Xuxiu Siku quanshu* 續修四庫全書 and *Siku jinhui congkan* 四庫禁毀叢刊 were

---

22. See Wang Liqi, "Preface to *Jiuyue ji*"《九籥集》序言 in his *Jiuyue ji* (Beijing: Zhongguo shehui kexue chubanshe, 1984).
23. Hu Shiying, *Huaben xiaoshuo gailun* (Beijing: Zhonghua shuju, 1980), pp. 422–5.
24. Wang Liqi, ed, *Jiuyue ji*.

published by Shanghai guji chubanshe and Beijing chubanshe in 1995 and 2000 respectively, it proved that Wang Liqi's edition is not the forty-seven-volume complete version of *Jiuyue ji*, but luckily it preserved a complete part of fiction, which includes "The Faithless Lover."

Differing from the story included in Feng Menglong's *Qingshi leilue*, the story in *Jiuyue ji* includes a short passage at the end talking about how the story was written:

> Song Youqing said: I heard this story from a friend in the fall of the *gengzi* year. As there was a lot of free time, I picked up a brush to narrate the story. While finishing the sentence "When her makeup was done, it was almost dawn," it was about midnight. I was tired and went to bed to sleep. I dreamed of someone with disheveled hair and of the voice of that woman who said to me, "I am ashamed of letting this event be known to others in the world. Recently the lord of the netherworld took pity on me and let me be in charge of wind and waves, participating in dealing with disasters and blessings in the human world. If you write this tale of me, I'll make you sick." The next day, that truly happened and lasted for several dozen days. Therefore I discarded it in a basket. In the *dingwei* year, when I was returning home southwards with my family, I checked my manuscripts in the basket, and found the one about this event was still there. Unable to bear letting it be forgotten, I grabbed a brush and finished it. I was only afraid that she would cause trouble once more, causing me to hold my belly [to relieve the pain] again.[25] Having written about this in order to record the anomaly, I left words for the girl: "The tale is finished now. Someday later when I pass Guazhou ferry, I hope you will not stir evil wind and waves to abuse me. If you don't forgive me, after crossing the river I will write it again. How can I break my brushes to behave like a blind man?" The time was the second day of the seventh month, in the fall of the *dingwei* year, and about eight years after the *gengzi* year, when my boat was traveling on the Wei River and reached a place more than a hundred *li* from Cangzhou. After several days, my maid servant Lutao suddenly fell into the river and drowned.

---

25. Pengfu 捧腹 means generally splitting one's sides with laughter, but that seems unlikely here.

宋幼清曰: 余于庚子秋闻其事于友人。岁暮多暇, 援笔叙事。至
"妆毕而天已就曙矣", 时夜将分, 困惫就寝, 梦披发而其音妇者谓
余曰: "妾羞令人间知有此事。近幸冥司见怜, 令妾稍司风波,间
豫人间祸福。若郎君为妾传奇, 妾将使君病作。"明日, 果然。
几十日而间。因弃置筐中。丁未, 携家南归, 舟中检筒稿, 见此
事尚存, 不忍湮没, 急捉笔足之, 惟恐其复祟,使我更捧腹也。既
书之纸尾,以纪其异; 复寄语女郎: "传已成矣,它日过瓜州,幸勿作
恶风浪相虐。倘不见谅,渡江后必当复作。宁肯折笔同盲人乎?"
时丁未秋七月二日, 去庚子盖八年矣。舟行卫河道中,距沧州约
百余里。不数日,而女奴露桃忽堕河死。

Song Maocheng, styled Youqing 幼清, was a native of Huating 華亭 in Songjiangfu, present-day Songjiang County, Shanghai. His family was a noble one (松江府望族, 《康熙松江府志》), and he had been a student in the Imperial Academy. He passed the imperial examination at the provincial level in the fortieth year of the Wanli reign (1612) but failed to achieve the metropolitan level though he took the examination several times. He was known for his talent in writing when he was young, and he became interested in writing tales. His *Jiuyue ji* is probably the first individual anthology to include tales. After being neglected for a long time, its value in the history of classical Chinese fiction gradually has become recognized in recent works, such as Zhang Peiheng's 章培恆 *Zhongguo wenxueshi* 中國文學史 and Wu Zhida's 吳志達 *Zhongguo wenyan xiaoshuoshi* 中國文言小説史.

II. Significance

The story of Du Shiniang occurred in the Wanli 萬曆 reign (1573–1620) of the Ming dynasty, and it was a sensational event. As mentioned above, Song Maocheng recorded how he finished his writing at the end of the tale: He heard the event from a friend in the fall of the *gengzi* year and started his writing at the end of the year; however, because of a strange dream in which the female protagonist threatened him if he wouldn't stop his writing she would make him sick, he didn't finish it until eight years later, the fall of *dingwei* 丁未 year.

Although it seems this tale is a record of a real story, it is significant in the history of Chinese fiction for its portrayal of the female protagonist, Shiniang. Shiniang is a lowly prostitute, but she values love instead of money. While vexed by Li's affection for her daughter, the mother starts provoking Li with bad words. "Unable to bear her mother's behavior," however, "the girl pledged to marry Scholar Li." To achieve her goal, Shiniang is also brave and wise:

> When her mother intended to break her pledge, the girl wept with grief, saying, "Previously you ordered my lover to raise three hundred *liang* of gold. Now the gold is ready, yet you broke your promise. I'll let the man leave with the gold, and I will kill myself right now!"
> Afraid of losing both the girl and the gold, her mother said, "I'll do whatever I promised; however, from your head to your heel, neither an inch of earring nor a foot of silk belongs to you." The girl happily accepted her mother's request.

When Li betrays her by selling her to a merchant, Shiniang's decisive act pushes the story to its climax: "the spectators on the boats and the riverbank all shed tears, cursing Scholar Li as an ingrate. The girl, holding the bright pearls, threw herself into the water and died."

The image of Shiniang is a brilliant one in the history of Chinese fiction. In numerous tragic love stories, almost all of the female protagonists are weak and passive, accepting whatever happens to them. Well-known examples include Yingying in the "Story of Yingying," Xiaoyu in "The Tale of Huo Xiaoyu," and Youyu in "The Record of Wang Youyu," etc. Unlike those passive female figures, Shiniang fights for her love and makes her own choice when tragedy befalls her.

III. Influence

Song Maocheng's "The Faithless Lover" was influential even during the Ming dynasty. In the fourth year of the Tianqi reign period (1624), Feng Menglong published his "Du Shiniang nuchen baibaoxiang" 杜十娘怒沉百寶箱 (Du Shiniang Sinks Her Jewel Box in Anger), a vernacular story derived from "The Faithless Lover," in his *Jingshi tongyan*警世通言 (Stories to Caution the World). Afterward, it was widespread and well received throughout the country, becoming one of the masterpieces of vernacular short stories.

While adopting the plot of "The Faithless Lover," Feng extended the work from 2,500 words to 10,000 words. The major changes Feng made in his work include the following: first, following the storytelling tradition, he added a short passage at the beginning as *ruhua*入話 (entering the story); second, Feng added more figures, such as the chivalrous man Liu Yuchun, to enrich the story; third, he added a didactic ending in which the faithless scholar goes crazy, the evil merchant dies, and the chivalrous man, Liu Yuchun, is rewarded with pearls for his generosity. Most importantly, however, Feng Menglong retold the story with much more detailed and vivid depictions, which raised the narrative to a new and advanced level; and, as its title indicates, the focus of the story changed from the faithless lover, Scholar Li, to the beautiful, smart, and unfortunate courtesan, Shiniang. The following passage at the end of the story shows the charm of Feng's writing:

> Turning to Li Jia, she went on, "In my years as a courtesan, I put away some private savings to support myself in the future. After we met, you and I took many a vow of lifelong love and fidelity. Before we left the capital, I had my sisters give me what were in fact my own possessions. The treasures hidden in the jewel box were worth no less than ten thousand taels of silver. I meant to add some grandeur to your return, so that your parents might act out of compassion and accept me as a member of the family. With the remainder of my life committed to you, I would have had no regret in life and in death. Little did I know that you would trust me so little that you followed some evil advice and abandoned me before the journey was even completed. You have betrayed my devotion to you. I opened the box and showed its contents in public so that you'll know that a mere thousand taels of silver are of little importance to me. I am not unlike a jewel box that contains precious jade, but you have eyes that fail to recognize value. Alas, I was not born under a lucky star. Having just freed myself from the tribulations of a courtesan's life, I find myself abandoned again. All those present will testify, by the evidence of their eyes and ears, that I have not failed you in any way. It's you that betrayed me!"
>
> There was not a dry eye among the onlookers, all of whom cursed Li for being the fickle ingrate that he was. Ashamed and exasperated, Li shed tears of remorse and was about to apologize to Shiniang when she threw herself into the middle of the current, the jewel box in her arms. The horrified onlookers cried out for her rescue, but with a heavy mist hanging over the raging waves, not the slightest trace of her could be seen. How tragic that a celebrated courtesan as pretty as a flower and as fair as jade fell prey to fish of the river![26]

26. Shuhui Yang and Yunqin Yang, trans., *Stories to Caution the World* (Seattle: University of Washington Press, 2005), pp. 563–4.

Through the revision by Feng Menglong, the story of Shiniang became a masterpiece among the best short stories of China.

Besides Feng Menglong's short story, dramas derived from this story include *Baibaoxiang* 百寶箱 (Treasure Box) by Guo Yanshen 郭彥深 of the Ming, Qing scholar Xia Bingheng's 夏秉恆 *Babaoxiang* 八寶箱 and Meichuang zhuren's 梅窗主人 *Baibaoxiang*.[27]

---

27. Hu Shiying, *Huaben xiaoshuo gailun*, p. 557.

Tale 10

"ZHU SHAN" 珠衫
(THE PEARL SHIRT)

By Song Maocheng
Translated by Jing Hu

A merchant from Chu,[1] aged 22 or 23, had a beautiful wife. He went to do business in Yue[2] and lived in a multistory building close to the marketplace. On one occasion, his wife stood by the window and looked outside from behind the curtain. Suddenly she saw a handsome man, who looked like her husband. She then lifted the curtain and peeked. The man saw that the lady's eyes were fixed on him; thinking that she was interested in him, his eyes fixed on her. She couldn't help blushing and put down the curtain.

The man was from Xin'an[3] and had been there as a visitor for two years. Seeing the beauty upstairs, he was so happy that he felt as if he had gone mad. He was thinking of telling the lady what he wanted, but he could not find any way. It suddenly occurred to him that he was familiar with the old woman selling beads in the east of the market. Using the pretext of selling beads, he told the old woman his thought.

The old woman said, "I have never met that lady. I dare not promise to help you with your request." The man took out a hundred *taels* of

---

This translation is based on the text in *juan* 2 of *Jiuyue bieji* 九籥別集, by Song Maocheng, photo-reproduced in the *Xuxiu Siku quanshu*, vols. 1373–4 (Shanghai: Shanghai guji chubanshe, 1995). I have also consulted the text in Huang Min's *Mingdai wenyan duanpain xiaoshuo xuanyi*, pp. 230–46. In Huang Min's version, the title "Zhu Shan" 珠衫 reads "Zhen Shan" 珍衫.

1. *Chu* 楚 is the name of a state in ancient times; it refers to modern Hubei, Henan, Anhui areas etc.

2. *Yue* 粤 is the abbreviation of Guangdong province.

3. The location of Xin'an is not clear. It may refer to present-day Anhui province, or it may also refer to modern Hong Kong and Shenzhen area.

silver and a few ingots of gold, laid them on the table, bowed to his knees and begged, "I will die soon because of missing that lady. The gold and silver on the table are just my tribute to you. When it is done, my reward will be doubled."

The old woman was pleasantly surprised and promised him, "Just wait in the hotel. I will gradually approach her. Our goal is for you two to have some fun; please don't expect this to happen in a short time." The man expressed his deep appreciation to the old woman and went back to his place.

The old woman then picked out large pearls and some rare jewelry such as hairpins and earrings from her pocket. The next morning[4] she went to the shop of the man from Xin'an. The shop faced the building where the lady lived. The old woman pretended to do business with the man for a long time, looking at and appreciating the color of pearls in the sunlight, playing with and wearing hairpins. All the people in the market scrambled to watch and made quite a hubbub, and the noise penetrated the lady's whole house. The lady went upstairs and peeked. Right then she ordered her maid to ask the old woman to come over.

The old woman rejected the price offered by the man from Xin'an and said, "No, no! you are really troublesome. At your price, I could have already sold them a long time ago." She put the jewelry into the bamboo-plaited box and went to the building across the street. She greeted the young lady and said:

> I have been living in the same lane with you for a long time. I know that you have a large collection of jewellery. In my humble opinion, those pieces of mine are treasures. The prices offered by the man downstairs are unreasonable. I think he does not have a girlfriend yet. I happen to have other things to do now; I would like to trouble you to keep them for me. I will come to talk to you about them in a short while.

With that, she hurried downstairs and didn't come back for several days.

One day, it was raining when the old woman came and said, "Something happened to my beloved daughter. I have been running around to take care of her these days and missed our appointment. But I have come here in the rain today, please show me all your jewellery,

---

4. For *mingdan* 明旦, the next morning, Huang Min's version reads *mingtian* 明天, the next day.

let me feast my eyes on them." The lady took out all kinds of rare and wonderful jewelry from the box, and the old woman expressed her admiration again and again. When the praise was over, the lady calculated the value of the old woman's goods and gave her a suitable price. The old woman said happily, "Given your assessment, I have no regret about selling."[5] The lady also asked whether half of the money could be paid after her husband came back home. The old woman said, "We are neighbours, why should we be suspicious of one another?" The lady was pleased with the low price and was also pleased with being able to pay half of the money later, so she invited the old woman to stay to drink wine. The old woman was clever and quick-minded. Their only regret was not getting to know each other sooner.

The next day, the old woman brought food and drinks to visit her. They drank their fill and had a lot of fun. After that, the lady couldn't bear living without the old woman's company for a single day. The old woman also said, "My house is a mess. Your place is very quiet. Please allow me to bring my bedding to sleep here to be with you. I'd like to act as your chambermaid.[6] The lady said happily, "I simply did not dare to invite you out of the blue; I will tidy up my place and wait for you to come." That night, the old woman moved to the lady's place to sleep. Their two beds were facing each other, so close that even a light cough or a quiet voice could be heard and a slight movement could be felt between them. Her maid slept in another room. The old woman brought wine and food with her, and she did not miss a single night. They shared intimate information and talked about sex in a romantic atmosphere.

5. *Han* 憾, regret, in Huangmin's version reads *gan* 感, feeling, in Song Maocheng's version.

6. The phrase *yujin shi'er* 鬱金侍儿 means to act as a maid who serves wine and helps her mistress get ready for sex. *Yujin* is literally aromatic turmeric, but this herb is often associated with sex. For example, Wang Dang's 王谠 (active in eleventh century) *Tang yulin* 唐语林 (Anecdotes of the Tang), Appendix 3 reads, "Since Emperor Xuanzong [r. 846–859] ascended the throne, in the palace, whenever the emperor favored a woman [i.e. has sex with her], camphor and turmeric would be put on the floor first. Emperor Xuanzong banned both of them [later]." 宣宗即位,宮中每欲行幸,先以龍腦、鬱金藉地上並禁止. *Yujin* 鬱金 is also the name of a good wine. See Li Bai's （701–762）poem "Ke zhong xing" 客中行, which refers to "the delicious *yujin* wine of Lanling" 蘭陵美酒鬱金香.

The man from Xin'an asked the old woman several times when he could see the lady. The old woman always said, "Not yet! Not yet!" When autumn came, the man came to visit the old woman and said:

> When I was first discussing this with you under the willow tree, the branches and leaves had not yet turned yellow. Since we reached our agreement, it has become the time for branches and leaves to droop and darken, and the seeds are now ripe. Further down, the willow branches and leaves will be gradually stripped away, and snow will soon cover the branches!

The old woman said, "Tonight come into her house with me. You must be in high spirits. The success or failure depends on you today. Otherwise, this half a year is wasted. She then told him her plan.

The old woman usually went to the lady's house after dark every day. That night, she secretly entered the lady's home with the man from Xin'an. She hid him outside the bedroom door. The old woman and the lady had a drink in the room and talked very affectionately.[7] The laughter grew louder and louder.[8] The old woman urged the maid to drink wine. The maid could not handle her liquor, so she became drunk and went to another room to lie down. Just then a moth was buzzing on the beam, and when the lady looked up at it, the old woman then put out the lights with a fan, saying, "Oh my! The light went out! I'll go out myself to get a fire to light the lamp!" She seized the opportunity to take the man into the room. She then faked a laugh saying: "I forgot to bring a candle!" Meanwhile, she secretly placed the man in her bed, and put down the bed-curtain to cover him. When the old woman came back with the fire, the man had covered his head with quilts.

The old woman drank with the lady for a long time. Both were a little tipsy and had no reservations in speaking. They took off their clothes and went to bed. The old woman described the situation when she was newly married at a young age. She then asked, "did you have the same experience?" The lady laughed loudly without answering. The old woman teased her with obscene words. After a long time, knowing

---

7. *Liang sheng xiang qi* 兩聲相戚 is in Huangmin's version, "the two talked affectionately." Song Maocheng's version reads *yu sheng xiang qi* 雨聲相戚. I think it should be *liang sheng xiang qi*兩聲相戚.

8. It reads *xiao ju jia yin* 笑劇加殷 in Song Maocheng's version, while Huangmin's version reads *xiao jia yin* 笑加殷.

10. The Pearl Shirt

that the lady was already aroused, she then said, "I still have the most sensitive story. But only across the pillow can I tell you." So she led the man to the lady's bed. The lady thought it was the old woman; she lifted the quilt and caressed his body and said, "Your skin turned out to be so smooth!" The man did not answer, but just jumped on her. The lady was crazy with lust, so she just let the man have his way with her. Since then, the two have been more in love than a married couple.

Soon the beginning of the summer had passed, the man from Xin'an needed to go back home together with some business partners. He said to the lady in tears, "After parting, it will hurt so much to miss you. May I beg an item to remind me of being with you?" The lady opened a box and took out a shirt made of pearls. Holding the collar and sleeves, she put it on him and said, "The way back will be fiercely hot. This pearl shirt will make you feel very cool and refreshed. I wish it would be your underclothes, as if it were me, clinging to your skin." The man accepted it, jumping up in great joy. The treasure he gave her was worth about a thousand *taels* of silver. When they parted the next day, they agreed to run off together to another place next year.

The man from Xin'an considered this fortunate encounter very romantic. Whenever he looked at his pearl shirt on the way back, it made him cry. Even when it became too cold for him in late autumn, he still did not take it off.

The next year, he was held back by things. The year after that, he visited Yue again and took the pearl shirt with him. During the trip, he happened to stay with a Chu merchant at the same inn. The two got along very well, joking about each other's private affairs. The man from Xin'an revealed his affair with a lady from the Chu merchant's hometown.

It turns out that the Chu merchant's relatives on the mother's side had a history of conducting business in Yue. And the people whom the Chu merchant was doing business with were old friends of theirs, so he used his mother's maiden name on the business trips. The man from Xin'an of course had no way of knowing this. The Chu merchant was very shocked to hear what the man from Xin'an said. He pretended not to believe it and asked, "Is there any proof of your story?" The man from Xin'an took out the pearl shirt and said in tears, "This is what my lover gave to me as a gift. May I have the fortune of putting my letter into your return trip luggage?" The man from Chu got up to leave and said, "she is my cousin, I dare not make trouble." The man from Xin'an also regretted that he had let this story slip out. He put away the pearl shirt and apologized to the man from Chu.

When the man from Chu finished selling his goods, he returned home and said to his wife, "I just passed your parents' home; your mother was very ill and eager to see you. I have already hired a sedan chair and parked it in front of the gate. You should go quickly." He also handed her a letter saying, "this is about funeral issues. After you go to your parents' home, discuss it with your father. I have just returned, and I am unable to go with you immediately."

When the lady arrived at her mother's home, she saw that her mother did not look sick, so she was very surprised. Opening the letter, they found that it was a divorce document. The whole family wept sorrowfully. They were not sure of the cause, so the lady's father went to his son-in-law's house to inquire about the reason. The son-in-law said, "if she can return me the pearl shirt, I will then meet her again." The lady's father returned home telling her what his son-in-law had said. The lady was ashamed almost to death. Since the parents did not know the details of the matter, they could do nothing but try to comfort her.

After a year, a Presented Scholar[9] from Wuzhong[10] came to Yue to be an official. When he passed through Chu, he wanted to select a concubine [to marry], and a matchmaker introduced this lady to him. The Presented Scholar spent fifty *taels* of silver to marry her. The lady's family told her ex-husband about this. The ex-husband gathered sixteen boxes, large and small, from the lady's room. All the boxes were full of gold and silver, silk and jewelry. He sealed them and sent them to his ex-wife. Those who heard about this were all amazed.

A year later, the merchant from Chu traveled to Yue again, and he remarried there. When he was about to take his wife home, he settled the account with his host backer, but he thought the host backer was unreasonable; following the old man's momentum, he shoved him. The old man fell to the ground and suddenly died. The old man's two sons sued him. The county magistrate happened to be the Presented Scholar from Wuzhong.

Late at night, when the county magistrate was examining the pleadings under the light, the concubine waited on him and saw her ex-husband's name. She cried and said, "He is my uncle; now he is

---

9. *Jinshi* 進士, a Presented Scholar, refers to a successful candidate in the highest level of imperial examinations.

10. *Wuzhong* 吳中 refers to the area of Wu State during the Spring and Autumn period, most of modern Jiangsu and part of Anhui and Zhejiang provinces.

suffering from misfortune. I beg you to spare his live, for the sake of all my service to you." The county magistrate said, "This case is reaching its conclusion."

The lady knelt for a long time and vowed to die. The county magistrate said, "Get up, let me think it over."

The next day, when the county magistrate was going out, the lady cried again and said, "If things don't go smoothly, I won't meet you alive!"

The county magistrate convened the court to handle the case and said to the two sons of the deceased: "there is no sign of fatal injury on your father, so a post-mortem examination needs to be performed. I am going to other counties to meet with relevant officials. The body can be moved to the morgue; wait until I come back to discuss the autopsy with you."

The deceased's two sons' families had accumulated thousands of *taels* of silver. To expose their father's bones (through autopsy) would be considered a disgrace. Besides, their father had been over sixty years old. It would be difficult to verify the marks of falling and injury. To prosecute the man from Chu for his crimes, the father's body must definitely be damaged.

They kowtowed and said, "The cause of our father's death is very clear. There is no need to gouge out his muscles and bones." The county magistrate said, "If we can't see the scars, what can be used to convict the man from Chu? "The two sons of the deceased continued to plead as before. The county magistrate said, "I have a suggestion that is enough to eliminate your regrets. Would you like to consider it?"

Both sons pleaded for his suggestion. The county magistrate said: "Let the Chu merchant put on mourning apparel, and address your father as his own. He will be responsible for all the funeral expenses. And he must help bear the coffin, cry and stamp loudly beside it, just as you do, and follow behind the procession. Would that please your late father?"

The two sons of the deceased kowtowed and said, "Yes, sir!"

The county magistrate asked the Chu merchant about this idea, and he was very happy to be able to dispense with the death penalty. He also kowtowed and took the offer.

After the matter was settled, the county magistrate then called the man from Chu to meet his concubine. They embraced and the intensity of their crying was beyond the relationship between uncles and nieces. The county magistrate noticed something unusual and said, "You two are not uncle and niece. You should tell me the truth." The two replied the same, "We are ex-husband and ex-wife."

With tears streaming down his eyes, the county magistrate said to the man from Chu, "I can't bear to see your situation, you can take her home." The county magistrate took out and returned the sixteen boxes that the lady had brought with her and escorted them out of his county.

It is said that the man from Xin'an visited Yue. He ran into bandits and all his goods were looted. He was unable to repay his debt. Worry and anger worsened his sickness; he thus called his wife to come to his house in Yue. By the time the wife arrived, the man had already died. The second wife of the man from Chu was the former wife of the man from Xin'an.

The author (of this story) concluded, "If this all were the case, then the Way of Heaven is so close to us that there would be no perverse people in the world."[11]

---

11. The author's conclusion is ambiguous. It sounds superficially like prosaic moralizing about how Heaven punishes the wicked and rewards the good, but it can also be interpreted to mean that the love and passion of the characters in the story is perfectly natural, even though it flouts conventional morality.

NOTES AND READING GUIDE

By Jing Hu

I. Text, Author, and Sources

"Zhu Shan" 珠衫 (The Pearl Suit), attributed to Song Maocheng, is found in *juan* 2 of his *Jiuyue beiji* 九籥別集.

Song Maocheng, styled Youqing 幼清, nicknamed Zhiyuan 稚源, was a native of Huating 華亭 (present-day Songjiang County, Shanghai). His life spanned the late Ming Wanli 萬曆 reign (1573–1620). "Zhu Shan" was written in 1595 when he was twenty-seven years old. He was a great literatus and was also one of the four famous bibliophiles [12] in Shanghai during that period. The building that housed his book collection was called the *Jiuyue* Building 九籥樓, and his substantial collected works were called *Jiuyue ji*.[13] The collection was supplemented

---

12. Other three bibliophiles are Wang Qi 王圻, Shi Dajing 施大經 and Yu Ruji 俞汝楫.

13. For more on the textual history of this work, see Lynn A. Struve, "Song Maocheng's Matrixes of Mourning and Regret," *Nan Nü*, Vol. 15.1 (2013): 69–108: Song requested a preface (from Li Weizhen 李維楨) for a collection of his works, self-titled *Jiuyue ji*, circa 1612, and copies (probably printed) were certainly in circulation by 1619. But manuscript and printed copies that survived into the twentieth century bear indications that the collection was supplemented after Song's death, and that portions were published or republished in the early Qing. See the introduction by Wang Liqi 王利器 (especially page 1) to a modern, typeset, punctuated edition of an incomplete manuscript formerly in Wang's possession (but lost during the Cultural Revolution), *Jiuyueji* (Beijing: Zhongguo shehui kexue chubanshe, 1984); and Zhu Honglin 朱鴻林, "Ji Song Maocheng Jiuyue ji" 記宋懋澄《九籥集》, in Zhu Honglin, *Mingren zhuzuo yu shengping fawei* 明人著作與生平發微 (Guilin: Guangxi shifan daxue chubanshe, 2005), pp. 75–85. Zhu studied not only a 33-*juan* 卷 copy at the Naikaku bunko 內閣文庫, but also a 47-*juan* "Wanli" imprint of the Jiuyue ji in several parts (the original of which is held by the Shanghai cishu chubanshe tushuguan 上海辭書出版社圖書館), as well as an early-Qing imprint of a *bieji* 別集 part, in 4 *juan* (original held by the Zhongguo kexueyuan tushuguan 中國科學院圖書館 and the Nanjing tushuguan 南京圖書館). These 51 *juan* have been photo-reproduced together in both the *Xuxiu Siku quanshu* 續修四庫全書, Vols. 1373–74 (Shanghai: Shanghai guji chubanshe, 1995) and the *Siku jinhuishu congkan* 四庫禁燬書叢刊, Jibu 集部, Vol. 177 (Beijing: Beijing chubanshe, 1997).

after Song's death, and one particularly important edition was edited by the great scholar Wu Weiye 吳偉業 (1609–1672). This early Qing work is titled *Jiuyue bieji*. It has a total of 4 *juan* 卷. *Juan* 1 is a collection of *chidu* 尺牘 (correspondence) written by Song; the other 3 *juan* are collections of *bai* 稗 (tales), which collects forty-four classical language tales. Among those stories, the most well-known are "Zhu Shan" and "Fuqing nong zhuan" 負情儂傳.

The *Jiuyue ji* was not widely circulated during the Qing dynasty. In fact, it was banned at some points (for reasons I'll discuss below). In recent decades, scholars have become increasingly aware of Song's importance in the development of traditional Chinese tales.

"Zhu Shan" was later included in *juan* 16 of *Qingshi* 情史 (History of Love), under the title "Zhenzhu Shan" (The Pearl Shirt), by Feng Menglong 馮夢龍 (1574–1646) with some minor modification. Later, Feng Menglong expanded "Zhu Shan" and changed this classical language tale to a vernacular story, titled *Jiang Xingge chonghui zhenzhu shan* 蔣興哥重會珍珠衫 (The Pearl Shirt Reencountered).[14] It became the first story in Feng's collection of vernacular short stories, *Gujin xiaoshuo* 古今小說 (Stories Old and New), which is also named *Yushi mingyan* 喻世明言 (Illustrious Words to Instruct the World).

II. The Significance of the Tale

Song Maocheng and his works greatly influenced his contemporaries, such as Feng Menglong, and the creation of later vernacular novels. It provided important source materials for subsequent vernacular fiction and the theater. As I mentioned before, Song's "Zhu Shan" was the source text of "The Pearl Shirt Reencountered" by Feng. And another of Song's tales, "Fuqing nong zhuan" was also the original version of the famous story "Du Shiniang nuchen baibao xiang" 杜十娘怒沉百寶箱 (Du Shiniang Sinks Her Jewel Box in Anger) in *juan* 32 of *Jingshi tongyan* 警世通言 (Stories to Caution the World) by Feng Menglong. Those two pieces are considered the greatest works in Feng's vernacular story collections, and later became so famous that they were better known and more influential than their source texts.

---

14. "Jiang Xingge chonghui zhenzhu shan" (The Pearl Shirt Reencountered), Feng Menglong, ed., *Yushi mingyan* (Beijing: Renmin wenxue, 1958), pp. 1–39.

Song was influenced by the thoughts of iconoclastic thinkers in the mid-late Ming dynasty such as Li Zhi 李贄, who attacked asceticism and hypocrisy and believed that it is human nature to pursue material benefits and sensory enjoyment. As a result, many of Song's works subvert traditional ethics and feudal moral concepts, resulting in the *Jiuyue ji* being banned during part of the Qing dynasty.

For example, "Pearl Shirt" completely contradicted traditional feudal ethical and moral concepts regarding women and marriage such as the "Three Obedience and Four Virtues"[15] and "Following only one man until the end of one's days" (*Cong yi er zhong* 從一而終). The tale gives a sympathetic portrayal of an adulterous wife who had an affair with a man when her husband was away on a business trip. Although the husband divorced her after he found it out, he did not publicize her adultery. Instead of being harshly punished and looked down upon by society, the lady was remarried to an official—a man with a higher social status than her ex-husband. Ironically, this enables her later to save her husband in a court case. The official then generously allows them to be reunited, and even returns the sixteen boxes of belongings that the woman had brought with her into the marriage. This completely contradicted the Neo-Confucian philosophy that was orthodoxy in Song's era, one of whose sayings was, "Preserve Heaven's principles and destroy human desires" 存天理, 滅人欲.

The characters and plot of this story also contrast sharply with those in classical tales, which typically feature a foolishly sentimental girl and a man with a cold heart.[16] In Song's tale, on the contrary, both the men and the woman are passionate and loving people. Although the lady fails to show "feminine virtue" because she failed to "follow only one until the end of her days", she still loved her ex-husband and saved his life after he divorced her.

---

15. These are Confucian principles that govern the behavior of women. The "Three Obedience" are "before getting married, she obeys her father; after getting married, she obeys her husband; if her husband dies, she obeys her sons" 未嫁從父,既嫁從夫,夫死從子. The "Four Virtues" that a woman should have are feminine virtue 婦德, feminine speech 婦言, feminine appearance 婦容, feminine industriousness 婦功.

16. Many famous stories such as "Yingying Zhuan" 鶯鶯傳 in Tang tales, "Wangkui Zhuan" 王魁傳 in Song tales and Song Maocheng's other tale, "Fuqing nong zhuan," all feature this theme.

Similar to Song, Feng Menglong supported the legitimacy of "feelings" in his writings too. In the preface to his *Qingshi* 情史 (History of Love), he makes the following observations:

> It has been my ambition to compile a history of *qing* ever since I was a young man, I have been known to be "love obsessed"; Whenever I see a person rich in emotion, I always desire to prostrate myself before him. 情史, 余志也。余少負情癡; 見一有情人, 輒欲下拜。[17]

We can also see Buddhist influence in the karmic retribution found in the story. The man from Xin'an took advantage of the young lady's loneliness, so he was punished: he died and his belongings were stolen and his widow married the divorced merchant from Chu. Even though the merchant from Chu divorced his wife, he generously returned her dowry. The reward for his good deed was being saved by his ex-wife, reunited with her, and regaining the "lost" pearl shirt. The lady also received some retribution: although she was reunited with her first husband, she was demoted to the status of a concubine, rather than a primary wife.

However, the retribution theme is mixed with the discourse of "feelings" in the tale. So the "Way of Heaven," *Tian Dao* 天道, that Song Maocheng mentioned in the last paragraph of the tale is ambiguous. Is his point that people are rewarded or punished by the universe in accordance with the laws of karmic retribution, or is it that even adulterous love, if it is sincere, is perfectly in accord with Heaven?

The story also reflects the changing social context in the Ming dynasty, as the role of commerce became more and more important in society. It would have been more unusual in earlier literature for the primary characters to be businessmen and their wives. During this period, the Confucian value of fidelity to one's spouse was weakening among the citizens, and also there was an awakening of respect for ordinary human desires and feelings.

III. From "Zhu Shan" to "Zhen Zhu Shan" to "Jiang Xingge chonghui zhenzhu shan"

"Zhu Shan" is a classical language tale, and it tells the story in a purely objective way without adding any comment. The author's point of view

---

17. *Qingshi*, p. 1. Translation from Hua-yuan Li Mowry, *Chinese Love Stories* (Hamden, CT: Archon Books, 1983), p. 12, with minor changes.

can only be inferred from the characters' own words and deeds. The structure is close to that of a historical biography.

In "Zhen Zhu Shan" from *Qingshi*, Feng Menglong made some small changes to better develop the story. For example, at the beginning of the story, Feng added "the love between the couple—the merchant from Chu and his young wife—is deep and strong" 夫妻之愛甚篤. This makes the following plot twists—the merchant of Chu returning all her dowry, the wife saving his life later and reuniting with him in the end—sound more reasonable. Feng also added in the later part of the story that "the man from Chu had already remarried, so now that his ex-wife had returned, she was lowered to the status of a secondary wife" 楚人已續娶, 前婦歸, 反為側室. This makes clear that the lady was punished in accordance with her karma. Feng also changed the fate of the man from Xin'an. In Song's original version, he went to Yue on business and died there. In Feng's version, he went to Chu again out of longing for the lady and died in Chu. Feng's version shows the man's intense longing and love for the lady.

In the vernacular story "Jiang Xingge chonghui zhenzhu shan" (The Pearl Shirt Reencountered), Feng Menglong gave each character a name, and added descriptions of the characters' complicated feelings and emotional changes. The plot and scene description are more detailed, too. More importantly, Feng adopted the style of "narration interspersed with comments" and expressed his opinions and comments in the form of verse.[18] For example, at the beginning of the story there was a comment: "If I do not debauch the wives of other men, they will not debauch mine" 我不淫人婦, 人不淫我妻, [19] which seems to remind readers that this story is about retribution. This version of the story ends with a verse which reads:

A loving couple were joined for a lifetime.
But how shameful when the wife returns as a concubine.
Blessings and misfortunes all come as a result of one's karma, no lie.
Heaven above is the just official easiest to come by.

18. See Mei Chun, "Garlic and Vinegar: The Narrative Significance of Verse in 'The Pearl Shirt Reencountered,'" *Chinese Literature: Essays, Articles, Reviews* (CLEAR), Vol. 31 (December 2009): 23–43.
19. Translation by Jeanne Kelly in Y. W. Ma and Joseph S. M. Lau, eds., *Traditional Chinese Stories: Themes and Variations* (Boston: Cheng & Tsui, 1994), p. 264.

恩愛夫妻雖到頭，妻還作妾亦堪羞。
殃祥果報無虛謬，咫尺青天莫遠求。[20]

We see that, compared to Song Maocheng's source text, Feng Menglong's vernacular version has a heavily moralizing voice. It also adds more details in support of the theme of karmic retribution; for example, the magistrate who reunited the couple was rewarded with three sons in succession and a smooth career. The old woman who arranged the affair was beaten by the lady's ex-husband's family and had to move out of the town. However, Feng also vividly describes the true love between the couple and highlights the appreciation of "feelings" in touching details. For example, when the merchant of Chu found out about his wife's adultery, he blamed himself: "At the beginning our love as husband and wife had no limits, but because of my craving for every bit of profit, I abandoned her, making her like a young widow, and creating this ugly situation. My regret is boundless!" 當初夫妻何等恩愛，只為我貪著蠅頭微利，撇他少年守寡，弄出這場醜事來，如今悔之何及。

Professor Hsia Chih-tsing 夏志清 speaks particularly highly of this vernacular short story by Feng, arguing that "it is a human drama of almost complete moral and psychological coherence."[21] He thinks this is the greatest short story in the Ming collections, with an open-minded and tolerant understanding of morality. He particularly comments on San Qiao'er 三巧兒, the name given to the "young lady" in Song's original story, arguing that she is natural and conforms to human nature: "she is able to reconcile the claims of virtue and passion precisely because she strives to be neither inordinately virtuous nor inordinately passionate."[22]

---

20. Ibid., p. 292, with changes.
21. C. T. Hsia, *The Classic Chinese Novel: A Critical Introduction* (Hong Kong: The Chinese University of Hong Kong Press, 2016), p. 287.
22. Ibid., p. 290.

SELECT BIBLIOGRAPHY

Texts

An Pingqiu 安平秋, et al., eds. *Jiandeng xinhua* 剪燈新話. Shanghai: Shanghai guji chubanshe, 1990.

Deng Shaoji 鄧紹基, ed. *Ming Qing xiaoshuo jingpin, fu lidai wenyan xiaoshuo jingpin* 明清小說精品附歷代文言小說精品. Changchun: Shidai wenyi chubanshe, 2018.

Feng Menglong 馮夢龍, ed. "Jiang Xingge chonghui zhenzhu shan" 蔣興哥重會珍珠衫 (The Pearl Shirt Reencountered), In *Yushi mingyan* 喻世明言. Beijing: Renmin wenxue, 1958, pp. 1–39.

Feng Menglong 馮夢龍. *Qingshi* 情史, *Feng Menglong quanji* 馮夢龍全集, Vol. 7. Nanjing: Jiangsu guji, 1993.

Liu Shide 劉世德, Chen Qinghao 陳慶浩, and Shi Changyu 石昌渝, eds. *Guoben xiaoshuo congkan* 古本小說叢刊, fifth series, Vol. 1. Beijing: Zhonghua shuju, 1991.

National Chengchi University Classical Fiction Research Center, ed. *Jiandeng xinhua*. Taipei: Tianyi chubanshe, 1985.

Qiao Guanghui 喬光輝, ed. *Qu You quanji jiaozhu* 瞿佑全集校注. Vol. 2. Hangzhou: Zhejiang guji chubanshe, 2017.

Song Maocheng 宋懋澄 (1569–1620). *Jiuyue bie ji* 九籥別集, *juan* 2, photo-reproduced in the *Xuxiu Siku quanshu* 續修四庫全書, Vols. 1373–74. Shanghai: Shanghai guji chubanshe, 1995.

Wang Liqi 王利器, ed. *Jiuyuebie ji* 九籥集. Beijing: Zhongguoshehuikexuechubanshe, 1984.

Xu Chenbang 徐振, ed. *Gudai aiqing xiaoshuo xuan* 古代愛情小說選. Beijing: Dazong wenyi chubanshe, 1998.

Xue Hongji 薛洪勣, Li Weishi 李偉實, and Wang Cuigang 王粹剛, eds. *Ming Qing wenyan xiaoshuo xuan* 明清文言小說選. Changsha: Hunan renmin chubanshe, 1981.

Yan Qing 言青 and Jing Ping 京平, eds. *Qingai yinyuan* 情愛姻緣. Ji'nan: Qi Lu shushe, 2002.

Zhou Lengjia 周楞伽, ed. *Jiandeng Xinhua, waierzhong*. Shanghai: Shanghai guji chubanshe, 1981.

Zhou Yi 周夷, ed. *Jiandeng Xinhua wai erzhong* 剪燈新話外二種. Shanghai: Gudian wenxue chubanshe, 1957.

Translations

Huang Min 黃敏, ed. *Mingdai wenyan xiaoshuo xuanyi* 明代文言小説選譯. Nanjing: Fenghuang chunmei chuban jituan, 2011.

Iizuka Akira 飯塚朗, trans. *Sentou shinwa* 剪燈新話. Tokyo 東京: Heibonsha 平凡社, 1965.

Jiang Ling 姜凌, ed. *Baihua lidai biji xiaoshuo daguan* 白話歷代筆記小說大觀. Beijing: Wenhua yishu chubanshe, 1995.

Ma, Y. W. and Joseph S. M. Lau, eds., *Traditional Chinese Stories: Themes and Variations*. Boston: Cheng & Tsui, 1994.

Zeitlin, Judith, trans. "The Regulator of the Ultimate Void by Qu You." *Renditions: A Chinese-English Translation Magazine*, No. 69 (2008): 35–40.

Studies

Brokaw, Cynthia and Kai-wing Chow. *Printing and Book Culture in Late Imperial China*. Berkeley: University of California Press, 2005.

Campany, Robert. "Ghosts Matter: The Culture of Ghosts in Six Dynasties Zhiguai." *Chinese Literature: Essays, Articles, Reviews (CLEAR)*, Vol. 13 (1991): 15–34.

Campany, Robert. *Signs from the Unseen Realm: Buddhist Miracle Tales from Early Medieval China*. Honolulu: University of Hawaii Press, 2012.

Chen Baowen 陳葆文. *Gudian xiaoshuo gushi leixing xuanxi* 古典小説故事類型選析. Taibei: Wunan tushu, 2019.

Chen Caixun 陳才訓. "Lun Li Changqi de Shujishi jiaoyu jiqi xiaoshuo Chuangzuo de xuancai yishi" 論李昌祺的庶吉士教育及其小說創作的炫才意識. *Zhongguo wenyan xiaoshuo yanjiu*, Vol. 4 (2009): 152–9.

Chen Caixun 陳才訓 and Shi Shiping 時世平. "Jiandeng yuhua: 'Weihuan gaoyi,' Lun Li Changqi de Shujishi jiaoyu jiqi xiaoshuo Chuangzuo de fengjiao yishi" 《剪燈余話》: 薇垣高議—論李昌祺的庶吉士教育及其小說創作的風教意識. *Zhongguo wenyan xiaoshuo yanjiu* 中國文言小說研究, Vol. 1 (2012): 150–60.

Chen Chao 陳超 and Wang Qiancheng 王前程. "'Hongmei ji' zhi gushi yuanliu jiqi yishu chaoyue" 《紅梅記》之故事源流及其藝術超越. *Beijing huagong daxue xuebao* 北京化工大學學報, Vol. 1 (2015): 63–6, 86.

Chiang, Sing-chen Lydia. *Collecting the Self: Body and Identity in Strange Tale Collections of Late Imperial China*. Leiden: Brill, 2005.

Chun, Mei. "Garlic and Vinegar: The Narrative Significance of Verse in 'The Pearl Shirt Reencountered.'" *Chinese Literature: Essays, Articles, Reviews (CLEAR)*, Vol. 31, No. 12 (2009): 23–43.

DeWoskin, Kenneth J. and J. I. Crump, Jr. trans. *In Search of the Supernatural: The Written Record*. Stanford: Stanford University Press, 1996.

Geng Xiangwei 耿祥偉. "Jiang Ji 'Furong ji' gaibian kaolun" 江楫芙蓉記改編考論. *Yuxi shifan xueyuan xuebao* 玉溪師範學院學報, Vol. 1 (2010): 61–4.

Guo Yingde 郭英德. *Ming Qing chuanqi shi* 明清傳奇史. Beijing: Renmin wenxue chubanshe, 2012.

Hanan, Patrick. *The Chinese Vernacular Story*. Cambridge: Harvard University Press, 1981.

He Mingxin 何明新. "'Jiaohong ji' he 'Lüyiren zhuan' de fan fengjian qingxiang" 《嬌紅記》和《綠衣人傳》的反封建傾向. *Chongqing shiyuan xuebao* 重慶師院學報, Vol. 4 (1986): 77–80.

Hsia, C. T. *The Classic Chinese Novel: A Critical Introduction*. Hong Kong: The Chinese University of Hong Kong Press, 2016.

Hu Shiying胡士瑩. *Huaben xiaoshuo gailun*話本小說概論. Beijing: Zhonghuashuju, 1980.

Huang Yonglin. *Narrative of Chinese and Western Popular Fiction: Comparison and Interpretation*. New York: Springer, 2018.

Hucker, Charles O. *A Dictionary of Official Titles in Imperial China*. Stanford: Stanford University Press, 1985.

Iizuka Akira 飯塚朗, trans. "Tengoku no saibankan ni natta otoko no hanashi" 天国の裁判官に なった男の話 (太虛司法傳) [The Story of the Man who Became a Heavenly Judge]. In *Sentou shinwa* 剪燈新話 [New Stories Told While Trimming the Wick]. Tokyo: Heibonsha 平凡社, 1965, pp. 206–14.

Liao Ying 廖穎 and Hu Yue 胡玥. "Qianxi 'Hongmei ji' he 'Lüyiren zhuan' de chayi" 淺析《紅梅記》和《綠衣人傳》的差異, *Mudan* 牡丹, Vol. 32 (2018): 62–4.

Lin Yiqing林宜清. "'Du Shiniang nuchen baibaoxiang' yu 'Fuqingnong zhuan' zhi bijiao yanjiu" 杜十娘怒沉百寶箱與負情儂傳之比較研究. *Mingdao tongshi luncong*明道通識論叢, Vol. 4 (2008): 23–42.

Liu Yongqiang 劉勇強. "Lishi yu wenben de gongsheng hudong: yi shuizei zhan qi (nü) xing he wanli xunqin xing wei zhongxin" 歷史與文本的共生互動:以水賊占妻（女）型和萬里尋親型為中心. *Wenxue yichan* 文學遺產, Vol. 3 (2000).: 85–99.

Louie, Kam and Louise Edwards, et al., eds. *Censored by Confucius: Ghost Stories by Yuan Mei*. Armonk, NY: M. E. Sharpe, 1996.

Lowry, Kathryn A. *The Tapestry of Popular Songs in 16th- and 17th-century China: Reading, Imitation, and Desire*. Brill Academic Pub, 2005.

Lü Xiang呂翔. "Song Maocheng xiaoshuo yanjiu" 宋懋澂小說研究, MA thesis, Shandong Normal University 山東師範大學, 2012.

Lu Xun 魯迅 (1881–1936). *Zhongguo xiaoshuo shilue* 中國小說史略. Beijing: Renmin wenxue chubanshe, 1973.

Luo Jintang羅錦堂. *Yuan zaju benshi kao* 元杂剧本事考. Xi'an: Shanxi shifan daxue chubanshe, 2017.

Luo Zongqiang羅宗強. *Mingdai wenxue sixiang shi* 明代文學思想史. Beijing: Zhonghua shuju, 2013.

Mair, Victor H. and Zhenjun Zhang, eds. *Anthology of Tang and Song Tales: The Tang Song chuanqi ji of Lu Xun*. Singapore: World Scientific, 2020.

Mowry, Hua-yuan Li. *Chinese Love Stories from the "Ch'ing-shih"*. Hamden, CT: Archon Books, 1983.

Nam, Nguyen. "Writing as Response and as Translation: *Jiandeng xinhua* and the Evolution of the Chuanqi Genre in East Asia, Particularly in Vietnam." Ph.D. dissertation, Harvard University, 2005.

Nienhauser, William H., Jr. *The Indiana Companion to Traditional Chinese Literature*. Vol. 1. Bloomington and Indianapolis: Indiana University Press, 1986.

Poo Mu-chou. "Ghost Literature: Exorcistic Ritual Texts or Daily Entertainment?" *Asia Major*, Third Series, Vol. 13, No. 1 (2000): 43–64.

Qi Yukun 齊裕焜. *Zhongguo gudai xiaoshuo yanbian shi* 中國古代小說演變史. Beijing: Renmin wenxue chubanshe, 2015.

Qiao Guanghui 喬光輝. "Li Changqi nianpu" 李昌祺年譜. *Dongnan daxue xuebao* 東南大學學報 (zhexue shehui kexue ban 哲學社會科學版), Vol. 4, No. 6 (2002): 103–111.

Qiao Guanghui 喬光輝. *Mingdai Jiandeng xilie xiaoshuo yanjiu* 明代剪灯系列小说研究. Beijing: Zhongguo shehui kexue chubanshe, 2006.

Shang Biwu. *Unnatural Narrative across Borders: Transnational and Comparative Perspectives*. Oxford: Routledge, 2019.

Shuhui Yang and Yunqin Yang, trans. *Stories to Caution the World*. Seattle: University of Washington Press, 2005.

Struve, Lynn A. "Song Maocheng's Matrixes of Mourning and Regret." *Nan Nü*, Vol. 15. 1 (2013): 69–108.

Sun Chang, Kang-I and Stephen Owen, eds. *The Cambridge History of Chinese Literature, Vol. II: From 1375*. Cambridge: Cambridge University Press, 2010.

Sun Kaidi 孙楷第. *Riben Dongjing suojian xiaoshuo shumu* 日本東京所見小說書目. Beijing: Renmin wenxue chuban she, 1981.

Tang Zhengang 趙振綱. "Hsia Chih-tsing zhongguo gudian xiaoshuo yanjiu zhong de daode pinping 夏志清中國古典小說中的道德批評." *Journal of School of Chinese Language and Culture at Nanjing Normal University* 南京師範大學文學院學報, Vol. 12, No. 4 (2010): 129–35.

Wang Qiancheng 王前程. "'Hongmei ji' yu *Qiantang yishi*— 'Hongmei ji' Zhong Jia Sidao shaqie deng gushi yuanliu kaoshu" 《紅梅記》與《錢塘遺事》—《紅梅記》中賈似道殺妾等故事源流考述, *Huazhong xueshu* 華中學術, Vol. 2 (2015): 115–26.

Wang Ruilai 王瑞來. "Jinggu shufei yinjiancheng – 'Qiantang yishi' kaoshu" 鏡古孰非殷監呈–《錢塘遺事》考述. *Sichuan shifan daxue xuebao* 四川師範大學學報, Vol. 4 (2013): 139–40.

Wu Zhida's 吳志達. *Zhongguo wenyan xiaoshuo shi* 中國文言小說史. Ji'nan: Qi Lu shushe, 1994.

Xiao Dan 蕭丹. "Bian Sangang 'Furong ping ji' yanjiu" 邊三崗芙蓉屏記研究. Master's thesis, Huaibei shifan daxue 淮北師範大學, 2014.

Xu Shuofang 徐朔方 and Sun Qiuke 孙秋克. *Mingdai wenxueshi* 明代文學史. Hangzhou: Zhejiang daxue chuban she, 2006.

Yu Yingshi. "The Radicalization of China in the Twentieth Century." *Daedalus, Journal of the American Academy of Arts and Sciences*, Vol. 122, No. 2 (Spring 1993): 126.

Zhang Peiheng 章培恆 and Luo Yuming 駱玉明. *Zhongguo wenxueshi* 中國文學史. Rpt. Shanghai: Fudan daxue chubanshe, 1999.

Zhang Yuling張玉玲. "Dui chanting lunli daode guannian de chedi dianfu – Song Maochen <Zhu Shan> jiedu 对传统伦理道德观念的彻底颠覆 - 宋懋澄《珠衫》解读. *Journal of Shandong University of Technology (Social Sciences)* 山東理工大學學報 (社會科學版), Vol. 22, Nos. 2, 3 (2006): 273–6.

Zhao Xiaohuan. *Classical Chinese Supernatural Fiction: A Morphological History*. Lewiston: E. Mellen Press, 2005.

Zhenjun Zhang 張振軍. *Chuantong xiaoshuo yu Zhongguo wenhua* 傳統小説與中國文化. Nanning: Guangxi daxue chubanshe, 1996.

Zhenjun Zhang. "On the Origins of Detached Soul Motif in Chinese Literature." *Sungkyun Journal of East Asian Studies*, Vol. 9, No. 2 (2009): 166–84.

Zhenjun Zhang. *Buddhism and Tales of the Supernatural in Early Medieval China: A Study of Liu Yiqing's* Youming lu. Leiden: Brill, 2014.

Zhenjun Zhang and Jing Wang, eds. *Song Dynasty Tales: A Guided Reader*. Singapore: World Scientific, 2017.

Zhenjun Zhang. *Hidden and Visible Realms: Early Medieval Chinese Tales of the Supernatural and the Fantastic*. New York: Columbia University Press, 2018.

Zhu Yangdong 朱仰東. "Li Zhen *Qiuqian huiji*: yi xiaoshuo xingshi zaixian yuandai mingzu ronghe jingxiang de dianfan"李禎《鞦韆會記》：以小說形式再現元代民族融合鏡像的典範. *Zhongguo gudai xiaoshuo xiju yanjiu* 中國古代小說戲劇研究, Vol. 16, (2018): 64.

Zhu Yangdong. "Li Zhen 'Qiuqian hui ji' Baizhu benshi bianyi" 李禎《鞦韆會記》拜住本事辨疑 In *Neijiang shifan xueyuan xuebao* 內江師範學院學報, Vol. 34, No. 4 (2019): 9–12.

INDEX

The following list includes only important names of figures (historical or fictional) and places, selected terms, and most relevant book titles, which appear in the footnotes. Personal names with little information, frequently mentioned place names, and general official titles are excluded.

"Ai fengwei ge" 哀鳳尾歌, 73
"Aiqing zhuan" 愛卿傳 (The Tale of Aiqing), 58
An Pingqiu 安平秋, 51

Bai Pu 白樸 (1226–ca.1295), 126
Bai Shouyi 白壽彞, 117n8
Baijia cuibian 稗家粹編, 76
Baizhu 拜住, 115, 117, 120–2, 124
Banxian tang 半閒堂 (Half Leisure Hall), 54
Bao yue 寶月, 98n40
Baopuzi 抱朴子, 51n4
Beiyong 北雍, 143n3
Benshi shi 本事詩, 125
Bian Sangang, 109
bianfeng 變風, 149n13
Bianjing 汴京, 76
biji 筆記, 62
bingdilian 並蒂蓮, 102
Biyu 碧玉, 26n22
Brokaw, Cynthia, 49n14
"Bu Qi zhuan" 卜起傳, 104

caizi jiaren xiaoshuo 才子佳人小說, 108
Campany, Robert Ford, 1n1
Cao Weiguo, 87, 99
Cao Zhi 曹植 (子建, 192–232), 25, 25n21
"Chang'an yexing lu" 長安夜行錄, 79
"Changgan xing" 長干行, 69n15
Chen Baowen 陳葆文, 16n11
Chen Caixun 陳才訓, 76n37, 79n44
Chen Guojun 陳國軍, 76n35
Chen Ping 陳平 (d. 178), 103
Chen Qiyou 陳奇猷, 73n30
Chen Xuanyou 陳玄祐 (fl. 780), 16, 70n23

Chen Xun's 陳循 (1385–1464), 78n40
"Chen Yilang" 陳義郎, 104
Chen Zilong 陳子龍 (1608–1647), 153
Cheng Junying 程俊英, 118n13
Cheng Minzheng 程敏政 (1445–1499), 77n39, 78n41, 79n43
Chizao Tang 摘藻堂, 77n39
Chong yuan 重圓, 98n40
Chow Kai-wing, 49n14
Chuanqi 傳奇 (transmission of marvels), 1, 1n3, 62
Chuguo xianxian zhuan 楚國先賢傳, 118n12
Chuke pai'an jingqi 初刻拍案驚奇, 113, 124n25
Chunqiu 春秋 (Spring and Autumn Annals), 49n14
Cipin 詞品, 70n21
Cong yi er zhong 從一而終, 169
Crump, J. I. Jr., 125n26
"Cui wei zi" 崔尉子, 104
Cui Yi 崔義, 109
Cui Ying 崔英, 87, 99, 106, 108, 110–11
"Cuicuizhuan" 翠翠傳 (The Tale of Cuicui), 3, 5, 19–32, 35, 58

da tuanyuan 大團圓, 110
Dadu 大都, 122n20
Danshan 丹山, 73n30
Danyang 丹陽, 10
Daozang 道藏, 84
Daozang jing 道藏经, 21n6
DeWoskin, Kenneth J., 1n1, 125n26
[*Hu*] *die fen* [蝴]蝶粉, 21n6, 67n9
Ding Daquan 丁大全, 61
Ditter, Alexei Kamran, 2n4
Donghuang 東皇, 66n7
Dongjun 東君 (god of spring), 20, 66

Index

Dongping 東平, 114
Du Fu 杜甫 (712–770), 118n12
Du Shiniang 杜十娘, 143, 153, 156–7
"Du Shiniang nuchen baibaoxiang" 杜十娘怒沉百寶箱, 156, 168
Du You 杜佑 (735–812), 102
Duke Jing 景 of Jin 晉 (599–581BCE), 42n6
Duke Mu of Qin 秦穆公 (r. 659 BCE–621 BCE), 74n34
Dushikou 獨石口, 121n19

Emperor Cheng 成 of Han (r. 32 BC–7 BC), 148n12
Emperor Chengzong 成宗 (r. 1294–1307) of Yuan, 7, 120n18
Emperor Lizong 理宗 of Song (r.1224–1264), 52n5
Emperor Qianlong 乾隆 (r. 1736–1795) of the Qing, 153
Emperor Renzong of Yuan (Ayurbarwada 愛育黎拔力八達; r.1311–1320), 51n2
Emperor Shenzong 神宗 of the Ming (Zhu Yijun 朱翊鈞 [r. 1573–1620]), 143n1
Emperor Shizu of Yuan 元世祖, *see* Kublai Khan
Emperor Shun 順 (惠宗; r. 1333–1370) of Yuan, 87n1, 123
Emperor Wen of Wei 魏 (Cao Pi 曹丕; r. 220–226), 25n21
Emperor Wu 武 (r. 141–87 BCE) of Han, 119n16
Emperor Wuzong's 武宗 (r. 1307–1311), 117n11
Emperor Yingzong 英宗 (r. 1320–1323), 115n6
Emperor Zhezong 哲宗 (Zhao Xu 趙煦; r. 1085–1100) of Song, 63n2
Empress Zhao 趙 (Feiyan 飛燕), 148
Erke pai'an jingqi 二刻拍案驚奇, 36, 139

Fan Shu 范攄, 125
Fannie 藩臬, 143n2
Fangxin 芳心, 67n10
Fei Qiong 飛瓊, 74n32
Feng Dayi 馮大異, 39–44, 45

Feng Menglong 馮夢龍 (1574–1646), 153–4, 156–8, 168, 170
fenghua 風化, 79
fenghuang 蜂黃, 21n26
"Fengweicai ji" 鳳尾草記 (The Record of a Phoenix-Tail Fern), 3, 63–75, 76, 82
Fu Fei 宓妃, 70n20
fude 婦德, 169n15
fumu guan 父母官, 100
"Fuqingnong zhuan" 負情儂傳 (The Faithless Lover), 5, 143–52, 153, 156, 168
"Furong ji" 芙蓉記, 109
"Furong ping ji" 芙蓉屏記 (The Record of the Lotus Screen), 3, 5, 87–98, 109

Gan Bao's 干寶 (fl. early 4th century), 124
Gao Nalin 高納麟 (1281–1359), 91, 100–10
Gao Yuhou 皋于厚, 79n45
Gao Yunwen, 51, 58
ganbang 桿棒, 58n21
"Gaotang fu" 高唐賦, 71n25
Ge Hill 葛嶺, 52n5, 54n9, 55n12
Ge Hong 葛洪 (283–343), 51n4
"ghost" (*gui* 鬼), 4, 4n5, 41
Glahn, Richard von, 55n11
gong'an 公案, 58n21, 100, 108
Gongsun Duan 公孫段, 42n7
Gongtian fa 公田法, 55n11
Gu Axiu 顧阿秀, 90
Guanyin 觀音, 90n11
Guazhou 瓜州, 10
Guben xiaoshuo congkan 古本小說叢刊, 63
Guhang zaji 古杭雜記, 61
Guixin zashi 癸辛雜識, 61
Gujin xiaoshuo 古今小說 (喻世明言), 168
Guo Qingchun 郭慶春, 91
Guo Tingbi 郭廷弼, 153
Guo Yingde 郭英德, 62n29
Guo Yanshen 郭彥深, 158
"Gushi shijiu shou" 古詩十九首, 68n13
Guxiaoshuo gouchen 古小說鉤沉, 15n9
Guyinxuebi 骨殷血碧, 150n14

Han Hong 韓翃, 97
Han Shou 韓壽 (d. 300), 74n33
Han Tuozhou 韓侂冑, 61
Han Yi 韓翊, 29n39
Hanwudi neizhuan 漢武帝內傳, 74n32
Hawkes, David, 70n20
He Mingxin 何明新, 58n19
Heisi 黑廝, 122
"Hejian jun nannü" 河間郡男女, 4, 125
Helin xiansheng 鶴林先生, 85n52
Helin yulu 鶴林玉露, 21n6
Hepu 合浦, 29n41
Hong Mai 洪邁 (1123–1202), 104
Hongfu 紅拂 (Lady of the Red Whisks), 30n43
"Hongmei ji" 紅梅記 (The Tale of Red Plum), 62
Hou Han shu 後漢書, 29n41
Hsia C. T. 夏志清, 126n29, 172
Hu Jing, 159, 167
"Hu Meiniang zhuan" 胡媚娘傳, 85
Hu Shi 胡適 (1891–1962), 115n6
Hu Shiying 胡士瑩, 153
huaben 話本, 2
Huaben xiaoshuo gailun 話本小說概論, 153
Huaisu 懷素 (737–99), 91
Huan Yan 桓焉, 118n12
Huang Min 黃敏, 49n15, 143
Huangchi nongbing 潢池弄兵, 28n31
huangquan 黃泉, 91n14
Huiyuan 慧圓, 89
"Huo Xiaoyu zhuan" 霍小玉傳, 156

Iizuka Akira 飯塚朗, 45n11
Inglis, Alister, 2

Jia Chong 賈充 (217–82), 74n33
Jia Qiuhe 賈秋壑 (似道; 1213–1275), 52–5, 59–62
Jia Wu 賈午 (260–300), 74n33
"Jia Yunhua huanhun ji" 賈雲華還魂記, 17
Ji'an 吉安, 76n36
jianchen 姦臣 (treacherous officials), 61
Jiandeng xinhua 剪燈新話, 2, 5–6, 6n8, 14, 45, 63, 138
Jiandeng yuhua 剪燈餘話, 3, 6n8, 17, 63
Jiang Ji 江楫 (fl. 1573), 109

Jiang Xingge chonghui zhenzhu shan 蔣興哥重會珍珠衫, 168, 170–1
jianghu 江湖, 90n12
Jiangyou 江右, 63n3
Jiankang 建康, 63, 76
Jiaofang 教坊, 143n4
Jiaohua 教化, 122
jiefu 節婦, 79
jieyi 結義, 128
Jin Cui hanyi ji 金翠寒衣記, 36
jinbuhuan 金不換, 139
"Jinfeng chai ji" 金鳳釵記 (The Golden Phoenix Hairpin), 4, 5, 7, 16
jingcheng 精誠, 125
Jingshi tongyan 警世通言, 111, 156
Jinling 金鈴, 66n6
Jinling 金陵, 76
Jinshi 進士, 164n9
Jishuitan 積水潭, 114n4
Jiuyue bieji 九籥別集, 159, 167–8
Jiuyueji 九籥集, 3, 143, 153–4, 167
Julu 巨鹿, 14

Kaiping 開平, 121
Kaiyun Tianbao yishi 開元天寶遺事, 66n6
Kao, George, 126n29
Kroll, Paul W., 7
Kublai Khan (r. 1260–1294), 117n8, 120n18, 122n21, 123n24
Kuokuochu 闊闊出, 120

Lady Houtu 后土, 12
Lady Zhuo 卓 (Wenjun 文君), 10
Lau, D. C. 劉殿爵, 129n35
Lau, S. M. 劉紹銘, 171n19
Lechang 樂昌, 25n20
Legge, James, 53n6, 81n46, 82n47, 118n13, 151n19
Lei shuo 類說, 102
Li Bai 李白 (701–62), 69n15, 161n6
Li Changqi 李昌祺 (1376–1452), 2, 6, 6n8, 17, 63, 76, 87, 99, 107–10, 113
"Li Changqi nianpu" 李昌祺年譜, 76n37, 78n40
Li Chaowei's 李朝威 (ca. 766–ca. 820), 69n18
Li Fang 李昉 (925–96), 15
Li Gongzuo 李公佐 (fl. 813), 104

Index

Li Hua 李華, 69n14
Li Huiniang 李慧娘, 62
"Li hun ji" 離魂記, 70n23
Li Jing 李靖, 30n43
Li Kui 李揆, 77
Li Mowry, 170n17
Li Wai-yee, 126n29
Li Weizhen 李維楨, 167n13
"Li Zhangwu zhuan" 李章武傳, 4
Li Zhi 李贄, 169
Liang Shanbo 梁山伯, 19n3
"Lianli shu ji" 連理樹記 (A Tree of Intertwining Limbs), 79
Liaozhai zhiyi 聊齋志異, 1, 62
"Lihun ji" 離魂記, 16
"Lisao" 離騷, 70n20
Lie xian zhuan 列仙傳, 118n12
Lienüzhuan 列女傳, 152n21
Liexian zhuan 列仙傳, 74n34
Liexian zhuan jiaojian 列仙傳校箋, 118n12
Liexian zhuan shiyi 列仙傳拾遺, 118n12
Lin Pu's 林逋 (ca. 967–1208), 70n21
Lin Xiangru 藺相如, 29n41
Ling Mengchu 凌濛初 (1580–1644), 17, 87n4, 107–8, 113, 139
"Lingbao liandu pushuo" 靈寶煉度普說, 84n50
lingguai 靈怪, 58n20
"Lingtou shu" 領頭書, 37
Lingyin Temple 靈隱寺, 57
Liu Bang 劉邦, 103
Liu Fu 劉斧, 60, 104
Liu Qian, 63, 76
Liu shizhuan" 柳氏傳, 29n39
Liu Xiang 劉向 (77 B.C.E.–6 B.C.E.), 74n34, 118n12, 152n21
"Liu Yi zhuan" 柳毅傳, 69n18
Liu Yiqing 劉義慶 (403–44), 14, 68n12
Liu Yuxi 劉禹錫 (772–842), 29n40
Longhu shan 龍虎山, 72n28
Lü Buwei 呂不韋 (d. 235 B.C.E.), 73n30
Lu, Tina, 139
Lu Xun 魯迅 (1881–1936), 1n2, 2n4, 5–6, 15n9
Lu Zhaolin 盧照鄰 (ca. 634–ca. 684), 98n40
Lu Zhaorong 盧昭容, 62
"Luanluan zhuan" 鸞鸞傳, 79

Luling 盧陵, 76
Lunyu yizhu 論語譯注, 129n35
Luo Dajing 羅大經 (1196–1252?), 21n6
Luo Zongqiang 羅宗強, 117n9
Luo Jintang 羅錦堂, 115n6, 125
Luo Ye's 羅曄, 2, 58
Luodai tongxin 羅帶同心, 70n21
"Luoshen fu" 洛神賦, 25n21
Lüshi chunqiu 呂氏春秋, 73n30
"Lüyiren zhuan" 綠衣人傳 (The Tale of the Lady in Green), 3–4, 33, 51–7, 58, 60, 62
Lüzhu 綠珠 (Green Pearl), 26n22
Lynn, Richard, 29n39

Ma Y. W., 171n19
Mair, Victor, 2n4, 29n39, 149n13
Mei Chun, 171n18
Meichuang zhuren 梅窗主人, 158
Meng Qi 孟棨, 125
Meulenbeld, Mark, 84n51, 86n53
Mideng yinhua 覓燈因話, 2, 138
Ming shi 明史, 100
Ming wen heng 明文衡, 77n39
Mingdai zhiguai chuanqi xiaoshuo xulu 明代志怪傳奇小說敘錄, 76n35
Moqi Xie 万俟卨, 61
Monggudai 忙古歹, 122
Mote, Frederick W., 122n21

Nam, Nguyen, 62n28
Nienhauser, William H. Jr., 1n1, 2n4, 62n28, 70n18
Ningbo fu 寧波府, 131n1
Nong Yü 弄玉, 74n34

Ouyang Xun 歐陽詢 (557–641), 70n22
Owen, Stephen, 49n13, 49n15

Pai'an jingqi 拍案驚奇, 17
Pang E 龐阿, 14
Pei Yu 裴禹, 62
Penglai 蓬萊, 80
pinghua 平話, 2
Pingkang 平康, 143n5
podao 朴刀, 58n21
Pu Songling 蒲松齡 (1640–1715), 1, 62
puliuzhizhi 蒲柳之質, 68n12
pushuo 普說, 84

Index

Qi Yukun 齊裕焜, 127n32
Qian Xili's 錢習禮 (1373–1461), 77
Qian Zhizhi 喬知之, 26n22
Qianniang 倩娘, 16
"Qiannü lihun" 倩女離魂, 16
Qiantang 錢塘, 51, 147
Qiantang yishi 錢塘遺事, 61
"Qiangtou mashang" 墻頭馬上, 126
Qiao Guanghui 喬光輝, 45n11, 51, 52n5, 76n37
qiaoyan ruhuang 巧言如簧, 151n18
Qidong yeyu 齊東野語, 61, 104
Qin'e 秦娥, 74n34
qing han 情憾, 76
Qingdi 青帝, 66n7
Qingluan 青鸞, 28n34
Qingming Festival, 8
Qingniang 慶娘, 9, 12–13
Qingshi 情史, 76
Qingshi leilue 情史類略, 153–4, 170
Qingsuo gaoyi 青瑣高議, 60, 104
Qinnü 秦女, 74n34
"Qiongnu zhuan" 瓊奴傳, 79
Qiu Jun 丘濬, 129
Qiu Zhao'ao 仇兆鰲, 118n12
"Qiuqianhui ji" 鞦韆會記 (The Tale of the Swing-play Gathering), 3, 113–23, 124, 126
"Qiuxi fang Pipating ji" 秋夕訪琵琶亭記, 84
"Qiuxiangting ji" 秋香亭記 (Autumn Fragrance Pavilion), 3, 33, 58
Qixia wuyi 七俠五義, 111
Qu You's 瞿佑 (1347–1433), 2, 6–7, 14, 17, 19, 39, 45, 49–50, 52, 58, 62, 113, 138
Qu You quanji jiaozhu 瞿佑全集校註, 45n11, 51, 52n5
Quhai zongmu tiyao 曲海總目提要, 37n52
Queen Mother of the West, 74n32

Red Turban Rebellion, 33
Riben Dongjing suojian xiaoshuo shumu 日本東京所見小說書目, 6n8, 153
Rongfu 榮甫, 114
Ruan Yuan 阮元 (1764–1849), 4n5
Ruan Zhan 阮瞻, 45n12
ruhua 入話, 156

san hun 三魂, 28n33
"Sanyuan chuandu pushu" 三元傳度普說, 84n50
Semu 色目, 122, 127
Sengjianu 僧家奴, 120
Seymour, Kelsey, 39, 45
Shanfang suibi 山房隨筆, 61
Shangdu 上都, 121n19
Shanglin 上林, 119n16
Shanglin Park 上林賦, 119n16
Shanhai jing 山海經 (Classic of Mountains and Seas), 28n38
Shanxi 剡溪, 117n10
Shao Jingzhan 邵景詹 (fl.1560), 2, 131, 139, 141
Shaoxi 苕溪, 27
Shazhali 沙吒利, 29n39
Shen Shao 沈韶, 84
Shenghuang 笙簧, 151n18
shenxian 神仙, 58n21
Shexiang chen 麝香塵, 21n7
Shi Chong 石崇 (249–300), 26n22, 31n48
Shi daxu 詩大序, 149n13
Shi Shiping 時世平, 76n37
Shi Songzhi 史嵩之 (1189–1257), 55n12
Shiji 史記, 128
Shijing 詩經 (Classic of Odes), 24n18, 42, 49n14, 53n6, 81, 118n13, 119n14, 149n13, 151n15, 151n17–19
Shijing yizhu 詩經譯釋, 118n13
Shiliemen 失列門, 123
Shisanjing zhushu 十三經註疏, 4n5
Shishu 詩書, 19
Shishuo xinyu 世說新語, 68n12
"Shoufa pushuo" 受法普說, 84n50
shuangling 爽靈, 28n33
Shuihu zhuan 水滸傳, 111
Si Dai 駟帶, 42n7
sifangwei 伺房帷, 67n8
Siku jinhui congkan 四庫禁毀叢刊, 153
Siku quanshu huiyao 四庫全書薈要, 77n39
siluo 絲蘿, 68n13
Sima Qian's 司馬遷 (ca. 145–90 B.C.E.), 128
Sima Xiangru 司馬相如 (178–117 B.C.E.), 10n6, 119n16

Index

Sondergard, Sidney, 19, 33
Song Maocheng's 宋懋澂 (幼清, 1569–1622), 3, 143, 153–4, 159
Song shi 宋史, 52n5, 55n12, 56n14, 61n27
Song Yü 宋玉 (ca. 298 B.C.E.–ca. 222 B.C.E.), 71n25
Soushen ji 搜神記, 124
Su Shi's 蘇軾 (1037–1101), 56n15
Sugeshili 速哥失里, 117, 128
Suiyin manlu 隨隱漫錄, 61
Sun Chang, Kang-yi, 49n13, 49n15
Sun Kaidi 孫楷第, 5, 153
Sun Keqiu 孫秋克, 6n9
Sun Yirang 孫詒讓, 120n17

taiguang 胎光, 28n33
Taihu lake 太湖, 27n26
Taiping guangji 太平廣記, 2n4, 15n9
"Taixu sifa zhuan" 太虛司法傳 (The Account of the Legal Administrator of the Grand Void), 39–44, 45
Taizhou Prefecture 台州府, 131n1
Tan Qixiang 譚其驤, 121n19
Tang Xianzu 湯顯祖 (1550–1616), 125
Tang Xianzu quanji 湯顯祖全集, 125n27
Tang yulin 唐语林, 161n6
Tangren xiaoshuo 唐人小說, 70n18, 70n23
Tao Qian 陶潛 (Yuanming 陶淵明, 365–427), 69n14
"Taohuayuan ji" 桃花源記, 69n14
"Taoyao" 桃夭, 118n13
"Teng Mu zuiyou Jujingyuan ji" 滕穆醉遊聚景園記 (Teng Mu's Drunken Excursion to Assembled Scenery Park), 5–6
Tian Dao 天道, 170
Tianshui 天水, 51
"Tiantai fangyin lu" 天台訪隱錄 (A Visit to Tiantai), 52n5
tiaonian 髫年, 69n14
Tiege 鐵哥, 120n18
Tiemuer Buhua 帖木而不花, 116
Tiyu youyun 殢雨尤雲, 21n8
Touxiang 偷香, 74n23
Tsao Joanne, 63, 76

Wanli 萬曆, 143, 155, 167
"Wang Daoping's Wife" 王道平妻, 125
Wang Dun 王敦 (266–324), 28
Wang Jing, 2, 59n22, 60n23, 76, 113, 124, 129n36, 148n12
Wang Liqi 王利器, 153–4, 167
Wang Pijiang 汪辟疆, 70n18, 70n23
Wang Qiancheng 王前程, 58, 61n25–6, 62n30
Wang Renyu 王仁裕 (880–956), 66n6
Wang Ruilai 王瑞來, 62n30
Wang Shixi 王士熙, 114n3
Wang Shizhen 王士禎 (1634–1711), 60n23, 153
Wang Shumin 王叔岷, 118n12
Wang Xingqi 王星琦, 62n29
"Wang Youyu ji" 王幼玉記, 156
Wang Zhou 王宙, 16
"Wangkui Zhuan" 王魁传, 169n16
Wanshou Mountain 萬壽山, 114n4
Wei Gao 韋皋, 30n42
Wei xingduolu 畏行多露, 151n19
Weiyang 維揚, 146
Wen qi lu 聞奇錄, 104
Wen Tingyun 溫庭筠 (812–866), 104
Wenxiao 文蕭, 98
wenyan xiaoshuo 文言小說, 1
Wu Chen, 131
Wu Qiuyan 吾邱衍 (1272–1311), 58
"Wu wangxiaonü" 吳王小女, 4
Wu Weiye 吳偉業, 153, 168
Wu Zhida 吳志達, 36n50, 155
Wushan 巫山, 71n25
Wuwei zi 無為子, 72n28, 84
Wuzhong 吳中, 164n10

Xia Bingheng 夏秉恆, 158
Xianquan ji 峴泉集, 84n50
Xiaoshi 蕭史, 118n12
"Xie Xiao'e zhuan" 謝小娥傳, 104
Xielipuhua 燮理溥化 (1295–1360), 101
Xihu 西湖 (West Lake), 52
Xin zeng bu xiang jiandeng yuhua Daquan 新增補相剪燈餘話大全, 76
xing 興 (stimulus), 81
Xingniang 興娘, 7–9, 13
Xingshi hengyan 醒世恆言, 111
Xinkan jiandeng yuhua 新刊剪燈餘話, 76
Xiyou ji 西遊記, 111

Xu Da 徐達, 36
Xu Deyan 徐德言, 25n20, 28n36
Xu Shuofang 徐朔方, 6n9
Xu Yaozuo's 許堯佐, 29n39
Xuelipuhua 薛理溥化, 94, 101
Xuxiu Siku quanshu 續修四庫全書, 153, 159, 167n13

yaksha, 40
Yandula 奄都剌, 114
Yang Bojun 楊伯峻, 129n35
Yang Rong's 楊榮, 77, 78n42
Yang Shen 楊慎 (1488–1559), 70n21
Yang Shuhui, 113, 157n26
Yang Su 楊素 (544–606), 28n36
Yang Yunqin, 113, 157n26
"Yao Gongzi zhuan" 姚公子傳 (The Tale of Young Master Yao), 131–7, 138–40
Ye Shaoweng's 葉紹翁 (fl. 1115), 115n5
Ye Xianzu 葉憲祖 (1566–1641), 36
yanfen 煙粉, 58
yaoshu 妖術, 58n21
Yi Jian xu zhi 夷堅續志, 104
Yi Jian zhi 夷堅志, 104
Yijing 易經 (Book of Changes), 41
yinbu 蔭補, 87n3
"Yingying zhuan" 鶯鶯傳 (Story of Yingying), 156, 169n16
yipu 義僕, 110
Yiwen leiju 藝文類聚, 70n22
"You xianku" 遊仙窟, 6
youjing 幽精, 28n33
Youming lu 幽明錄, 14, 45n12
youqi 幽期, 76
Yu Yingshi 余英時, 130
Yuan hua ji 原化記, 104
Yuan Sheng 袁聲 (fl. 1692), 37
Yuan shi 元史, 91n15, 99, 116n7
Yuan zaju benshi kao 元雜劇本事考, 126n28
"Yueye tanqin ji" 月夜彈琴記, 79
Yunpizi yuhua 運甓子餘話, 76
Yunxi youyi 雲溪友議, 125
Yushi mingyan 喻世明言, 111
Yutang xianhua 玉堂閒話, 104

zaju 雜劇, 2
zaokang zhiqi 糟糠之妻, 102

Zeng Zao 曾慥 (fl. 1126), 102
Zhang Chang 張敞, 90
Zhang Peiheng's 章培恆, 155
Zhang Qianniang 張倩娘, 70n23
Zhang Qingzhong 張清種, 68n13
Zhang Shicheng 張士誠 (1321–1367), 22, 26
Zhang Yi 張鎰, 16
Zhang Yuchu 張宇初 (1361–1410), 72n28, 84
Zhang Zhengchang 張正常 (1335–1378), 84
Zhang Zhenjun, 1n1, 2, 2n4, 4n6, 15n9, 15n10, 19, 29n39, 33, 45, 59n22, 60n23, 129n36, 143, 148n12, 153
Zhang Zhuo's 張鷟, 6
Zhangtai 章台, "Zhang Terrace," 29
Zhangzhou 漳州, 56
Zhao Gongfu 趙公輔 (fl. 1280), 16
Zhao Hede's 趙合德 (d. 7 BC), 148n12
Zhao Yuan 趙源, 51–7, 59–61
Zhedong 浙東, 131
Zhen Ji 貞姬, 109
Zheng Guangzu 鄭光祖 (fl. 1295), 16
Zheng Huchen 鄭虎臣 (1219–1276), 56n14
Zheng Xuan 鄭玄, 120n17
Zhengshuo 正朔, 22n13
Zhengtong Daozang 正統道藏, 84n49
Zhengyi Dao 正一道, 72n28, 84
"Zhenshan" 珍衫 (The Pearl Shirt), 5
Zhenze 震澤, 147
zhiguai 志怪 (accounts of anomalies), 1, 1n1, 45, 124
zhiren 志人 (records of people), 1
Zhongguo wenyan xiaoshuo yanjiu 中國文言小說研究, 76n37
Zhongguo wenyan xiaoshuoshi 中國文言小說史, 155
Zhongguo xiaoshuo shilue 中國小説史略, 1n2, 5
Zhou Chaojun's 周朝俊, 62
Zhou li 周禮, 119n17
Zhou Mi 周密 (1232–1298), 104
Zhou Xuanchu 周玄初, 85
Zhou Xuanzhen 周玄真 (1328–?), 85n52
Zhou Yi's 周夷, 51, 113
Zhou Yibai 周貽白, 36n51

Zhouli Zhengyi 周禮正義, 120n17
Zizheng 子政, 152
Zhu Honglin 朱鴻林, 167n13
"Zhu shan" 珠衫 (The Pearl Shirt),
    159–66, 167, 170–1
Zhu Yangdong 朱仰東, 114n3, 116n6, 127

Zhu Yingtai 祝英臺, 19
Zhuti 朱提, 146
zifu 紫府, 22n9
Zou Xin 138
Zuiwengtanlu 醉翁談錄, 2, 58
Zuozhuan 左傳, 31n49, 42